MW00620241

Look up Jim Collins
Ann Rev of Anthro
Article

1500 words
Spring 96
6/97

Literacy continues to be a central issue in anthropology, but methods of perceiving and examining it have changed in recent years. In this study Niko Besnier analyzes the transformation of Nukulaelae from a non-literate into a literate society using a contemporary perspective which emphasizes literacy as a social practice embedded in a socio-cultural context. He shows how a small and isolated Polynesian community, with no access to print technology, can become deeply steeped in literacy in little more than a century, and how literacy can take on radically divergent forms depending on the social and cultural needs and characteristics of the society in which it develops. His case study, which has implications for understanding literacy in other societies, illuminates the relationship between norm and practice, between structure and agency, and between group and individual.

Studies in the Social and
Cultural Foundations of Language No. 16

Literacy, emotion, and authority

Studies in the Social and Cultural Foundations of Language

The aim of this series is to develop theoretical perspectives on the essential social and cultural character of language by methodological and empirical emphasis on the occurrence of language in its communicative and interactional settings, on the socioculturally grounded 'meanings' and 'functions' of linguistic forms, and on the social scientific study of language use across cultures. It will thus explicate the essentially ethnographic nature of linguistic data, whether spontaneously occurring or experimentally induced, whether normative or variational, whether synchronic or diachronic. Works appearing in the series will make substantive and theoretical contributions to the debate over the sociocultural-functional and structural-formal nature of language, and will represent the concerns of scholars in the sociology and anthropology of language, anthropological linguistics, sociolinguistics, and socio-culturally informed psycholinguistics.

Editorial Board

LITERACY, EMOTION, AND AUTHORITY

READING AND WRITING ON A POLYNESIAN ATOLL

NIKO BESNIER
Yale University

CAMBRIDGE
UNIVERSITY PRESS

1995

Published by the Press Syndicate of the University of Cambridge
The Pitt Building, Trumpington Street, Cambridge CB2 1RP
40 West 20th Street, New York, NY 10011-4211, USA
10 Stamford Road, Oakleigh, Melbourne 3166, Australia

© Cambridge University Press 1995

First published 1995

Printed in Great Britain at the University Press, Cambridge

A catalogue record for this book is available from the British Library

Library of Congress cataloguing in publication data

Besnier, Niko.
Literacy, emotion, and authority: reading and writing on a
Polynesian atoll/ Niko Besnier.
p.   cm. – (Studies in the social and cultural foundations of
language; no. 16)
Includes bibliographical references and index.
ISBN 0 521 48087 6. – ISBN 0 521 48539 8 (pbk.)
1. Literacy – Tuvalu.   2. Language and culture – Tuvalu.   I. Title.
II. Series.
P211.3.T88B47   1995
302.2/244/099682–dc20   94-34107   CIP

ISBN 0 521 48087 6 hardback
ISBN 0 521 48539 8 paperback

For Guy Besnier
and to the memory of Faiva Tafia

CONTENTS

ILLUSTRATIONS AND TABLES

Figures

Maps

Tables

ACKNOWLEDGMENTS

My interest in everyday forms of literacy first awoke while sojourning on Nukulaelae at various times between 1979 and 1982. I returned in mid-1985 to conduct a focused investigation of literacy practices on the atoll. The main thrust of this research was of a sociolinguistic nature, and it became the basis of a 1986 dissertation on stylistic aspects of Nukulaelae literacy, a summary of which appeared later (Besnier 1988). Backgrounding these early endeavors was a substantial store of ethnographic materials on Nukulaelae reading and writing practices, which I came to realize was of equal if not greater value than the more stylistic material. This book originated in this corpus of field observations, which was initially the by-product of my research. Field work in 1990 and 1991 enabled me to refine further these materials and sharpen their focus.

My greatest debt for making my field research possible goes to the Nukulaelae community. I suspect that few anthropologists have been as lucky as I have been to be able to conduct ethnographic research in such an idyllic setting. However, what makes the setting idyllic is not so much the beauty and bountifulness of the atoll, but the unfailing generosity and warmth of its inhabitants. Among the numerous people who have made my sojourns on Nukulaelae pleasant, interesting, and comfortable, I must single out Sina Faiva and the late Faiva Tafia, who, along with Lamona and Semolina, took me into their family. Kelese Simona, Lenese Telava, the late Mataua Akelei, Tausegia Tafia, and Valoa Samuelu (in alphabetical order) all provided invaluable insights on matters related to the topic of this book, and so did the numerous individuals that I cannot mention for lack of space. My assistants Mele Alefaio and Pesega Toomu (in 1985), and Tufue Niuioka and Avanoa Luuni (in 1990–91), contributed labor and enthusiasm, without which my research could not have been conducted. I also thank the Government of Tuvalu, and the atoll's Council of Elders and Island Council, for allowing me to spend a total of approximately three and a half years on Nukulaelae since 1979. Funding for field research on Nukulaelae was provided, over the years, by the National Science Foundation (grants No. 8503061 and 8920023), the Harry Frank Guggenheim Foundation, the Wenner Gren Foundation for Anthropological Research, and the Fondation de la Vocation.

This book could not have been written without the unwavering support I received over the years from Elinor Ochs, Harold Conklin, and Brian Street. At Yale, I have had the good fortune of being surrounded by exemplary colleagues, friends, and students: Susan Brownell, Mike Coe, Ian Condry, Mickey Dietler, Micaela di Leonardo, Joe Errington, Angelique Haugerud, Miki Makihara, Nicole Polier, Hal Scheffler, Jan Simpson, and John Szwed, as well as visiting scholars like Michael Lambek, Mahir Şaul, and Jackie Solway, have all had an impact on this work. I cannot fail to mention the collegiality of fellow scholars of Tuvalu, particularly Ivan Brady, Michael Goldsmith, Doug Munro, and Peter McQuarrie, whose insights pepper this book. I received advice and comments on specific details of this project from Philip Bock, René Galindo, Deborah Gewertz, Mike Goldsmith, Mary Hussey, Doug Munro, and Harry Stout. Shirley Brice Heath and Alessandro Duranti read and commented on the entire manuscript, as did David Bloome. My heartfelt thanks to all.

This book was written principally in Honolulu, Albuquerque, and New York City. The luxury to write in Honolulu's superb surroundings was made possible by a Rockefeller Fellowship at the Center for Pacific Islands Studies, University of Hawaii. In Albuquerque, I benefitted greatly from Rex Swanda's hospitality and company, and from his occasional queries regarding the nature of my control population for this study. In Manhattan, Richard Ogust kept me on my toes. During the final throes of writing, Charles Briggs, Joe Errington, Julia Hough, Bambi Schieffelin, and Brian Street offered advice, shared their wisdom, and patted me on the hand. Rachel Schofer provided invaluable assistance in manuscript preparation. For the maps, I am indebted to the artistic talents of Robert Williams and Tom Decker.

Parts of this book were presented in talks and colloquia at the University of Sydney, University of New England, University of Hawaii, Bond University, University of Sussex, University of Massachusetts at Amherst, the 1987 Boston University Conference on Language Development, the First International Conference on Oceanic Linguistics (Vila, Vanuatu, 1993), and the 1994 Symposium About Language and Society in Austin. Several paragraphs of the introductory chapter are revised from "Aspects of Literacy," co-authored with Brian Street, in *Companion Encyclopedia of Anthropology: Humanity, Culture, and Social Life*, edited by Tim Ingold (Routledge, 1994). Parts of Chapters 4 and 5 have appeared as "Literacy and Feelings: The Encoding of Affect in Nukulaelae Letters," *Text* 9:69–92 (1989), and portions of Chapter 7 as "Christianity, Authority, and Personhood: Sermonic Discourse on Nukulaelae Atoll," *Journal of the Polynesian Society* 103:339–78 (1994). Relevant passages are reprinted here with permission kindly granted by Routledge, Mouton de Gruyter, and the Polynesian Society.

TRANSCRIPTION CONVENTIONS AND ORTHOGRAPHY

The arguments developed in this book rest heavily on the empirical analysis of both written texts and transcripts of spoken discourse produced in the Polynesian language in common use on Nukulaelae Atoll, Tuvalu Group, Central Pacific. This approach foregrounds two questions of particular concern: how spoken discourse should be transcribed; and what orthographic conventions should be adopted in light of the fact that there is no standardized orthography for the language in question. I have adopted a number of conventions in answer to these questions, which are described here. *literacy questioned at all levels.*

Transcripts and written texts

Transcribing spoken discourse is an analytic act, as many scholars have demonstrated (e.g., Edwards 1993, Gumperz and Berenz 1993, Ochs 1979a, Tedlock 1983); the selection of linguistic and extra-textual information to be included in the transcript from a very broad range of possibilities, as well as their visual presentation, involve decisions that predetermine how the transcripts are read and what categories become the focus of analytic scrutiny.

Many spoken excerpts cited in this book are not the object of detailed grammatical analysis, although I do pay attention to formal features in my analysis of the meaning of many excerpts. I have therefore adopted transcription conventions that represent a compromise between the fine-grained transcription system used in Conversation Analysis (e.g., Atkinson and Heritage 1984) and the selectively translated paraphrases with which social anthropologists are commonly satisfied. Thus I have found it expedient in most cases to exclude from the transcripts descriptions of prosody (e.g., pitch, loudness, duration) and of cooccurring non-verbal events (e.g., gestures, facial expressions). However, transcripts include all the segmental "noise" audible on tape, such as hesitations, false starts, and other types of repairs. On occasion, I analyze a stretch of spoken discourse in greater structural detail, focusing for example on pitch variations and intonational contours. In such cases, the relevant linguistic categories are noted in the transcript, and the applicable transcription conventions are explained in the text. The orthography used throughout this book is based on phonemic principles, as discussed below, but the phonological structure of the language is such that this phonemic orthography is very close to the phonetic form of discourse.

Transcripts in the original language are provided first, and are followed by their translations. In the translations, I strive to keep the general "flavor" of the original, sometimes at the expense of English idiomaticity, particularly when the exact wording of the original is consequential for my analysis. However, I have also paid attention to the dangers of "exoticizing" the translation beyond what is required, by ignoring the polysemy of certain words for example.

Following is the list of miscellaneous conventions used in the transcripts:

(words in parentheses)   conjectured or inaudible string
[. . .]   untranscribed string of words
words in bold   illustrative material
word-   abrupt cut-off

In addition, when additional wording or contextual information must supplement the translation for the sake of intelligibility, this information is provided in square brackets.

I generally provide a recording reference (e.g. [sermons:P 1991:2:A:271–277]) between the original transcript and its translation. A typical reference consists of the name of the tape (sermons:P 1991:2), the side of the tape (A), and tape-recorder counter references (271–277). References to written discourse excerpts (e.g. [sermons:P 1991:10]) consist of a file name (sermons:P 1991) followed by a page number (10) where relevant.

In most cases, personal names have been changed to pseudonyms or initials to protect the identity of named individuals. The use of initials is not ideal, although it is often rendered necessary by the finite range of personal names on Nukulaelae. When citing particularly sensitive material, I have changed the initials of individuals to X, Y and Z, and have sometimes left out details in transcript excerpts or background notes.

Writing system and orthography

In the insular Pacific (i.e., Melanesia, Micronesia, and Polynesia), no autochthonous tradition of literacy had developed before contact with the West, and reading and writing were introduced at the time of Europeans influx into the region in the eighteenth and nineteenth centuries. Like the inhabitants of other Pacific Islands, Nukulaelae Islanders use roman characters when writing their own language, mostly confining themselves to the eleven consonant symbols (f, g, h, k, l, m, n, p, s, t, v) and five vowel graphemes (a, e, i, o, u) needed to represent the basic phoneme inventory of their language.

How Nukulaelae Islanders developed historically the orthographic system that they currently use to write their language is undocumented. One can surmise that they tailored it on the orthography that London Missionary Society missionaries devised in the early nineteenth century for Samoan. The orthographic transfer from one language to the other was facilitated by the commonalities in the phonological structures of Samoan and Tuvaluan. However, there are also significant differences between the two systems (e.g., Tuvaluan has phonemically geminated consonants), and difficulties inevitably arose during the borrowing process.

Like other Polynesian languages, the dialects of Tuvaluan (including the Nukulaelae dialect) have a small inventory of basic phonemes. However, they differ from better known Polynesian languages in one major respect: both consonants and vowels can be geminated, whereas only vowels undergo gemination in most other Polynesian languages. This feature, which was first described systematically by Milner (1958), is also found in a few languages of Outlier Polynesia (i.e., small Polynesian-speaking enclaves in Melanesian and Micronesia). It has different phonetic consequences for different consonants: oral stops are heavily aspirated when geminated (there is no aspiration in the ungeminated forms); nasal stops become syllabic; and other consonants are articulated for a longer period of time than their ungeminated equivalents.

In this study, I employ the same orthographic system for spoken and written utterances, and this system is based on phonemic principles. Double graphemes indicate geminated segments. The letter *g* represents a velar nasal stop, *l* is either a lateral or central flap (in free variation), and all other letters have their approximate IPA value. Conveniently, there are only very few differences between phonemic representations and phonetic realizations, and the language exhibits relatively few "fast-speech" phenomena that increase the "distance" between spoken and written forms of the language. An inventory of the graphemes in the orthographic system used in this book is provided in Table 1.

I have deviated from these orthographic norms in a few instances. First, I have preserved the original orthography of some written materials when it seemed appropriate to do so, in which case this is indicated in the text. Second, I have rendered most contemporary personal names (be they pseudonyms or not) and place names in their most common written form when these names occur in the English text (e.g., Funafuti, phonemically *Funaafuti*), but have provided a phonemic version of the name where it first occurs in the book. However, names that appear in transcripts and the place names on Map 1· are all in phonemic orthography. When citing words or texts in Gilbertese and Samoan, I have followed the standard orthographies used in these languages, except where I expressly state otherwise.

There is no standardized orthography for writing Tuvaluan. There have been several attempts to impose orthographic standards, most recently by a

Table 1. *Grapheme inventory*

p			t		k	pp		tt		kk
m			n		g	mm		nn		gg
		f	s		h		ff	ss		hh
		v					vv			
			l					ll		
	i			u			ii		uu	
	e			o			ee		oo	
			a					aa		

governmental committee based on Funafuti, the capital of the country, called the Tuvalu Language Board. This committee has issued several mutually contradictory decrees on Tuvaluan orthography (e.g., Tuvalu Language Board 1980, 1991). Significantly, these decrees concern only the representation of vowel gemination, the one suprasegmental feature that Tuvaluan shares with Samoan: the concern is whether geminated vowels should be indicated with superscript macrons, as in Samoan, or with double graphemes, and whether they should be marked in all instances, only when ambiguity arises, or under no circumstances. The virtual silence over how to treat consonant gemination is probably due to the historical association of Samoan with literacy in Tuvalu, which has shaped what counts as an orthographic problem and what does not (Samoan does not have geminated consonants, so writers of that language are not faced with the problem of how to represent them). For the most part, the Board's decrees have no impact on everyday literacy practices, and as such their fate is the same as other overt attempts to exert authority from above (see Chapter 7 and Besnier 1991a, 1993 for further discussion).

The orthography I have adopted here diverges from the common orthographic practices extant on Nukulaelae and in the rest of Tuvalu, principally because few writers of Tuvaluan mark segmental gemination consistently. I have thus modified the orthography of written texts I cite in this book for the sake of consistency. I have also altered the punctuation of written texts, in that Nukulaelae writers use punctuation sparingly and haphazardly (cf. Chapters 4 and 6). The decision to edit the form of written texts was a difficult one to make. On the one hand, a methodological perspective that focuses on the relationship between texts and their contexts dictates that any modification of the form of textual data constitutes tampering with the evidence. On the other hand, there are practical motivations for the solution I have adopted. First, part of my purpose here is to make selective microscopic comparisons between written texts and genres, and between speaking and writing. Such comparisons would be unwieldy if the orthography of written texts differed significantly from that of spoken transcripts. Second, there is evidence that the multiplicity of orthographic and punctuation practices and their characteristics sometimes hinder the comprehension of written texts, even for native users of the language, as I discuss in Chapter 4. While the lack of standardization is tied to social factors that are of considerably greater import than processing ease (e.g., a basic suspicion of acts of authority), the reading difficulties that result from the resulting diversity are problematic for the type of analysis I endeavor to present here.

The lack of standardization in written Tuvaluan does not preclude the fact that there is some systematicity within and across orthographic practices, a topic that deserves more attention than I am able to give to it here. Briefly, in the various orthographic systems that Nukulaelae Islanders utilize, geminate vowels are sometimes indicated with two vowels in one of two cases. In the first case, the two morae of the geminated segment belong to two different morphemes, as in words like *fakaasi* "show" (from the causative prefix *faka-* and the root *asi* "appear") and *faiika* "fish" (phonetically *faaika*, from the verb *fai* "harvest" and the noun *ika* "fish"). In the second category fall words in which the second mora of the geminated vowel receives primary word-stress (i.e., is the penultimate mora of the word), e.g., *niisi* "some" and *paala* "wahoo." In addition, there are two minor situations in which double vocalic graphemes are sometimes found. First, geminate vowels may be indicated in borrowings from Samoan words in which a glottal stop occurs between the two vowels, as in *faameo* "to ask a favor" (from Samoan *fa'ameo*) and *vii* "praise song" (from Samoan *vi'i* "to praise," apostrophes in Samoan indicate glottal stops). Second, some writers use double vocalic graphemes in certain contexts to indicate that the consonant preceding the vowel sound is geminated, as in *ttau* "must," written *taau*, and *ssuga* "honorific particle," written *suuga*. These cases suggest that writers are clearly aware of consonantal gemination, but that they mistakenly attribute the locus of gemination to the vocalic segment that follows. Generally speaking, consonant gemination is otherwise not indicated, although a few writers do mark it intermittently with an apostrophe either before or, more rarely, after the consonant (e.g., *'mao* or *m'ao* for *mmao* "far away"). On occasion, writers mark consonant gemination by reduplicating the entire syllable (e.g., *mamao*); indeed, many (but not all) geminate consonants originally derive from reduplicated syllables that have undergone a reduction process, although non-reduced forms are never used in the spoken form of the southern dialects of Tuvaluan. It is also very possible that the use of reduplicated syllables in writing is borrowed from written Samoan (the Samoan word corresponding to Tuvaluan *mmao* is *mamao*). Again, one perceives the influence of Samoan orthographic conventions in these various patterns, although the apostrophe has a completely different meaning in the written form of that language.

Word boundaries are where most variation is encountered, although some consistency does emerge. Certain one-mora function words that are homophonous with either the last segment of the previous word or the first segment of the following word are frequently omitted in writing. Such is the case of the possessive prepositions *a* "alienable possession" and *o* "inalienable possession" (in the following illustrative sentences, I provide the version as originally written on the first line, the version in phonemic orthography on the second line, the word-by-word glosses on the third line, and the idiomatic translation on the last line):[1]

Fai a   **muna**   tagata.
Fai a   **muna a**   ttagata.
say Cnt word of the + man
     "The man [then] says."

Ia tela   te   mea   mo   togi meakai **au**   tama.
Ia, teelaa te   mea   moo   ttogi meakkai **a au**   tama.
Itj that   the thing Cmp buy food   of your child
     "Here, here's something with which [you] can buy some food for
     your children."

Ate   **taeao**   tatou tai   nofoaki foki e lo.
A   te **taeao**   o taatou tai nofoaki foki eeloo.
Cnt the morning of we-3-i quite present also indeed
     "This morning we have quite a few [important people] present."

One-mora function words that occur in sequence are usually written as one word. For example, the conjunction *mo* "and," the ergative case marker *nee*, and the locative preposition *i* "at," when followed by the definite singular article *te*, are written as *mote*, *nete*, and *ite*. Similarly, the verb *oti* "finished" and the inceptive aspect marker *koo*, which together mark perfective aspect, are frequently written together as *kooti* or *koti*, and the anaphoric pronouns *ei* coalesces in writing with the locative preposition *i* or the directional preposition *ki*, yielding *iei* and *kiei*. These patterns reflect stress-assignment rules, according to which stress is assigned to these sequences as if they formed single words. But some word strings are commonly written as one word simply because they frequently occur in sequence in discourse. For example, the quantifier *soo* "any" is very frequently followed by the indefinite article *se*, and as a result the sequence is frequently written as one word, *sose*; for the same reasons, the universal tense marker *e* and the existential verb *isi* appear as *eisi*, and the demonstrative *teelaa* and the downtoning adverb *laa*, which together form a discourse conjunct *teelaa laa* "thus," are written as *telala*.

In contrast to these mergers, one also encounters splitting tendencies. Certain monomorphemic words, such as the durative aspect marker *koi* "still" and the deictic adverb *aka* "up," are frequently found written as two words (*ko i* and *a ka*), probably because they thus resemble more common morphemes in written form. Dual and plural possession pronouns, as well as indefinite singular possessive pronouns, are usually written in two words, the first of which is homophonous with the article from which the possessive pronoun is formed. For example, *nemaa* "some [of] our" (dual exclusive) is usually written as *ne ma*, *telotou* "their" (plural) as *te lotou*, and *seaku* "one [of] my" as *se aku*. Dual second-person possessive pronouns are often broken up in the middle of the possessive morpheme, so that *teaulua* "your" (dual) can appear as *teau lua*.

Some more or less idiosyncratic patterns of variation result from the homophony between single morphemes and morpheme sequences. The conditional conjunctions *kaafai* and *maafai* and their allomorphs are sometimes written as two words, *ka fai* and *ma fai* respectively, because they thus resemble the tense-aspect markers *kaa* and *maa*, which can also have conditional meanings. In contrast, the verb *fai* "do," which is also related to the form of the conjunctions, is sometimes written in one word with the tense-aspect markers *kaa* and *maa*, even when it clearly functions as the main verb of a conditional clause:

Kafai te fatele pela seai mai fua ne tino.
Kaa fai te faatele, peelaa seeai mai fua ne tino.
Fut do the dance thus Neg Dxs just some person
"When there is a dance, it's as if no one were here."

One interesting case is that of the verb *iloa* "know" preceded by the universal tense marker *e*, and the intensifying adverb *eiloa*, which itself is compounded from the anaphoric pronoun *ei* and the intensifier *loa*. The strings *e iloa* and *eiloa* are homophonous, and they are written either as two words, *ei loa*, or as one word, *eiloa*:

Telala **eiloa** ne au ko koe e alofa mai.
Teelaa laa, **e iloa** nee au ko koe e alofa mai.
thus Nps know Erg I Foc you Nps feel-empathy Dxs
"So I know that you have empathy for me."

Seai **ei loa** se tino **ei loa** ne ia te mea tena.
Seeai **eiloa** se tino **e iloa** nee ia te mea teena.
Neg indeed a person Nps know Erg he the thing that
"No one knows what this is."

A handful of additional orthographic details are worth noting. Reduplicated words or portions of words of more than one mora are often written with a "squared" sign following the base string, e.g., *Nukulaelae* is rendered as *Nukulae²*, *laulau* "to [continually] tell" as *lau²*. This practice is associated with "informal" written styles (e.g., letter writing) or with writing done under time constraints (e.g., minute taking), and is particularly conspicuous with high-frequency words, and with words in which the reduplication has a predictable meaning (e.g., when it marks continuative or iterative aspect).

Finally, in telegrams, Nukulaelae Islanders use a modified orthography whose features are to a certain extent predictable. Telegraphic orthography has the following general characteristics: articles, prepositions, tense-aspect markers, conjunctions, and negative particles are written together with the following word, while postponed deictic adverbs (*mai* "hither," *atu* "thither," *aka* "up," *ifo* "down") are written together with the preceding string if the latter is not already too long. The text of the following telegram illustrates these various patterns:

TECHEQUE	FAKAMULI	SETALIA		OFULI		ITEBANK
te cheque	fakamuli	see	talia	o	ffuli	i te bank
the cheque	last	Neg	authorize	Cmp	change	at the bank

FAIMAI	KEFAITALI	ISE	2/3	MASINA	KEMAUA	MAI
fai mai	kee faittali	i se	2/3	maasina	kee maua	mai
say Dxs	Sbj wait	at a	2/3	month	Sbj get	Dxs

SETALIAGA	ITEBANK		NEUMAI	IEI	
se taliaga	i	te bank	ne aumai	i	ei
a authorization	from the bank		Pst bring	from Anp	

ALOFAATU	
alofa	atu
feel-empathy	Dsx

"The bank is not willing to exchange the last cheque[,] [they] say that [we have to] wait 2/3 months for [it] to clear at the bank from which it originated[.] Love [signature]"

As in other parts of the world, these conventions are obviously geared to minimize the word-count and hence the cost of transmitting the message.

I

INTRODUCTION

Anthropological perspectives on literacy

Literacy has occupied a central position in the historical development of anthropological thought. During the formative decades of the field and its allied disciplines, literacy was implicated, more or less explicitly, as a determinant of differences between "civilized" and "primitive" thought and action (Durkheim and Mauss 1903, Maine 1873, McLennan 1876, Tylor 1874), scientific mentalities and prelogical thinking (Cassirer 1946, Lévy-Bruhl 1910, Luria 1976), open and closed systems (Popper 1959), *pensée domestiquée* and *pensée sauvage* (Lévi-Strauss 1962), and context-free and context-bound cognitive processes (Vygotsky 1962). Until the turn of the twentieth century, pointing to literacy as the pivot between "us" and "them" was a relatively simple task: literacy was defined as a more or less exclusive feature of Western life. Where it existed in the non-Western world, it had characteristics that gave it an inferior quality: for example, it was thought that learning to read and write in China required years of apprenticeship because of the apparently complex and unwieldy nature of the writing system. Similarly, in much of the Islamic world, literacy was described as being in the exclusive hands of a social élite, which prevented it from giving rise to an enlightened society. Only in the West, early anthropologists maintained, did literacy reach its apogee and thus enable the "general improvement of mankind by higher organization of the individual and of society, to the end of promoting at once man's goodness, power, and happiness," as Tylor defined the rise to "civilization" (1874:1:27).

While modern anthropologists, for the most part, eschew the overarching determinism of their nineteenth- and early-twentieth-century predecessors, the contrast between literacy and pre-literacy remains a major preoccupation in contemporary anthropological theory. The historical persistence of this nineteenth-century preoccupation is hardly unique among questions of concern to the field: as Kuper (1988) demonstrates, major patterns of continuity over time underlie anthropological thinking on many issues, despite cosmetic changes in how they are approached.

1

Many contemporary scholars, among whom Jack Goody figures prominently (1968, 1977, 1986, 1987, Goody and Watt 1963), have continued to maintain that the historical advent of literacy plays a crucial role in bringing about fundamental changes in the makeup of culture, society, and the person, and that cross-cultural differences in modes of thought can be attributed to the presence of literacy in some societies, and its absence elsewhere. Goody, whose stance has become significantly more tentative and mitigated with each restatement (Halverson 1992), originally took to task the contrasts that previous scholars had proposed between, for example, domesticated and undomesticated thought. Criticizing the dichotomies that had been advanced earlier for their lack of explanatory power, Goody proposed to demonstrate that "many of the valid aspects of these somewhat vague dichotomies can be related to changes in the mode of communication, especially the introduction of various forms of writing" (1977:16). This deterministic view of literacy and its subsequent restatements represent what has come to be referred to as the *autonomous model* of literacy (Street 1984).[1] The persistent popularity of the model across different traditions of inquiry demonstrates that it strikes a particularly enduring chord in Western thinking.

According to early versions of the autonomous model, certain inherent properties of literacy, particularly alphabetic literacy,[2] cause basic changes in the structure of societies, the makeup of cultures, and the nature of individuals. (In subsequent versions, the word "cause" is replaced by "facilitate," "make possible," or "encourage," but the basic tenets of the model remain largely unchanged.) For example, writing enables its users to keep permanent records that can be subjected to critical scrutiny, in contrast to orally transmitted information, which is inherently ephemeral and unreliable. As a result, writing gives rise to (or facilitates) standards of historical and scientific verifiability and concomitant social designs. Similarly, bureaucratic institutions and complex state structures depend crucially on the type of long-distance communication that literacy makes possible. While the emergence of literacy does not necessarily engender bureaucratic institutions, it greatly facilitates their work (Goody 1986). According to other versions of the model, bureaucracy cannot survive long without the presence of writing (see Larsen 1988 for a critical discussion).

Literacy is also said to alter individual psychological functions: a written text, particularly if written in an alphabetic script, is claimed to be less context-dependent than a comparable spoken text, and the ability to produce and process written texts presupposes (and hence gives rise to) context-free thinking. Literacy is also thought to affect memory in significant ways, as it makes possible rigorous recall of lengthy texts, compared to the imprecise, pattern-driven memory of pre-literate individuals. The central role that the autonomous model accords to literacy as a causal (or, later, enabling) factor thus helps to *explain* the differences between pre-literate and literate individuals, societies, and cultures that earlier researchers had described but not explained (Goody 1977).[3]

The premises and claims of the autonomous model have been subjected to severe critical scrutiny by researchers in a variety of fields, including social anthropology (Street 1984), sociolinguistics (Heath 1983), cultural psychology (Scribner and Cole 1981), rhetoric (Pattison 1982), folklore (Finnegan 1988) and history (Clanchy 1993, Graff 1979, W. Harris 1989). For these critics, literacy should be viewed not as a monolithic phenomenon but as a multi-faceted one, whose meaning, including any consequences it may have for individuals, groups, or symbolic structures, is crucially tied to the social practices that surround it and to the ideological system in which it is embedded. Proponents of an *ideological model* (Street 1984, 1988, 1993) find highly suspect the uncanny resemblance between middle-class academic ways of viewing literacy in post-industrial societies and the social, cultural, and cognitive characteristics purported to be the consequences of literacy. They criticize the fact that proponents of the autonomous model invariably present these purported consequences as inherently superior to the characteristics of pre-literacy (while also romanticizing certain aspects of pre-literacy).[4] Advocates of the ideological perspective view literacy as a sociocultural construct, and propose that literacy cannot be studied independently of the social, political, and historical forces that shape it. They point out, for example, that literacy is found in many societies of the world that do not display the social and cognitive characteristics which the autonomous model predicts should accompany literacy. Proponents of the autonomous model have attempted to meet these objections by proposing that these cases are situations of *restricted literacy*, i.e., literacy which somehow has not reached its fullest potential (Goody 1968:11–20). However, these qualifications more or less explicitly equate non-restricted literacy with Western middle-class standards, and it is highly questionable whether any form of literacy is ever non-restricted in one way or another (see Chapter 8 for a fuller discussion).

The parameters of inquiry that the ideological model introduces into the discussion highlight the serious problems associated with the category "pre-literate society" that proponents of the autonomous model invoke unproblematically. Under what conditions should a group be considered to be literate? At what point in history can a society be considered to have made the transition from pre-literacy to literacy (cf. Howe 1992:74, O'Keefe 1990:190–4, Stock 1983:9)? If pre-literate societies are groups whose members do not individually control reading and writing skills, ambiguous cases abound. For example, does the category include communities in which a handful of writers act as "literacy brokers" for other members of the group, by writing letters, filling out bureaucratic forms, and interpreting written directions for them (e.g., Weinstein-Shr 1993 on Hmong immigrants in the United States, Baynham 1993 on Moroccan immigrants in London, Wagner, Messick, and Spratt 1986 on Morocco)? How does one characterize communities in which men define women as "illiterate" despite the fact that women do read and write, because the type of literacy that women engage in is confined to the private world of the household, and hence remains invisible to men (e.g., Rockhill 1987 on urban Hispanic California)? Are groups that are the target of efforts by outsiders to make them literate, but whose majority resists these efforts, literate or not (e.g., E. Brandt 1983, Guss 1986, Leap 1991, Schieffelin and Cochran-Smith 1984, Scollon and Scollon 1981)? In each of these situations, the persons or groups in questions are familiar, sometimes intimately so, with the nature, purposes, and social evaluations of reading and writing. Yet they do not fall under the classic definition of "literate people." An adequate model of literacy must somehow capture this discrepancy, something which a narrow deterministic definition of literacy fails to do.

A cursory overview of the current state of the world indicates that most societies of the world in fact fall between the categorical cracks of the autonomous model. Today, it is highly doubtful that any community remains untouched by literacy, despite anthropologists' persistent invocation of the category "pre-literate society."[5] Political globalization, highly organized missionizing efforts that place literacy in the foreground of their endeavors, and the penetration of capitalism into the most remote corners of the globe have all contributed to the erasure from the ethnographic spectrum of groups that have never come into contact with reading and writing. Of course, the literacy experiences of various groups and persons can differ significantly, but where does one draw the line between literacy and pre-literacy? It is impossible, in today's world, to define the pre-literate condition without imposing a value-laden, a priori, and arbitrary standard for what it means for a person or group to be literate. And indeed, works of scholars like Wallerstein (1974) and Wolf (1982), which demonstrate that political and economic globalization is not a recent process, make one wonder about the historical reality of the pre-literate condition even in centuries past. The sobering examples of the spread of literacy into insular Southeast Asia several centuries before the rise of European and American hegemony over the area (Conklin 1949, 1991, Rafael 1988, Reid 1988) and of the multiple cases of "invented literacies" in various parts of the world (Harbsmeier 1988, Smalley, Vang, and Yang 1990) retrospectively call into question whether the "pre-literate society" as a category even existed in the early days of anthropology and other social sciences.[6]

The ideological reaction to autonomous approaches to literacy thus represents a call away from facile categorizations, a retreat from hasty generalizations, and a return to the ethnographic drawing board. Underlying it is the belief that generalizations are much more likely to be discovered in the relationship between literacy and its sociocultural, political, and ideological context than in the inherent properties of literacy itself. The ideological model takes as its object of inquiry the diversity of literacy experiences that emerges within and across societies (cf. K. Basso 1974, Szwed 1981). Within societies, diversity may be tied to differences between contexts, to distinct religious traditions, or to patterns of inequality between groups. Across societies, the heterogeneity of literacy can result from a host of possible factors, including the nature of pedagogical practices tied to literacy, its origin and historical relationships, and the attitudinal underpinnings of reading and writing. Rather than seeking an overarching and context-free characterization of the cognitive and social consequences of literacy, proponents of the ideological model focus on the *activities*, *events*, and *ideological constructs* associated with particular manifestations of literacy.

Ethnographic approaches to literacies

This book takes as its point of departure the premise that literacy is a fundamentally heterogeneous phenomenon, whose shape can be determined by many aspects of the sociocultural context in which it is embedded. The first aim of an ethnographically informed approach to literacy is descriptive: before claiming to understand the general meaning of literacy for a particular social group, one must characterize the range and diversity of literacy experiences and contextualize each one of them in its historical antecedents, its contemporary associations, and its links to other forms of literacy. Central problems for such an analysis include the question of who has access to what type of literacy, in what social context each literacy activity is learned and used, and what social values are foregrounded in the social context in which acts of reading and writing take place.

Two analytic concepts emerge as particularly important tools for the ethnographic investigation of literacy: *literacy event* and *literacy practice*. The concept of "literacy event" refers to a strip of social life in which literacy plays a central role, which can be broken down into its various components, such as settings, participants, and genres (Heath 1983:386).[7] The notion of "literacy practice" is grounded in several disciplinary traditions, including social theory (Bourdieu 1977), psychology (Lave 1988), history (de Certeau 1984), and anthropology (Ortner 1984). Sherry Ortner's tongue-in-cheek definition of "practice" is a heuristically useful point of departure: "Anything that people do" (1984:149). "What people do" should be understood to include recurrent, socially patterned, culturally informed ways of acting and evaluating, as well as what people think they do and why. A practice-oriented approach is thus interested in experience, performance, and interaction, particularly when these have sociopolitical implications. In addition, a focus on practice entails that close attention be paid to persons as social agents, as loci of understanding, and as intentional or (more commonly) unwitting mediators between social structure and everyday action, the macroscopic and the microscopic, and the past and the present. It is in the practice of everyday life that social structures and cultural constructs are reproduced and sometimes altered. An analysis of social practice hence focuses on the social, political, cultural, and economic nature of institutions and other settings in which everyday social action takes place, and on how the nature of these settings informs social action. David Barton summarizes the relationship between literacy event and practice succinctly: "Literacy *practices* are the general cultural ways of utilizing literacy that people draw upon in a literacy event" (1991:5, also Barton 1994:33–52). Both concepts are rather broad, but this quality is a reflection of the diversity of the phenomena they are aimed to capture. In developing a conceptual vocabulary for an analysis of social life, what one loses in precision, one gains in flexibility, malleability, and descriptive power.

Among ethnographic accounts concerned with the relationship of literacy to its social context, two broad methodological trends can be identified. One, which I call *comparative-ethnographic*, contrasts the characteristics of various literacy events and practices in a particular society, and seeks to characterize the relationship between the diversity of literacies and aspects of the communicative ideology extant in the group. The other approach, which I call *event-centered*, focuses on a particular type of literacy practice, and investigates its characteristics in the context of the social and cultural processes at play in associated literacy events. A sample of particularly successful ethnographies best illustrates the potentials of each of these approaches.

Comparative-ethnographic studies

Scribner and Cole's (1981) analysis of literacy among the Vai of Liberia is a classic example of a comparative-ethnographic study of the heterogeneity of literacy experiences in a specific community. While it primarily addresses psychological issues, the study also offers a rich ethnography of Vai literacy practices. Among the Vai, three different literacy traditions coexist, each associated with different languages, institutions, and social activities. Qur'anic literacy is learned in religious schools and used to read Muslim scriptures; English literacy is learned in Western-style schools and used in transactions with the outside world; and Vai literacy, which exploits a locally devised syllabary, is learned informally and used to write letters and keep records of economic transactions. A small percentage of the Vai population is proficient in all three literacies, while others know only one or two, and a substantial number are illiterate. In this ideal comparative laboratory, Scribner and Cole set out to test two claims put forward by proponents of the autonomous model: that significant cognitive consequences can be ascribed to literacy; and that alphabetic writing in particular fosters analytic thought. They adapted to the Vai situation a battery of psychological tests, such as syllogistic problems, memory tasks, and rebus games. The results of these tests demonstrate that literacy itself is not a good predictor of cognitive skills. Rather, the cognitive performances of different Vai subpopulations can be explained in terms of the psychological and social accompaniments of each literacy tradition, particularly those that are given salience during literacy apprenticeship. For example, Qur'anic literates perform well on incremental recall tests, a reflection of the importance of memory work in Qur'anic schools. Subjects literate in the Vai syllabary perform well in rebus-solving tests, because learning and using the Vai syllabary involves rebus-like problems. Vai persons literate in English, who have attended Western-style schools, do well on tests that resemble school activities, like syllogisms. Thus the pedagogical practices that characterize each literacy experience, rather than literacy itself, shape the individual's cognitive makeup: "particular practices promote particular skills" (Scribner and Cole 1981:258).

Learning how to read and write is not simply a process of developing cognitive skills associated with the decoding and encoding of visual symbols, but also involves learning how these skills are used in their social context. Heath (1983) investigates the implications of this proposition in three communities of the rural American South: Maintown, a white middle-class community; Roadville, a white working-class town; and Trackton, a black working-class community. She found strikingly divergent patterns across these three communities in how children are socialized with respect to such language-related activities as story-telling and book-reading. In Maintown, preschool children are taught to pay attention to books from an early age. Bedtime stories are accompanied by pedagogical practices like question–answer and "initiation–reply–evaluation" sequences. In particular, questions like "What did you like about the story?" resemble the sort of analytic questions that children are expected to answer early on in school contexts. Maintown children also learn the particular turn-taking mechanisms (i.e., when to be silent, when to speak) and fictionalization skills that are valued in schools. In contrast, Roadville children learn to find connections between literacy and "truth." Roadville parents, who are predominantly fundamentalist Christians, use literacy for instruction and moral improvement, and explicitly value the "real" over the "fictional." Reading to children in Roadville is an uncommon event, during which children are taught to be passive participants and the content of written materials is not connected to everyday life (compare Zinsser 1986). Finally, Trackton children learn early in life how to defend themselves orally and to engage in verbal play. Young children receive attention from adults if they can offer a good verbal performance. Adult Trackton residents, who are not literacy-oriented, do not read to children. Children are not asked pedagogical questions about their surroundings; Trackton adults assume that they will learn through their own efforts and by observing adults. In these three communities, pre-school children are exposed to different pedagogical practices and learn to attach different values to literacy, which will accompany them to middle-class-dominated schools and in large part determine their academic performance when it is evaluated according to middle-class standards.[8]

Distinct literacy practices may be associated with different contexts of use, and may thus play divergent roles in the lives of members of a society. Street (1984:132–80), for example, focuses on a rural community in pre-revolutionary Iran, and describes three sets of literacy practices: *maktab* literacy, commercial literacy, and school literacy. Before state schools were introduced into the rural areas, villagers learned reading and writing in Qoranic schools, or *maktabs*. *Maktabs* have traditionally been denigrated by Western commentators and educators because of their emphasis, in good Islamic tradition, on rote learning and repetition. However, in the community in which Street conducted field research, villagers transferred the literacy skills learned in the *maktab* to other contexts. During the boom years of the early 1970s, there was a growing demand from urban areas for village produce, and villagers developed entrepreneurial skills in marketing and distributing their fruit that required making out bills, marking boxes, using checkbooks, and so on. These literate skills were particularly evident among those who had attended *maktabs* and had continued Qoranic learning in their homes; they were able to use literacy skills for commercial purposes, while at the same time extending the range, content, and social function of these skills. In contrast, school literacy acquired in the context of Western-style village schooling did not provide an entry into commercial literacy. It did, however, provide a novel social and economic route to urban professional employment, notably through entry to urban secondary schools. While *maktab* literacy, commercial literacy, and school literacy belonged to different social domains, a single individual might learn more than one of them.

Situations abound in which different literacy practices compete for the same or for closely related intellectual and social spaces in the lives of members of a group. In Seal Bay, an Aleut village in Alaska, one finds two sets of literacy practices, having different historical antecedents, and conflicting social and symbolic associations: a "village" literacy, associated with the Russian Orthodox church, conducted in Aleut using the Cyrillic alphabet; and "outside" literacy, associated with English, schooling, economic transactions, and Baptist missionaries (Reder and Green 1983). These two literacies, which until recently remained functionally separate, have begun to compete in certain contexts. Characteristically, the competition between literacies is both a reflection and an enactment of conflicts between "tradition" and "intrusion," between different economic systems, and between competing religious ideologies.

As the four case studies I have presented here illustrate, competing or coexisting literacy traditions and practices may be associated with different social contexts, different subgroups of a society, or distinct historical antecedents. The resulting tensions across literacy practices frequently become a focus of struggle between contexts, groups, and individuals. Studies of literacy in the comparative-ethnographic tradition can illuminate the ways in which literacy symbolizes and encodes social conflicts of various types.

Event-centered studies

An event-centered approach to literacy typically focuses on one particular social setting where literacy plays a key role and investigates how the social characteristics of the context shape the nature of literacy as it is practiced in that setting. The context may be a social event, e.g., a church service, a class in a religious school, or the session of a court of justice; it may be a social institution, e.g., a school, in which literacy permeates both "on-stage" and "off-stage" activities; or it may be the context of production or consumption of a particular genre, such as personal letter writing or book reading. In all cases, the central object of ethnographic investigation is the way in which literacy derives its meaning from the broader context in which it is practiced, and how other aspects of the situation acquire meaning from acts of reading and writing.

How legal documents are drawn up and evaluated in a particular society is an example of the type of question that event-centered ethnography is particularly well suited to investigate. Messick (1983, also 1993) describes the production and use of written contracts and deeds associated with the ownership of land in a North Yemeni provincial capital prior to the 1962 revolution. These documents are drawn up by members of a class of traditionally educated scholars, or *'ulamā'*. While the documents are rarely dispensed with, their presence does not guarantee the effectiveness of the legal claims they purport to represent, however carefully prepared they might have been. Rather, if these claims are brought to justice, what is examined is the "honor" (i.e., background, demeanor, reputation, and training) of the scholar who prepared the documents. Literacy plays an important role in Yemeni society, and has done so for many centuries; yet the meaning of legal literacy is specific to this society, and is defined in terms of locally salient categories like the honor of the writer. Messick further shows that this meaning can be generalized to other literacy practices in that society, in that literacy and its non-textual context are intermeshed with one another in non-legal settings in ways that resemble the patterns associated with the practice of legal literacy.

Print literacy can be subjected to comparable investigation, as demonstrated in Radway's (1991) study of the romance in Middle America. The romance, probably the single most important literacy genre to enter the lives of many Americans, is an immensely popular but devalued genre that supports a huge industry and that has been the subject of much disagreement among literacy critics and analysts of popular culture (Modleski 1984, Radford 1986). Radway demonstrates that the romance plays a variety of roles in the lives of its readers, who are predominantly women. For example, many readers, who typically lead a rather dreary existence, derive vicarious pleasure in identifying with the heroine of the romance. More importantly, romance reading enables readers to claim a space of their own, in which they are not required to play the nurturing role that husbands and children expect of them. Thus romance reading has a critical character, albeit a covert and non-threatening one. The resistant nature of romance reading does not reside in the text of the novels (which, in fact, often depict women as subservient and powerless), but in the social context in which the novel is consumed.

While it was not designed specifically to do so (and despite its less-than-ethnographic methodology), Radway's research opens up important avenues for an anthropological understanding of literacy consumption in post-industrial societies. First, it demonstrates that, in Western contexts as elsewhere, the meaning of literacy resides in the sociocultural context in which it is embedded, and not in any inherent property of literacy itself: the cultural meaning of a written text must be understood in terms of its relationship with this context, i.e., in terms of who the readers are, what their position is in society, how they use and judge the texts, and so on. Second, literacy can serve to sustain and reproduce certain power relations in society (e.g., between genders or social classes), but it can also help members of society to distance themselves from disadvantageous positions in these relations, and thus resist them in small but significant ways. Finally, Radway's study is a call for greater attention to be paid to mundane and devalued literacy practices like romance reading. The common narrow focus on literacy practices that are "officially" considered legitimate is probably the reason why traditional anthropological paradigms have presented hegemonic attitudes toward literacy as the "natural" consequences of literacy itself.

Shuman's (1986) ethnography of oral and written communication in an inner-city junior high school in the Eastern United States documents the rich literacy culture that adolescents can develop more or less independently of "approved" school literacy. While reading and writing are the primary focus of on-stage pedagogical activities, adolescents also build a complex literate culture of their own, which is only remotely related to official school literacy. For example, they keep diaries, write letters to one another for a variety of purposes, and forge notes to school authorities. Rather than viewing these literacy practices as poor peripheral imitations of writing approved by and intended for adults, Shuman treats them in their own right, and finds them to be governed by complex social rules of interaction. For example, forged "hall passes" to the school authorities are frequently written collaboratively to avoid detection; who one chooses as one's collaborators presupposes a complex social organization of interpersonal alignment, which collaborative writing can either reinforce or modify. An important function of the adolescents' uses of literacy is the negotiation of social distance. For example, threatening notes stuffed into the recipient's locker are less "on record" than verbal challenges to fight, and recipients often ignore them in a manner that would not be possible in face-to-face challenges. In contrast, love notes or "best friend" notes often express intimate feelings that the writer would otherwise feel embarrassed to verbalize. Relative commitment or social distance is thus not a function of the mode of communication (i.e., speaking vs. writing), but is determined by local social norms. The same genre, in different contexts and for different purposes, can either have a distancing function or serve as a token of intimacy. Shuman's ethnography illustrates the potential complexity of the relationship between literacy practices and interactional norms in contexts that, at first glance, appear trivial and dismissable.

Towards methodological synthesis

While the distinction I am drawing between comparative-ethnographic and event-centered approaches reflects broad tendencies in methodological emphasis, it is to a certain extent artificial. Indeed, the cross-contextual comparison of literacy practices presupposes some understanding of the meaning of literacy in each context. Thus the relationship of literacy to the setting in which it is practiced can be most fruitfully studied by first locating the particular literacy practice in the full range of literacy practices extant in the society under scrutiny. Far from being mutually exclusive, these two approaches complement one another, in the sense that a communicative event must be understood both paradigmatically (i.e., in contrast to other communicative events) and syntagmatically (i.e., in terms of its relationship to sociocultural processes). Many of the more effective ethnographic investigations on literacy in particular communities have emerged from a judicious combination of approaches. Interestingly, a certain polarization emerges between the ethnographic settings in which these two methodologies are commonly employed: while many investigations of literacy in post-industrial societies take an event-centered perspective, ethnographers of non-Western settings frequently attempt to describe literacy in those societies in one fell swoop. Considerably more detailed descriptions are thus available on particular literacy events in Western societies than in non-Western settings. In this book, I attempt to remedy this imbalance by approaching the ethnographic materials from both perspectives: I will first investigate various literacy events in detail, and then complement this investigation with a more general assessment of the similarities, differences, and tensions across literacy practices and across the sociocultural and ideological dynamics with which they are associated.

A successful ethnographic investigation of literacy must also be "comparative" in a different way: it must investigate the relationship between literacy and orality. As Keith Basso points out, "writing, wherever it exists, is always only one of several communication channels available to the members of a society. Consequently, the conditions under which it is selected and the purposes to which it is put must be described in relation to those of other channels" (1974:426). Literacy and orality are frequently intertwined in social life, and the relationship between the two must be examined before the meaning of literacy (and of orality, for that matter) can be understood in all its complexities.

The relationship between literacy and orality has been the focus of a substantial body of literature emanating from two subfields of linguistics, namely sociolinguistics and discourse analysis. Primarily concerned with the structural comparison of spoken and written language, investigators working in this tradition have typically taken particular linguistic structures (e.g., subordinate clauses) and analyzed their distribution across various types of spoken and written texts (useful overviews of this research are Akinnaso 1982, Barton 1994:81–94, and Chafe and Tannen 1987). The resulting correlations are then explained in terms of what the researcher perceives as the natural "adaptation" (Pawley and Syder 1983) of language users to various communicative environments (see Chafe 1992 for a pithy statement of this stance). For example, certain types of subordinate clauses are more frequent in many forms of writing than in speaking; this pattern is said to result from the greater amount of leisure that communicators have in typical writing situations to plan and revise the texts they produce, in comparison to spoken communication, which is more immediate and less readily planned. This type of reasoning leads to the identification of oral and literate "strategies," i.e., the structural and stylistic "choices" that language users make to adapt to such factors as the presence or absence of an immediate audience, and the degree of personal "involvement" or "detachment" that they experience *vis-à-vis* the text (Tannen 1985).

Works in this vein recognize that spoken and written communication are neither structurally nor functionally opposed, but lie on a continuum from most literate-like (e.g., academic writing) to most oral-like (e.g., informal conversation); most registers, or situational varieties of language use, fall between these two extremes. Thus the pitfalls of autonomous dichotomizing are to a certain extent overcome. However, problems remain. For example, there is evidence that a unidimensional continuum is inadequate to accommodate the variations in linguistic behaviour across contexts of oral and written communication (Biber 1988).[9] Furthermore, in order for there to be a continuum, there must be well defined extremes, the most literate-like of which is pre-theoretically associated with such features as the effacement of the authorial voice, structural complexity, and informational "repleteness" (for the text to be amenable to processing with little knowledge of the extratextual context), i.e., with the very social stance that the Western academic subculture idealizes (cf. Bailey 1983, Gilbert and Mulkay 1984, Goffman 1981, Mulkay 1979, Prelli 1989). Yet sociolinguists and discourse analysis explain the responses of communicators to different communicative contexts along this continuum in terms of cognitive rather than social processes; in this respect, this tradition of work does not differ from other areas of mainstream linguistics (Ochs 1979b), which defines its task as a search for universal cognitive explanations for language (of course, there are many different accounts of what "cognition" consists of).

While they have suffered from the lack of a social perspective on spoken and written communication, sociolinguistic and discourse analytic studies have nevertheless provided valuable information on structural aspects of literacy, and have contributed the important insight that literacy can be contextualized in orality. However, I am proposing that this contextualization be done in a more specific and cautious manner than is commonly done in sociolinguistics. Rather than attempting to compare widely divergent manifestations of literacy and orality, as I have done elsewhere with some of the material I analyze here (Besnier 1988), I argue here that particular literacy practices be compared with oral practices that bear clear social and cultural affinities to them (cf. Chapter 6).

There is another way in which orality provides a context for literacy. Talk frequently provides a contextual frame for literacy and, as Heath points out, "literacy events have social interactional rules which regulate the type and amount of *talk* about what is written, and defines ways in which *oral language* reinforces, denies, extends, and sets aside the written material" (1983:386, emphasis in original). An investigation of literacy as social practice must therefore pay attention to oral dimensions of literacy events, whose meaning is an integral part of the social definition of literacy, an issue which the autonomous model, incidentally, is ill-equipped to address. Again, I will demonstrate the importance of contextualizing literacy in orality in the ethnographic setting I focus on in this book (cf. Chapter 7 in particular). I will be drawn to explore patterns of oral practice (including styles of singing) that may seem at first glance rather remote from an immediate concern with literacy, and will show that these forays into orality can greatly enrich one's understanding of the social value of certain literacy events.[10]

Beyond dichotomies

The autonomous model of literacy continues to have a strong impact in sociocultural anthropology and on other disciplines that seek inspiration from anthropology. Yet its usefulness as an ethnographic approach and a theoretical construct has been seriously undermined, if not completely disproved, in many works that take the ethnographic description of literacy events and practices as a necessary stepping stone to any serious theoretical statement on literacy. Thus, while this book is not designed to be yet another challenge of the assumptions of the autonomous approach, I will nevertheless point out periodically the difficulties that the autonomous model runs into in the face of empirical evidence.

The main purpose of this work is to further our understanding of literacy in its ethnographic context. Indeed, ethnographic approaches such as Street's ideological model have been justifiably criticized for their particularism, sociological determinism, and emphasis on diversity (e.g., Clanchy 1987, Cole and Nicolopoulou 1992, Miyoshi 1988). An approach that centralizes the particular clearly runs the risk of losing track of the general. Furthermore, the description of single literacy events and the comparison of literacy practices within the same society do not constitute adequate ends for a research agenda that professes to be a theoretical endeavor.

This work is aimed in part to address these criticisms and to provide the foundation of a more ambitiously theoretical program for an ethnographically based approach to literacy. From a theoretical perspective, contemporary approaches to literacy must now move away from defining themselves in negative contrast to earlier deterministic models, and must seek generalizations that will be of use in our understanding of literacy as a human phenomenon, albeit a very heterogeneous one. To date, much work on literacy has been devoted to demonstrating the fact that literacy must be understood in terms of its sociocultural context. While this point is of utmost importance and bears repeating (I will do so periodically throughout this study), research questions must now be posed more precisely. Specifically, the challenge that faces the study of literacy in its social context is to identify *which* aspects of context are most likely to affect and be affected by acts of reading and writing, and *how* modes of communication are embedded in society and culture. Broader comparative questions must be addressed, and bridges established between the concerns of the ethnography of literacy and other traditions of inquiry that have focused on related ethnographic problems. This study explores various avenues for a comparative understanding of the relationship between literacy and its sociocultural context, and identifies ways in which generalizations can be sought in the study of literacy from an ethnographic and critical perspective.

Several avenues can be pursued in theorizing literacy. One line of research that has been fruitfully followed is to locate literacy in the structures of power, broadly speaking, extant in society. Works in this vein investigate how certain forms of literacy are used as an instrument or justification for the maintenance of structures of social inequality; how different forms of literacy (e.g., school literacy vs. home literacy, "official" forms vs. grassroots forms, print literacy vs. non-print literacy, etc.) become associated with various social groups, contexts, and purposes that occupy different positions in hegemonic structures; and how specific literacy activities can become the vehicle for resistance and contestation. Several examples of works that address these issues have already been discussed. This body of research can make important contributions to social theory by demonstrating how everyday reading and writing practices (as examples of everyday social practices in general) contribute to the maintenance of power or the emergence of resistance. It can also denaturalize the ideological makeup of schools, religious ceremonies, legal institutions, and bureaucracies, as well as everyday domestic settings. The bulk of the research that has addressed issues of literacy and power has focused on educational institutions in post-industrial societies, one of the most obvious sites of sociocultural reproduction (see Bloome and Green 1992 for a review). However, ethnographically informed works on literacy and power in other settings are beginning to emerge (e.g., Lambek 1993, Lindstrom 1990, Messick 1993, Street [ed.] 1993, to name only a few).

In this study, I will explore aspects of the relationship between literacy and social inequality, particularly in the form of gender hierarchy and religious authority. However, in the context that this book focuses on, this relationship is not as compelling a focus of ethnographic inquiry as in many other societies, for reasons that I discuss more fully in Chapter 8. In the pages that follow, I will therefore pay more attention to the relationship between literacy and other social and cultural processes, whose connections to literacy are less well described cross-culturally, and are certainly under-theorized. I will document, for example, the intimate and complex connection that can exist between certain forms of literacy (e.g., personal letters) and certain aspects of emotionality. I will show that this connection must be understood both as a material and symbolic phenomenon. In the ethnographic setting described here, economic transactions with the outside world are monitored and negotiated through letters, and because economic transactions are generally understood as emotion-driven social actions, letters become mediating tools between emotions and material transactions, and the site where emotionality and economic transactions are "translated" into one another. This example illustrates one way in which an in-depth ethnographic investigation of literacy, by identifying areas of social life and culture in which written communication is likely to play a pivotal role, can contribute to more general anthropological concerns. The validity of the hypotheses I present here, of course, will have to be tested further in light of comparative data from other societies, once these data become available.

As I have already argued, the socio-cultural context of literacy is what gives reading and writing activities their meaning. To rephrase this point metaphorically, society and culture "bleed" onto literacy. Of theoretical concern is the nature of this "bleeding" process: how do literacy activities acquire meaning from the extra-communicative context in which they take place? This question will be of particular interest here when I consider the gendering of literacy, a theme that I invoke intermittently throughout the book and address in a more focused manner in Chapter 8. The ethnographic situation lends itself well to investigating how literacy and a social category like gender are linked, because there is no obvious gender-based asymmetry in access to literacy in the community, even though the various literacy activities that members of the community engage in do have gendered qualities. The argument I will develop necessitates that I cast a wide ethnographic net over this particular society and culture, because it invokes widely divergent issues, including emotionality, personhood, and political power, as well as issues of norms and their transgression. I will demonstrate that gender and particular literacy practices are related indexically, and thus that their relationship is non-determining, open to divergent interpretations, and contingent on context. Furthermore, the characteristics of literacy activities contribute to the gendering of persons who engage in them as much as gender gives a social shape to literacy activities, and thus the relationship between the literacy and gender is constitutive.

A final question of theoretical interest for an ideological approach is how literacy develops when it is first introduced to a previously "non-literate" society (I use this term bearing in mind the caveats discussed earlier). Here, unfortunately, very little comparative information is available. With a few exceptions, studies of incipiently literate situations are ethnographically thin, and are predominantly concerned with ill-defined and theoretically problematic notions like the "acceptance" of literacy by pre-literate peoples. However, the historical stance that I adopt in this study suggests a number of interesting avenues. First, the situation I describe in the following pages illustrates the discrepant intentions that the introducers and the recipients of literacy often have, and centralizes the issue of who has control over literacy both within and across groups. Recent (and all too few) ethnographic studies of contemporary efforts to introduce literacy to areas of the world like Papua New Guinea bear witness to struggles over what literacy should be for, and in what contexts and for what purposes it should be consumed or produced. This book will highlight the particularly important role that letter writing appears to play in the history of literacy in many societies as a pivotal genre that people readily "latch onto," and from which other genres emerge. Unfortunately, the dearth of comparative information on incipiently literate situations precludes the articulation of anything but the most tentative of hypotheses on this topic at this time.

Plan of this study

This book focuses on the social uses of literacy on Nukulaelae Atoll in the Central Pacific. The approach I adopt has a strong empirical base: I will describe in detail the roles that reading and writing play in the daily life of Nukulaelae Islanders, and how literacy, in the course of the atoll's history, developed the characteristics it has nowadays. In particular, I will seek to understand the meaning that literacy has for the members of this society in terms of the social contexts in which it occurs, its symbolic associations, and its historical antecedents.

In Chapter 2, I describe the ethnographic and historical background of this study, many details of which become relevant to the analysis of literacy I present in subsequent chapters. I first describe the social and political organization of the atoll community, its links with the outside world, its economic conditions, and its ideological makeup, particularly in reference to internal politics. I then turn to the history of the atoll, which can only be reconstructed from rather fragmentary records. I emphasize the circumstances that formed a backdrop to the introduction of literacy to the atoll in the nineteenth century, namely the missionization of the community, its victimization by slavers, the establishment of a German-owned plantation, and the beginning of British colonial rule. These events shaped the historical evolution of Nukulaelae's relationship with the rest of the world, an understanding of which is an important prerequisite for an analysis of the evolution of letter writing. I close the chapter with a discussion of the problematics of boundary setting in ethnography.

In Chapter 3, I first discuss the languages relevant to life on the atoll, focusing in particular on the two extraneous languages of particular importance to literacy activities, namely Samoan and English. I then turn to schooling and its historical background. While many authors have stressed the importance of disentangling schooling from literacy in ethnography (e.g., Akinnaso 1992, Cook-Gumperz 1986, Scribner and Cole 1981, Street and Street 1991), I nevertheless show that an understanding of their ideological relationship is important, particularly since they are taken to be one and the same in both historical and contemporary representations. However, most of this study is devoted to literacy events conducted outside pedagogical settings, and my discussion of school literacy is necessarily brief. I then turn to the historical development of literacy itself, insofar as it can be disassociated from the history of education and religious conversion. Chapter 3 closes with a survey of social contexts in which Nukulaelae Islanders engage in reading and writing activities; in this survey I emphasize "non-textual" literacy practices, i.e., those that do not use or give rise to continuous written texts. In the rest of the book, I focus primarily on textual literacy practices.

The most prominent of these practices is letter writing, to which I devote Chapters 4 and 5. In the first of these chapters, I describe the context in which letters are written, who writes and reads them, and the form that they take. My discussion is based on a fine-grained analysis of a large corpus of letters, as well as observations of the way Nukulaelae Islanders write and read letters, how they perceive them in comparison to, say, oral forms of communication, and how they theorize about them in ethnographic interviews. The second chapter analyzes the same ethnographic materials in greater depth, and investigates the social and cultural meaning of letter writing and reading. I show that members of the community use letters to monitor economic transactions with the rest of the world, nurture geographically dispersed networks of reciprocity, and transmit information. Letters are thus deeply embedded in patterns of exchange of both material and symbolic commodities (e.g., goods and gossip), and, as such, they are but one link in communicative networks that straddle the boundary between literacy and orality. Above all, letter writing is the locus of emotional displays of a certain kind, a characteristic that permeates many of the social roles that letters play. I demonstrate that letter writing is a means through which Nukulaelae Islanders display a particularly vulnerable and emotional facet of their personhood to their interactors, which they do not generally do in face-to-face interactions. I explain this attribute in terms of the symbolic associations between letter writing and separation, an emotionally charged phenomenon in Nukulaelae society.

Reading and writing figure prominently in religious activities on the atoll. More specifically, sermons, the core element of the church service, are written out ahead of time, and their oral delivery is based on this prepared written document. In Chapter 6, I describe the church service as a social event, and compare the sermon with secular oratory, a genre with which it shares many features. I then investigate the similarities and differences between written sermons and their oral versions, and identify the textual transformations that take place at the time of oral delivery. Next, I investigate the puzzle that the very existence of written sermons presents: why do preachers prepare their sermons in advance, when they can engage in elaborate oratorical performances in other contexts without written prompts? There are several answers to this question, some of which are explicit in Nukulaelae Islanders' explanations, while others are more covert: written sermons are embedded in a system of knowledge trans- mission; and they contribute to the sense of order that Islanders particularly value in religious contexts. Further insight into the problem can be obtained through an investigation of sermons as oral performances, which I present in Chapter 7. In this chapter, my analysis takes a methodological turn, as I investigate oral sermons as performance events and analyze the role that written sermons play in the performative aspects of the genre: because the essence of sermon deliveries "resides in the assumption of responsibility to an audience for a display of communicative skill" (Bauman 1986:3), sermons are performance events *par excellence*, much more so than letters. Approaching sermons from a performance-centered perspective, I demonstrate that the genre occupies a privileged position with respect to truth-seeking. However, truth-seeking can only be performed successfully if one has the authority to do so. This prerequisite is of special concern on Nukulaelae, where all forms of authority are by nature suspect, and where the performance of sermons is accompanied by powerful displays of authority. I demonstrate that written forms of sermons help ground this authority, and do so by relying on their privileged relationship to the truth and on the fact that they potentially have multiple coauthors. I also discuss how these dimensions shed light on the gendered nature of written sermons, which are produced almost exclusively by men. Thus, rather than merely serving as mnemonic devices, written sermons have a complex meaning that can only be understood by considering the ideological associations of the context in which they are composed and performed.

In the conclusion, I analyze the implications of the Nukulaelae material for theoretical concerns. I first deconstruct the category "restricted literacy," which is commonly invoked to describe similar ethnographic contexts. Characterizing Nukulaelae literacy as restricted leads to a contradiction. Rather, Nukulaelae literacy is better understood as an instance of "incipient literacy," a notion that, unlike "restricted literacy," makes no claim of internal homogeneity or unified theoretical status. After briefly comparing the Nukulaelae material with several other cases of incipient literacy, I present hypotheses about the trajectory of reading and writing following their initial introduction.

My discussion then turns to the implications of the ethnographic description for a theoretical understanding of how reading and writing practices articulate with the contexts in which they take place. I highlight several specially significant social and cultural categories. I first investigate how hegemonic structures are imposed and maintained through literacy practices. The case of Nukulaelae is particularly interesting because today literacy is not used as a hegemonic tool in any obvious manner. While it did emerge as an instrument of domination in its very early history, literacy soon was empowered by the dominated. Today, literacy is conspicuous in contexts where social asymmetries are prominent, but several of its characteristics also make it a means through which the community's egalitarian ideology is reinforced. Thus, rather than being a tool for either domination or resistance, literacy can have a multiplicity of seemingly contradictory meanings that depend crucially on the social contexts of reading and writing practices. I demonstrate how this context-dependence operates with respect to one specific hegemonic formation, namely gender asymmetry. Recapitulating the ethnographic particulars of the interaction between gender and literacy, I show that this relationship is not a simple symbolic correlation, since both women and men in principle have equal access to reading and writing. Rather, Nukulaelae literacy practices are indexically gendered. More precisely, the relationship between reading and writing activities on the one hand and the attributes of men and women on the other is mediated by the semiotic associations between particular types of emotion and gender groups. Finally, I demonstrate how local definitions of the person help define literacy on Nukulaelae and elsewhere, and isolate personhood as a category whose role in giving meaning to literacy practices must become the focus of a context-sensitive approach to reading and writing.

2

THE ETHNOGRAPHIC CONTEXT

Nukulaelae

Nukulaelae is an atoll in the South-Central Pacific, part of the island group and nation of Tuvalu, formerly known as the Ellice Islands. This chain of nine low-rising coral atolls and islands spans 400 miles, between the latitudes of 5°S and 11°S, and the longitudes of 176°E and 180°. The group is situated on the outskirts of Triangle Polynesia, close to the Gilbert Islands (Kiribati), which lie to the north and are the easternmost island group of Micronesia (see Map 1). Tuvalu can be subdivided geographically into a northern group, made up of Nanumea, Nanumaga, Niutao, and Nui (phonemically, *Nuui*), and a southern group, which includes Vaitupu, Nukufetau, Funafuti (phonemically, *Funaafuti*), Nukulaelae, and the southernmost and smallest island of the group, Niulakita. This last was not settled permanently until the twentieth century and is used today as copra-producing grounds by Niutao Islanders. The group's total land area is 10 square miles.

As a typical atoll, Nukulaelae consists of an oval-shaped string of islets that surrounds a lagoon and is itself surrounded by a coral-reef ring (see Map 2). Submerged reef platforms and sand bars bridge the breaks between the islets. The entire atoll, including the lagoon, is about 2 miles at its widest and 6 miles long. Even by atoll standards, it is very small: its dry-land area is 449 acres, and its maximum elevation rests a few feet above sea level. It is surrounded by deep seas, which provide rich harvesting grounds for pelagic fish. The nearest land is Funafuti atoll, 70 nautical miles to the North; Fiji, the closest larger land mass and cosmopolitan center, is 600 miles to the South. Nukulaelae and the rest of the group lie outside of the main belt of tropical westerly winds, and thus hurricanes are rare. However, the morphology of the atoll makes it vulnerable to the occasional storm (cf. Brady 1978, McLean and Munro 1991). Droughts are also a problem, although they generally do not last long, compared to the devastating and frequent dry periods that islands closer to the Equator, such as the Southern Gilberts, experience. Nukulaelae offers no safe anchorage for sea crafts, and reaching land from the ocean involves a dangerous reef crossing

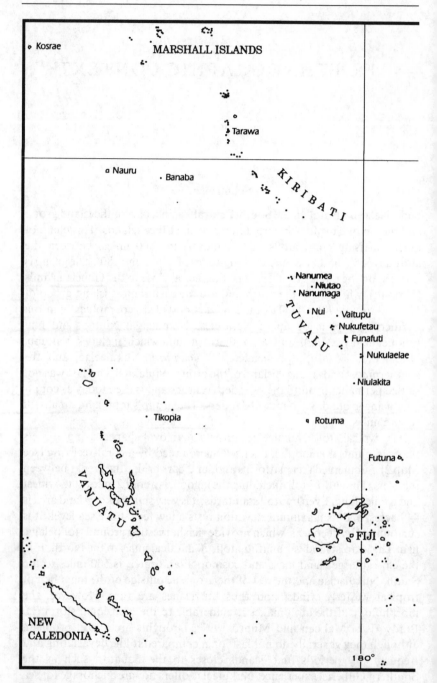

Map 1   *The Central Pacific*

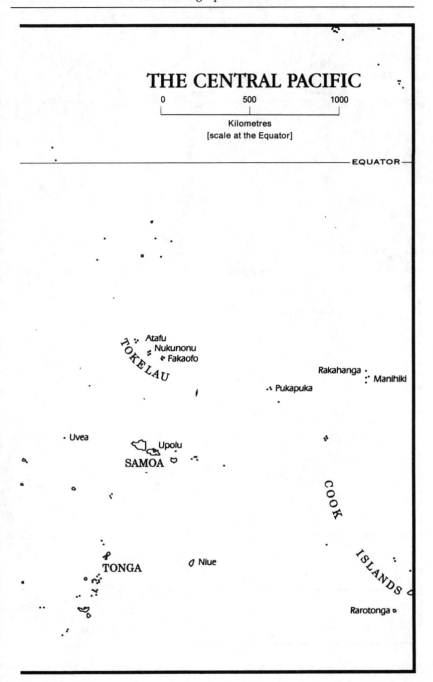

THE CENTRAL PACIFIC

0   500   1000

Kilometres
[scale at the Equator]

EQUATOR

Atafu
Nukunonu
Fakaofo

TOKELAU

Rakahanga
Manihiki

Pukapuka

Uvea

Upolu

SAMOA

COOK

TONGA   Niue

ISLANDS

Rarotonga

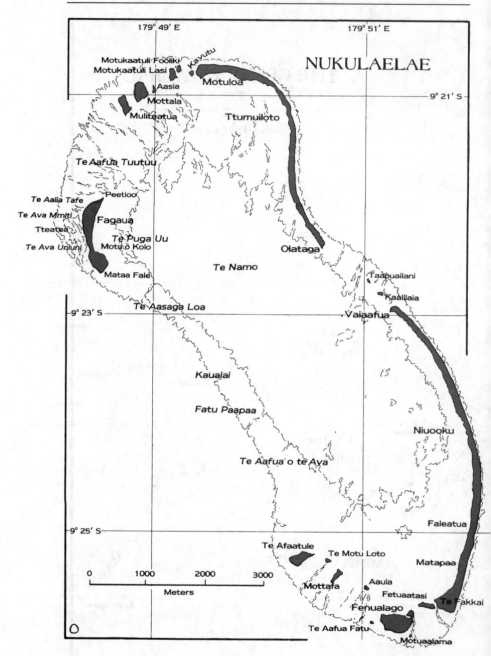

Map 2 *Nukulaelae*

Figure 1   *Partial view of the atoll from the lagoon side of Fagaua Islet,*
showing on the horizon, from left to right, Mottala, Aasia, Motukaatuli Lasi,
and part of Motuloa Islet.

which can only be accomplished in a shallow canoe or barge and only at
certain times of the day.

People and movements

In 1979, at the last census prior to my field work (Iosia and Macrae [eds.]
1980), there were 347 residents on Nukulaelae, out of a total population of
7349 for Tuvalu. The atoll's population in the second half of the twentieth
century fluctuated between 300 and 350, but it remained well below 200
between the 1860s and the 1930s (Munro and Bedford 1980, Bedford,
Macdonald, and Munro 1980). In addition, a substantial number of
persons who identify themselves as Nukulaelae Islanders reside more or less
permanently on Funafuti, the country's capital, and periodically visit
Nukulaelae.[1]

   The inhabitants of the atoll speak a Polynesian language, and they are
generally identified as a Polynesian people. However, as I will discuss
presently, this identification obscures the complex human intermixing from
which the atoll's contemporary inhabitants descend. Nevertheless, both
culturally and linguistically, Nukulaelae does have strong affinities to the
rest of Polynesia. The only permanent settlement today is located on

Fagaua, a small, crowded islet that bounds the lagoon to the West. The reason for this settlement pattern is that the fresh-water lens that "floats" under the surface of the porous coral soil, pushed on each side by the heavier ocean water (the so-called Ghyben-Herzberg lens, found beneath all atolls), is less brackish on Fagaua than on other islets.

The soil of the atoll consists essentially of alkaline coral sand, upon which a layer of vegetable sediment has accumulated naturally or artificially since the formation of the atoll. The quality of the soil is poor, and it must constantly be nurtured by hand: for generations, Nukulaelae Islanders have been harvesting leaves and other vegetable materials for compost, which is applied strategically to the bases of food plants. This laborious task requires regular trips to the uninhabited islets of the atoll across the lagoon, where wild leafy plants are plentiful, and where coconuts are also harvested. Land resources are limited, particularly when contrasted with the extreme fertility of volcanic and continental islands of the Pacific (which Nukulaelae Islanders never cease to marvel at when they go abroad). Besides the coconut tree (*niu*, Cocos nucifera) and the pandanus (*fala*, Pandanus pulposus), two very early imports, the only food plant that grows readily in this type of environment is the swamp taro (*pulaka*, Cyrtosperma chamissonis). It is a hardy plant recognizable by its very large leaves, whose starchy corm (i.e., the bulbous underground core to which the leaf stems are attached) is the main staple of the atoll diet. It is cultivated in gardens at the bottom of large pits (*vai pulaka* or *umaga*), of which there are two on the atoll, one on Fagaua, the other on Mottala islet. The first is the largest of the two; it is approximately 300 yards long and 100 yards wide. Dug by hand over several generations, the pit reaches down 15 to 20 feet to the fresh-water lens.

Other than swamp taro, the various edible products of the ubiquitous coconut tree (e.g., meat, milk, sap, spongious kernel of the mature nut) figure prominently in the atoll diet. Other vegetable foods that are gathered or more or less successfully cultivated include breadfruits (*mei*, Artocarpus altilis), bananas (*futi*), papayas (*oolesi*), sugar cane (*tolo*), a few small taro plants (*talo*, Colocasia esculenta) and sweet potatoes (*pateta*), ficus (*felo*, Ficus tinctoris), edible ferns, and some pumpkins (*panikeni*), all of which were imported in historical times. In contrast to produce, sea resources are abundant, varied, and readily accessible both on the shallow reef and in deeper ocean waters, and Nukulaelae Islanders are a skillful fisherfolk. Products from the sea are supplemented by coconut crabs (*uu*, Birgus latro) and small edible birds, both special delicacies, and domesticated pigs and fowl, both post-contact introductions. Imported foods, mainly rice, flour, tea, and sugar (and, occasionally, canned fish and meat), are also available at the small cooperative store, and are well established in the Nukulaelae diet, although stocks run out periodically because of erratic shipping.

Figure 2   *The path leading from the village to the bush on Fagaua Islet, with the swamp-taro pit in the background. The leaves of swamp taro and banana trees growing in the pit are visible.*

Oral history bears witness to early contacts between Nukulaelae and other islands of Tuvalu. Pre-historical contacts with other Pacific islands (e.g., Gilbert Islands, Rotuma, Tonga, Samoa, Futuna, Uvea, Tokelau and Polynesian Outliers) are also not improbable. Traditionally, Nukulaelae Islanders and other Tuvaluans traveled between the islands of the group on large sailing outrigger canoes (see Kennedy 1931 and Koch 1961 for descriptions of canoes on other islands of the group). Smaller versions of these crafts are still in common use, though many have been replaced since the early 1980s by dinghies with outboard motors. Voyages between the islands involved high risk and required sophisticated navigational skills. Nukulaelae oral traditions include stories of many trips to and from the atoll, and their sometimes tragic outcomes. One such instance concerns a canoe captained by Makaga, a historical hero. In the mid-nineteenth century, Makaga and his crew missed Nukulaelae while returning from Funafuti and drifted 85 nautical miles south to Niulakita, where the remains of a canoe believed to be theirs were discovered several decades later (Kelese Simona, personal communication, also in Roberts 1958). However, by the end of the nineteenth century, Tuvaluans had lost much of the art of long-distance navigation, which the colonial administration forbade anyway from the 1890s on. Since World War II, Nukulaelae and all other atolls of Tuvalu have been visited with varying degrees of regularity by a government vessel, which called once a month on average during my field work. In the 1980s, Tuvalu had only one combined passenger and cargo ship, the M.V. *Nivaga II* (phonemically, *Niivaga*). It is on this vessel that the transmission of letters, the writing and reading of which is one of the major Nukulaelae literacy activities, depends (cf. Chapter 4).

Despite the infrequency of interisland communications, Nukulaelae Islanders have always yearned to travel, and many today have visited or migrated to other parts of Tuvalu and the Pacific. Within Tuvalu, Funafuti is the most common destination of temporary and permanent migratory movements from Nukulaelae and the other outer islands of the group (Connell 1986, Wit 1980, 1984). In return, there are always a number of non-Nukulaelae Islanders in residence on the atoll at any time. They include persons with kinship and affinal ties to the community, the pastor, and a handful of government employees, including the Island Executive Officer (IEO), the Telegraph Operator, and a couple of primary-school teachers.

Various social factors have traditionally facilitated interisland migration. Land tenure, an important determiner of an individual's allegiance to and status on a particular island, is based on a complex pattern of shared ownership and claims to membership of corporate groups of kin. This system allows individuals to claim rights on several islands at once. Kinship ties between islands are created through adoption, fosterage, and exogamous marriages (*aavaga ki tai*, literally, "to marry seaward"), which are frequent and can be either virilocal or uxorilocal. Descent is reckoned bilaterally, which helps to maximize the economic options of individuals, although patrilineal descent is stronger than matrilineal descent: patrilineal ties are referred to as *toto maalosi* "strong blood," in opposition to *toto vaaivai* "weak blood" on the mother's side. The land crunch (*oge manafa* "land famine") typical of life on other atolls is somewhat less of a problem on Nukulaelae than elsewhere in Tuvalu: in 1979, the average number of claims per acre of land was lowest on Nukulaelae than on any other island. That same year, 91 percent of Nukulaelae's population had land claims on at least one island of the group other than their home island (the highest percentage for all of Tuvalu), although the pattern is reversed for local land claims: only 45 percent of all land claims on Nukulaelae were made by non-local people, the second lowest figure for the group (Chambers and Chambers 1980). However, it is well understood that in the hypothetical case of all non-resident Nukulaelae Islanders returning to the atoll to live, the carrying capacity of the atoll's resources would be far exceeded. Land matters remain sensitive issues, particularly when unreasonable claims are pressed by "outsiders," i.e., persons whose kin ties to the atoll are judged to be tenuous (e.g., through an illegitimate line, adoptive ties, or too much "weak blood"). All island communities in Tuvalu have traditionally minimized the legitimacy of inter-island land claims by integrating affinal outsiders into the local socioeconomic system, thus ensuring that their descendants' strongest allegiance is to the local community rather than to their island of origin (Brady 1970, 1972, 1974, 1976, Butinov 1982, and Koch 1963 describe Tuvaluan kinship, land tenure, and adoption in detail).

The effect of personal friendship bonds is sometimes comparable to kinship ties in that they may be sealed with gifts of land or lead to temporary or permanent migration from one island to the other (Koch 1963). Furthermore, the islands of Tuvalu are "paired" together (*fakasoa*, literally, "make friends") in a pattern of community-wide friendship. Such a tie binds together Nukulaelae and Vaitupu. These enduring and non-exclusive bonds are consolidated through regular exchanges or *malaga* "traveling parties," which consist in large groups of individuals from one island visiting the other island for several weeks at a time. During these visits, competitions of all kinds (games, food exchanges, etc.) take place, and they usually result in several inter-island marriages and a couple of illegitimate children. Davies (1873:2) reports finding on his mission visit to Nukulaelae ninety Vaitupu Islanders, including the "king" of Vaitupu, and G.A. Turner (1874:7) the following year describes the reciprocal *malaga* from Nukulaelae to Vaitupu, which included the Nukulaelae "king," the Samoan pastor, and twenty islanders. We do not know if this tradition predates conversion to Christianity (the term *malaga* is a borrowing from Samoan, which suggests a post-missionization innovation), but we do know that it was firmly established by the end of the nineteenth century.

Economic life

The most consequential patterns of migration away from the atoll are economically motivated. Like other outer-island Tuvaluans, many Nukulaelae Islanders migrate to Funafuti primarily because all employment opportunities in the country are located there. However, between the end of World War II and the last decades of the century, the most important migratory destinations were Ocean Island, or Banaba (phonemically *Paanapa*), and Nauru (Wit 1984, Munro and Bedford 1990). In both cases, Tuvalu citizens, as well as islanders from the Gilberts and other parts of the Pacific, were hired to work for a couple of years at a time in the phosphate industry as laborers, petty office and service-industry workers, and occasionally nurses and foremen.[2] Workers with families were generally allowed to bring their spouse and one child with them. In the heyday of phosphate extraction, up to 200 Tuvaluans from various islands resided on Ocean Island; the 1979 census reports 35 Nukulaelae Islanders on Nauru, out of a total of 400 Tuvaluans. Wages were very modest, and rights and

In the context of widely spread social & economic ties.

benefits restricted. At the time of writing, Nauru's phosphate supply is virtually depleted, and the influx of labor from Nukulaelae and the rest of Tuvalu is about to cease. In the same way, the British Phosphate Commission ended wage labor in 1980 when phosphate reserves were depleted on Ocean Island. Employment on Nauru and Ocean Island provided one of the few sources of cash for Nukulaelae. Remittances from relatives on Nauru and the savings that workers brought back with them enabled Nukulaelae Islanders to meet the increasing need for money. Sojourns on Nauru enabled Nukulaelae Islanders to stock up on high-prestige items like tools, radios, dinghies, outboard motors, fish nets, and clothing, many of which are not readily available in Tuvalu. Nukulaelae workers on Nauru and Ocean Island also provided most of the financing for large-scale communal development projects, such as the construction of sea walls to protect the swamp-taro pits from sea-water seepage, the building of a new meeting house, the erection of water-catchment tanks to alleviate chronic water shortages, and so on. As discussed in Chapter 4, the demands placed on the Nukulaelae people on Nauru were considerable.

There are virtually no commercially exploitable resources on the atoll. Copra (dried coconut meat), the major Pacific Islands industry since the first moment of contact, ceased to be produced in any quantity in the 1970s, as the decreasing demand for the product made prices plummet; and attempts over the years to introduce such cash-generating industries as mother-of-pearl cultivation, bêche-de-mer processing, and fish drying have consistently failed for many different reasons. Yet, despite the appearance of self-sufficiency, the atoll's economy has depended on imports for many decades, and money has a well-established history in this society. Small items like soap, cloth, fishing line, fish hooks, pots and pans, and paper and writing implements have long figured on the list of items sold at the trading store, and later the cooperative store; most of these items are now considered necessities, with the addition of modern items like kerosene and batteries. Most store-bought food is generally dispensable, but many on the atoll find it hard to live without tea, sugar, and rice for any length of time. Regular customary gifts to the pastor have long included cash, and the sums involved in fund-raising competitions and other forms of gift transactions have increased dramatically in recent years. In the early 1980s, all houses in the village, which until then had been open thatched structures, were rebuilt with wooden frames, cement bricks, and corrugated iron roofs; this innovation suddenly created an unprecedented demand for money, aggravated by the simultaneous appearance of fuel guzzling outboard motors brought back from Nauru. As a result, Nukulaelae is fast becoming desperately cash hungry. The absence of commercially exploitable resources other than labor puts great strain on the economic viability of the community.

Fortunately, since the mid-1980s, Tuvalu has gained access to sources of cash: a few contract workers from Tuvalu have been allowed to go to work in New Zealand each year, but more importantly, Hong Kong and German shipping companies have begun hiring young Tuvaluan men. The pattern is not new: Tuvaluans have worked as sailors on Western ships since the earliest days of contact. However, the new wave of seamen has acquired a prominence that their predecessors did not have. Not only is the new crop numerically more important, but it has access to considerably more money than any group of Nukulaelae migrant laborers that preceded it (even though seamen's salaries are generally well below international standards), and it will soon become the sole substantial source of monetary income for Nukulaelae and the rest of the country. The structure of this labor force differs significantly from that of wage labor on Nauru. While the latter included women, older men, and children, only younger men who have successfully completed rigorous training at Funafuti's Amatuku Marine Training School can become seamen. Furthermore, while Nukulaelae people formed a community on Nauru, seamen are relatively isolated from one another. Finally, the income from seamen's salaries greatly exceeds the sums which Nukulaelae Islanders were used to handling up until now. The implications of these changing circumstances for the future of Nukulaelae and other islands of Tuvalu remain to be investigated (but see Besnier 1991 for the beginning of an analysis).

Tuvalu's economy, in which Nukulaelae's economy is embedded, has been described as a MIRAB economy, an acronym coined from terms referring to the four cornerstones of such systems: migration, remittances, aid, and bureaucracy (Bertram and Watters 1985; see also Munro 1990a). MIRAB economies are also found in other Pacific micro-states and, despite their apparent inviability, are surprisingly stable and resilient. Among the various characterizing factors of Tuvalu's MIRAB economy, migration and remittances are directly relevant to Nukulaelae. By and large, the effects of foreign aid and bureaucracy are confined to Funafuti. However, bureaucracy affects Nukulaelae and the other Outer Islands of Tuvalu indirectly, in that it is because of employment opportunities in government that many Nukulaelae Islanders migrate to the capital. All in all, Tuvalu's MIRAB economy has important consequences for the purposes of this study: it results in the creation of geographically dispersed but cohesive kinship networks whose members maintain a lively system of economic exchanges, in which reciprocity figures prominently. As discussed in Chapter 5, these relationships of reciprocity are nurtured principally through letters.

Spacial and social organizations

Nukulaelae oral traditions suggest that the pre-contact population was dispersed in hamlets scattered around the lagoon. Its consolidation into a single village was implemented either by the Samoan religious teachers who missionized Nukulaelae, or by the British colonial authorities, or both. A site called Te Fakai (phonemically, *Te Fakkai*, literally, "the settlement") at the southern end of Niuoku islet (see Map 2) was the location of a main early settlement. Coral house foundations, probably of post-contact manufacture, are still visible, and there are remnants of shrine-like structures at Fale Atua (literally, "House of Gods") just north of Te Fakai. Older persons describe the main village as having migrated gradually around the atoll in a counter-clockwise fashion from site to site. The modern village on Fagaua islet is built around several important structures. The imposing coral-lime church building towers in the center, and south of it is the *maneapa*, a house in which all major community events (e.g., feasts and political meetings) are held. The maneapa is the center of "traditional" life for the community, although the concept of a community house is clearly a post-conversion innovation (Goldsmith 1985); the name itself is a borrowing from a Gilbertese word, *m'aneaba*. The church building and the maneapa are surrounded by an empty grassy area, the *malae*, or "village green," also likely to be a post-contact concept (despite the antiquity of cognate institutions in many other Polynesian societies). At the northern end of the village, in an area called Petio (phonemically, *Peetioo*, after Betio, the islet of Tarawa Atoll in the Gilbert Islands that housed the headquarters of the Gilbert and Ellice Islands Colony), is the Fakai o te Malo (phonemically, *Fakkai o te Maaloo*, literally, "Government Settlement"), where the Island Council building, the telegraph office, the primary school, the dispensary, the rest house for visiting dignitaries, and the homes of government employees are located. The pastor's house and its adjoining meeting house is also in the same area, separated from the rest of the village by an empty lot and a coconut grove.

On each side of the *malae*, maneapa, and church, houses are neatly aligned in two main rows along the two parallel and very straight village paths. These rows define the "village sides" (*feituu ala*), named *Pepesala* and *Nukualofa*, that function as important organizational units in community activities. The main houses are generally close together and uniform in construction. Either adjacent to them or closer to the shore are cooking huts, in which much of daily life actually takes place. Cooking huts often double as sleeping huts, particularly if they are close to the lagoon or ocean where the breeze blows and mosquitos are fewer. At the edge of the village, the two paths narrow down and begin meandering as they circle the swamp-taro pit and join up into a single path to the southern end of the islet, through coconut groves and past an unobtrusive cemetery.

The inhabitants of the atoll organize themselves in approximately sixty-five residential units (*fale*, literally "house"), the number and composition of which can vary across time and space, and thirty land-holding groups of kin (*pui kaaiga*). For many purposes (e.g., the distribution of communal

Figure 3   *The maneapa.*

labor, representation to the Council of Elders), the household is the most
important social unit. However, Nukulaelae society is divided into multiple
social groups of all kinds (some of which are more fundamental to the
organization of daily life than others), whose membership criss-crosses the
community in extremely complex ways. These groups are frequently (but
not always) organized according to principles of binary complementarity, a
very familiar pattern on Polynesian atolls (Hooper 1969, Sahlins 1958). For
example, every individual belongs to one of the two *feituu ala* "village
sides," which sponsor communal work parties, fund-raising activities, and
feasts and dances on various occasions. Usually, membership is determined
by residence: one belongs to the village side associated with the village
"half" where one lives. However, one may also change village side if one
moves (e.g., after marriage) or for more trivial reasons. An individual may
also belong to a dancing club, the island choir, the Youth Group, an
organization of young agriculturalists, and so on. Membership in some
groups is individually based, while in others it involves entire households or
families. Groups constantly emerge and disappear, and some manage to
monopolize an enormous amount of time, attention, and resources, even
surpassing in importance, for a brief moment, the most fundamental social
institutions. Competition between rival groups has also been known to
bring the community to the brink of civil war. All organizational units,

including more enduring ones, can vary widely in composition and size across time and space, a symptom of the overall malleability of the atoll's social organization (cf. Brady 1970).

Since the beginning of the 1980s, the atoll has been under the political leadership of a Council of Elders (*taupulega*) headed by an elected chief (*ulu fenua*).[3] The exact function of the Council and the chief, and the extent of their authority, are hotly contested topics, which I have analyzed elsewhere (Besnier 1991). Briefly, much of the controversy surrounding leadership and authority on the atoll is embedded in the complexity of its inhabitants' political ideology. Two broad strands can be discerned in the Nukulaelae prescriptive schema for political organization. On the one hand, one finds a yearning for an iron-fisted leadership which, when it operates legitimately, brings *manuia* "prosperity, fortune," *gali* "beauty," and *fiileemuu* "peace, quiet" to the community, and nurtures the spirit of harmonious communalism, unity, and consensus that Nukulaelae Islanders emphasize so insistently in self-characterizations. This ideology, which echoes many quintessential Polynesian themes (cf. Marcus 1989), is thought to have characterized the community in *aso taumua* "the days bygone," when the chief's authority over the atoll was absolute. This *discourse of nostalgia* is at the root of the reestablishment, in the early 1980s, of a "traditional" chiefly structure, comparable to inventions of tradition witnessed in many other parts of the Pacific (White 1992).

However, Nukulaelae Islanders also articulate a fierce spirit of egalitarianism, according to which everyone in the community is on the same footing and no one is entitled to exert authority over others. Within this discourse, the possibility of one individual effectively engaging in meaningful political action is limited. (The importance of this discourse for literacy is explored in Chapter 8.) Not surprisingly, the *discourse of egalitarianism* is most explicitly articulated in off-stage, private contexts, although it also can surface in on-stage settings, where it is frequently used to sabotage front-end political action. The resulting ideological schema presents severe problems for political action, in that it leaves very little basis for the successful exercise of authority. Power and status are thus painfully temporary, and as such are not very desirable in the eyes of the wise. Even though the appearances of a highly stratified political structure are maintained, the exercise of leadership is constantly subverted (Besnier 1991, 1993). In Chapter 7, I will demonstrate the importance of these political dynamics for an understanding of church-related literacy practices.[4]

Besides the Council of Elders, the most important political body on the atoll is the Island Council, in charge of relations between the island community and the central government, and presided over by an Island President. Established by the colonial authorities in 1965, the Council is assisted by an Island Executive Office appointed by the Ministry of Local Governments on Funafuti. Even though the Island Council administers most of the grant money for island development that the national government provides, its authority and prestige have slowly eroded since the reestablishment of the Council of Elders. Other high prestige positions in the atoll community include the member of parliament (Nukulaelae's MPs have played key roles in the government since Tuvalu's independence), and the pastor.

Despite the basic suspicion with which acts of leadership are viewed, daily life on Nukulaelae is replete with microscopic forms of authoritarianism. More or less organized surveillance is very much part of daily routine, and is thoroughly grounded in patterns that Samoan pastors and colonial administrators instituted in the late nineteenth and early twentieth centuries (Goldsmith and Munro 1992a). Rules, regulations, bylaws, and patrols (called *aasiga* "inspections") of many different types regulate both minute details and more important aspects of everyday life (and give rise to written notices, summonses, minutes, and other miscellaneous tokens of literacy). For example, at the end of 1990, the Council of Elders commanded that all young men assemble 500 ripe coconuts and 300 solid kernel coconuts each for the use of their respective households, to ensure that each household be covered over the Christmas season without there being a need to make coconut gathering trips to the islets. Throughout the year, the Island Council's cleanliness patrol makes a weekly inspection of house interiors, porches, latrines, pig sties, and chicken coops, and fines the household if there is any evidence of uncleanliness or untidiness. During the two Sunday church services, a patrol roams the village to ensure that everyone except the sick and invalid is in church (see Chapter 6). Some forms of control are more ephemeral and circumstantial than others. In 1990 the Health Subcommittee of the Women's Committee had a daily patrol that inspected food larders to ensure that everyone was eating a balanced diet, but these inspections only lasted a few months. In 1991, the Women's Council decreed that all women should attend Women's Day celebrations wearing new undergarments; an inspection team went around the maneapa during the feasts lifting each woman's skirts to check that she had complied with the decree, and a fine of one dollar was assessed for non-compliance (see Besnier 1991 for further discussion).

These coercive practices can coexist ideologically with the egalitarian spirit described earlier, because great pains are taken to present them as manifestations of this egalitarianism: the enforcing authority is always *te fenua* "the island community," a structured subset of the community whose membership is evenly distributed across kin groups (e.g., women of the community), or an authoritative body considered to be a synecdoche of the community (e.g., the Council of Elders, the Island Council, or the

Nukulaelae Church). Thus, according to the logic of communalism and consensus, the very objects of surveillance are also in charge of enforcing it. In fact, according to the "official" version of Nukulaelae society (i.e., the version presented in public speeches or in answer to the ethnographer's queries), the enforcement of rules and regulations *ensures* that everyone is subjected to similar demands and that everyone's contribution to the communal of resources is identical. Because they are manifestations of the "dictatorship of the people," everyone is expected to accept these inspections good-naturedly. However, the reality is often different: despite their benign appearance, these multiple inspections and regulations can engender serious hardships for many people, and are met with much grumbling. In particular, whether these coercive actions are indeed manifestations of communal authority or of the whim of a few players is the topic of constant gossip and, occasionally, of fierce struggle in public forums. The discontent and anguish that they generate are also abundantly clear in letters: to acquire new undergarments, for example, a woman has to write a letter to an off-island relative and hope that this person will be able to afford the item and to find a way to send it on the monthly ship in time for Women's Day. The requesting party thus runs up symbolic and material debts within her reciprocity network, and the logistics involved in procuring the required items are complex. However, most inhabitants of the atoll also see in these patterns of community intrusion a way of ensuring equality, safeguarding community cohesion, and, paradoxically, protecting the interests of each individual. They thus tolerate a high level of community intrusion into their daily affairs, even by Polynesian standards.[5]

The overwhelming majority of Nukulaelae's population adheres to a congregationalist brand of Protestantism. However, in recent years (particularly since the late 1970s), some islanders have converted to various other religions, including the Seventh-Day Adventist Church, the Baha'i Faith, and the Jehovah's Witnesses. Mormonism, various brands of charismatic Christianity, and Islam have also gained converts on Funafuti and are known to Nukulaelae Islanders. At the time of my field work, one family on the atoll had joined the Baha'is and a few community members living on Funafuti had become Jehovah's Witnesses, while several Nukulaelae people on both Nukulaelae and Funafuti wavered in and out of these "new faiths" (*talitonuga ffoou*), as they are commonly referred to. (There is no clear case of anyone embracing agnosticism or paganism.) For converts, there is much to be said to living off-island: converts who stay on Nukulaelae are tormented for their religious beliefs, and quickly become ostracized from the community because of the tight bond between the Church and political, economic, and "traditional" life on the atoll. In many ways, leaving the Church is tantamount to betraying the community, and it closes many doors to traditional forms of political life. Changing economic conditions are nevertheless making it increasingly easy for single families to survive without relying on traditional exchange networks, and changing religion is consequently becoming somewhat easier.

Historical context

The period of the atoll's history most relevant to this study is the second half of the nineteenth century, during which contacts between the atoll and the rest of the world began intensifying and literacy was first brought to the atoll. The historical picture that can be reconstructed for that period demonstrates that Nukulaelae experienced major demographic, social, political, and probably cultural discontinuity.[6] However, a few words about the atoll prior to the 1860s are in order. My description will be very brief out of necessity: very little is known about the atoll's pre-contact history and pre-historical social organization and culture. For instance, we do not know when the atoll was settled or from where. Contemporary oral traditions are silent on this subject (but see Roberts 1958), and no archeological research has been conducted on Nukulaelae (whether archeological data are retrievable is an open question, given the geological instability of atoll environments). Furthermore, because Nukulaelae was not missionized by Westerners (as I will explain presently), and because of its isolation from major Pacific trade routes, it was never subjected to the large influx of Western eyewitnesses from whom we have inherited voluminous accounts of life in other parts of Polynesia around the time of contact. Consequently, information on the atoll's pre-contact social organization is extremely scant. Even oral traditions are remarkably uninformative on the topic; contemporary Nukulaelae Islanders' representations of their pre-contact past is heavily laden with Christian ideology. Events reported to have taken place in pre-Christian days are all presented as "preparations" for the advent of Christianity: Nukulaelae accounts, be they oral or written (e.g., Tinilau 1983 and other chapters in Laracy, ed., 1983), bear suspicious resemblance to the type of discourse one finds in journals of the more rigid and ethnocentric missionaries who roamed the frontiers of the Pacific in the nineteenth century.

What can be pieced together of Nukulaelae's pre-contact past suggests a loosely hierarchical social structure headed by a chief, selected from among the members of one particular clan or kin group, who ruled in conjunction with some sort of a council, probably made up of the heads of kin groups. The chief was seconded by a second-in-command (*tao aliki*), whose status and function resembles that of the Samoan *tulāfale* "talking chief." Chieftainship was based on a mixture of ascription and achievement. In short, Nukulaelae society was structured like other atolls of Western

Polynesia (cf. Sahlins 1958), exhibiting the least amount of hierarchical elaboration in the spectrum of Polynesia's systems of social organization.

What is known about pre-contact cosmology and religious practices is even more meager. The journals of a handful of late-nineteenth-century missionaries (who rarely visited the islands for more than a few hours and were hardly unbiased observers) suggest that Nukulaelae Islanders practiced an ancestor cult of some sort. A number of deities manifested themselves in natural events like lightning and shooting stars, and were iconicized in the form of unworked stones. The coexistence of different supernatural entities, some associated with the kin group and others with the entire atoll community, is congruent with the fluidity which character- ized Tuvalu's social structure (Goldsmith 1989a:87–95). Individuals called *vaka atua* (the term *taulaaitu*, a post-missionization borrowing from Samoan, is also sometimes used today) are said to have functioned as religious practitioners, although nothing is known about their social status and about the extent to which they differed from other power-holding entities in the island community.

Nukulaelae Islanders' first contact with Westerners took place in 1821, when the whaling ship *Independence II*, registered at Nantucket, Massachu- setts, and under the command of George Barrett, called at the atoll and christened it Mitchell's Group. This first contact date is rather late in Pacific history: by the second decade of the nineteenth century, Euro-American encroachment in the rest of the Pacific was already well under way, and missionaries, colonizers, and traders were beginning to flood other island groups like Samoa, Tahiti, Tonga, and Hawaii. In contrast, Nukulaelae and the rest of Tuvalu are geographically isolated, and the difficulties involved in spotting low-lying atolls even from a short distance further contributed to this isolation. More importantly, the atolls had little to offer to most Westerners compared to the larger and more fertile island groups of the Pacific. That Westerners viewed this area of the Pacific as unattractive is clearly reflected by the fact that two atolls of the group, Nui and Niulakita, had been known since 1568 and 1595 respectively, when they were sighted by the Spanish explorer Mendaña; yet between these dates and 1819, only two ships are recorded to have ventured into Tuvalu waters, and had only the briefest of contacts with the inhabitants of the group (Munro 1982:25–8).

From the 1820s to the 1860s, American, Australian, and European whalers roamed the oceans surrounding Tuvalu, but hardly ever had any contact with the inhabitants, for many complex reasons (Munro 1982:30– 56). The few contacts that Nukulaelae Islanders had with passing vessels were uniformly brief and peaceful. Because they had little to offer of interest to Westerners, Nukulaelae and surrounding communities were spared the specter of encroaching Euro-American colonialism that was rapidly descending on more desirable areas of the region.

However, by mid-century, conditions had changed, and the atoll entered a period of extreme turmoil. From the momentous events of which Nukulaelae Islanders were either agents or victims, three stand out as particularly significant: the introduction of Christianity; a raid by Peruvian slavers; and the lease of the largest islet of the atoll to a German plantation venture. It is in the midst of these events that literacy made its appearance, and this troubled historical context contributed to providing Nukulaelae literacy with a specific meaning, as I will demonstrate in this study.

Missionaries

Despite their sporadic and fleeting nature, early contacts with Westerners gave Nukulaelae Islanders the opportunity to become acquainted with the technologies, priorities, and beliefs of the visitors. In particular, they began to catch glimpses of Christianity, as the crews of ships in transit would somehow communicate to them the rudiments of their beliefs and of the rituals associated with it. Their first close acquaintance with some form of Christianity was through a certain Tom Rose (today remembered as *Taumeesi*, a coalescence of his first and last name), "a colored man" whose ship was wrecked off Nukulaelae (*Boston Daily Journal*, August 8, 1865, cited in Ward, ed., 1967:261). During the four years he spent there, he conducted rudimentary Christian services, which would later be described as follows: "They met about 8 A.M. A hymn was sung, and then Thomas read a portion from his English Bible, and afterwards told the people in their own language what he had read. When he had finished doing so, all went away; there was no prayer" (Elekana 1872:148). The Bible that Rose used was apparently one that the islanders had bought from a passing ship.

According to early Western testimonies, subsequent missionary records and modern Nukulaelae representations, the islanders' interest in the subject was intense, prefiguring the thoroughness and rapidity that would characterize conversion a few years later. While some of the imputed fervor to find out about the Westerners' religion should be understood as ideologically motivated exaggeration by those who recorded it, the enthusiasm with which it was eventually embraced is nevertheless noteworthy. Many motivational factors for this attitude probably came into play, including the association of Christianity with desirable goods and technologies and with the promise of divine protection (cf. Brady 1975, Goldsmith 1989a:121–5, 1993, Goldsmith and Munro 1992a, 1992b, Munro 1982:80–161). Significantly for my purposes, Christianity was closely linked to literacy, and the enthusiasm for the former came hand-in-hand with a comparable enthusiasm for the latter.

In 1861, a fortuitous event gave Nukulaelae Islanders direct access to the foreigners' religion: that year, a lay deacon from Manihiki Atoll (Northern Cook Islands) by the name of Elekana was beached on Nukulaelae with half a dozen people, after having been blown off course by unexpected bad weather during a passage from Manihiki to nearby Rakahanga, and drifted 1500 miles in a small canoe for several weeks (see Map 1). Elekana spent two months on the atoll, during which he initiated the missionization process. The story of Elekana's "miraculous" drift voyage quickly acquired the status of a parable in the annals of the London Missionary Society (LMS), which at the time dominated missionary efforts in the Pacific, and it was used as propaganda in England on several occasions (Murray 1865, G. Turner 1865, Elekana 1872).[7] It plays a significant role in contemporary Nukulaelae Islanders' oral historical canon and understanding of the historical antecedents of modern-day Nukulaelae culture. The various representations of Elekana's story are analyzed in detail by Goldsmith and Munro (1992a).

Systematic missionization began in 1865, when LMS authorities in Samoa, alerted by Elekana of Nukulaelae Islanders' eagerness to convert, dropped off the first Samoan religious teacher, Ioane. By the 1860s, the LMS had been established in the Pacific for seven decades, and had reached the acme of its influence. The Society had begun to delegate the task of converting new island groups to Pacific Islanders who hailed from already heavily missionized island groups, such as Samoa, Tonga, and Hawaii.[8] In the case of Nukulaelae and the rest of Tuvalu, the LMS thought it particularly advantageous to abide by this norm. Pacific Islanders, it was reasoned, would feel more at home in environments that resembled that of their own native lands, whereas Europeans would not adapt well to atoll living. Needless to say, LMS authorities greatly overestimated the similarities between Samoa and Tuvalu, since in fact many Samoan teachers found it difficult to deal with such factors as the atolls' isolation, small size, and restricted diet (Munro 1978). British missionaries also invoked linguistic similarities as a further motivation for leaving the conversion of island communities in the care of Pacific Islanders.[9] In the case of seven of the eight islands and atolls of Tuvalu, this argument had some legitimacy. However, Samoan teachers based on Gilbertese-speaking Nui Atoll had as difficult a time acquiring the local language as English speakers would have had. Even on Tuvaluan-speaking islands, it was not the pastors who adopted linguistically to the community, but the reverse. Samoan quickly became the language of the Church and of all formal contexts, and left a strong imprint on the structure of the Tuvaluan dialects.

The LMS's envoys to Tuvalu were known as "native teachers" because LMS authorities did not deem Samoans fit to be ordained as pastors; they reluctantly agreed to ordain them after 1875 but this was a political gesture made in the context of a power struggle in which the English missionaries and Samoan envoys were locked.[10] These teachers were trained at Mālua Seminary, a missionary training center founded on the island of Upolu, in what is now Western Samoa, in 1844 (G. Turner 1861:124–41, Gilson 1970:88–94). Once posted on Nukulaelae and elsewhere in Tuvalu, they were overseen by English missionaries, who would visit for a few hours once a year or less on missionary ships, the *John Williams III* and *IV*. During these very brief visits, the British missionaries would assess the Samoan teachers' progress and perform all the important ritual work, testing potential new converts, baptizing them, and so on. While they seldom set foot on Nukulaelae, the British church authorities kept a tight rein on the missionization process (Goldsmith and Munro 1992b).

On Nukulaelae and other islands of Southern Tuvalu, the relationship between Samoan teachers (and later pastors) and their adoptive communities quickly acquired a highly hegemonic façade: traditional tokens of chieftainship, such as the right to wear pearl-shell fish lure necklaces (*paa kasoa*) and eat the head of any turtle caught, are said to have been bestowed upon him. All the pastor's and his family's worldly needs were taken care of by the community, as they still are today. In true Samoan fashion, many of the early pastors had a healthy sense of their own and their home islands' superiority over the rest of the world, and had little regard for the atolls' slim resources, their tiny size and population, their lifestyles still tainted by heathenism, and the downplaying of stratification and concomitant lack of decorum that characterized their political institutions. At the same time, there is evidence that the community carefully and subtly controlled the pastor's authority and influence on community politics and everyday affairs. In Chapter 7, I will demonstrate that the complex relationship between early missionary-pastors and the community left a strong imprint on church-related literacy practices.

Furthermore, it is unclear whether the social changes associated with the pastors' arrival were locally motivated or instigated by the pastors. In addition, the control that British missionaries maintained at a distance over the Samoan teachers left little power of any consequence to the latter even in religious matters. The Samoan teachers' ultimate subservience to their overseers is unlikely to have escaped the attention of the Nukulaelae community. In Chapter 3, I will speculate on the implication of these questions for the history of literacy on the atoll.

The LMS's reliance on Samoan teachers and later pastors to missionize Tuvalu, which lasted until 1958, had many other lasting consequences. One of these consequences is that European missionary presence in the group was always minimal.[11] In this respect, Tuvalu differs from areas of Polynesia (e.g., Tonga, Samoa, and Tahiti) that were exposed to Christianity earlier and through direct influence from the West. In particular, the Western missionizing agents with whom these other societies came into contact had access to significantly greater resources than the Samoan teachers sent to Tuvalu. These resources enabled missionaries to translate books (first and foremost the Bible), import printing presses, establish schools, and organize complex organizational infrastructures in other areas of the Pacific. In contrast, Tuvalu never gained access to these resources (e.g., printing presses) or has gained access to them only recently (as in the case of the translation of the Scriptures into the local language).

Nukulaelae also differs from other areas of the Pacific in an antithetical way: while church personnel were soon localized in other areas of Polynesia, in the Outer Islands of Tuvalu the religious hierarchy has retained a strong alien flavor. Since the Church of Tuvalu broke its ties with Samoa in 1969, all pastors have been Tuvaluans; however, they are always posted to islands other than their home island. There is an explicitly articulated motivation for this practice. As the guardian of spiritual peace in the community, the pastor must remain detached from worldly issues. Since Tuvaluans go to great lengths to shield high-status outsiders from community internal affairs, posting pastors on islands where they remain honored guests of the community minimizes the chances of their getting involved in island politics and displaying favoritism towards close relatives. The success of this strategy depends on the personality of the pastor and on the rapport that the host community establishes with him. Every so often, serious conflicts arise between particular pastors and their congregations over issues of religious vs. secular authority, or allegations of secular transgressions; in fact, the Nukulaelae community, with its infamous love of contention and propensity to foment conflict, has gained a certain reputation for keeping its pastors under close watch in these respects. Church authorities usually resolve these difficulties by removing or even defrocking pastors, a practice that LMS authorities instituted in the early days. The net result is that the pastor is always a liminal member of the community:[12] while his role as the guardian of the spiritual welfare of the community accords him high personal status and much prestige, he remains at the margin of the community, as an "honorary" member who has to be careful not to become too involved in the internal affairs of the island.

The missionization of the atoll had one particularly important economic consequence: it created an unprecedented need for cash among Nukulaelae Islanders. Before conversion, the community was not unacquainted with money (and, indeed, its intimate affiliation with Christianity on the one hand and literacy on the other): a few years before Elekana's landfall, the islanders had purchased an English Bible from the captain of a passing ship, for which they obviously had required money (Elekana 1872:148). The barter trade that they initially conducted with passing ships gradually gave way to monetary transactions, particularly as the coconut-oil trade became more systematic and as resident traders began establishing themselves (Munro 1990b:31–3). By the early 1860s, Nukulaelae Islanders were familiar with money (although not familiar enough with it to protect themselves from fraud; see Iosefa, Munro, and Besnier 1991:33–4). However, the need for a steady cash income became crucial after the atoll received its first pastor. First, the pastor and his family needed to be paid (in addition to being fed and housed), a condition that the LMS imposed on the community. Still today, the pastor accepts substantial gifts of money from the community on a regular and circumstantial basis, and there is fierce competition between individuals, groups, and islands over who donates most. Second, on its yearly visit, the mission ship expected that each community would contribute food, copra, and, more importantly, money. The mission preferred currency because it did not want to look like it was operating a trading ship when it returned to Samoa. Third, the mission ship sold Samoan Bibles to the islanders; for example, book purchases from the missionary ship amounted to $8.45 in 1872, $11.75 in 1873, $8.50 in 1875, and 8/- in 1876 (different currencies were in use concurrently), sums that somehow had to be raised (Iosefa, Munro, and Besnier 1991:44). Fourth, the pastors' insistence on everyone being "properly" clothed meant that cloth had to be purchased from traders. Finally, churches eventually had to be built, and only imported materials were deemed suitable for the purpose; Nukulaelae would have to wait until 1928 to have a "proper" church, built with remittances from workers on Ocean Island. These emerging needs ensured Nukulaelae's increasing economic dependence on the outside world, first through the copra and coconut-oil trade, and subsequently through labor migration (Munro 1990b). As I demonstrate in Chapters 4 and 5, one form of literacy, letter writing, has long played a prominent monitoring role in the maintenance of Nukulaelae's economic ties with the rest of the world.

Slavers

In 1863, namely two years after Elekana's landfall and two years before the arrival of the first Samoan teacher, three Peruvian slave-ships or "blackbirders" anchored off the atoll. Initially the slavers had difficulty convincing Nukulaelae people to come on board. However, according to missionary accounts, the beachcomber Tom Rose (mentioned earlier) alerted one of them of the islanders' interests in Christianity.[13] With the help of a member of his crew posing as a missionary, he told them "that they were missionary ships and invited them on board to receive the holy sacrament" (Moresby 1876:73). Once they were on board, the ships set sail and left. According to a missionary who visited Nukulaelae in 1870, most able-bodied adults were taken away, leaving only women, children, and older people, including the chief, Tafalagilua: "[T]he strong men and women were advised to leave their small children in charge of the aged. In some cases they did not; in others the men went, and left their wives and children behind" (Whitmee 1871:11). Other islands of the Pacific suffered great losses in comparable circumstances between 1862 and 1864, when the Peruvian labor trade was active, but probably none were as devastated as Nukulaelae. The blackbirders took their captives to the island mines of Sala y Gomez, off the coast of Peru. None ever returned (Maude 1981:74–82, Munro 1982:63–79), and this single event probably explains in large part the historical discontinuity observable in the atoll's collective memory.[14] There are numerous divergent estimates of the number of islanders that the blackbirders took, ranging from 100 to 400 (Munro 1990c). What is certain is that Nukulaelae's work force was so seriously decimated that the community's very survival would remain in doubt for many years to come.

How the severely diminished community managed to rebuild itself can only be reconstructed from historical fragments. For example, the land tenure system needed to be completely revised. Significantly, this task was accomplished by two strangers. According to a record of genealogies (*tusi gafa*) I was fortunate to be able to consult on Nukulaelae, two men from Funafuti, Vave and Taupo, arrived on Nukulaelae in the years following the Peruvian raid, and the task of dividing up the land among twenty-eight remaining Nukulaelae men was entrusted to them. Following is the relevant passage from this document, in the original orthography, which appears to have been compiled around 1945 from earlier documents:

Vave se tagata Funafuti laua mo Taupo. Taupo ne fakafolau kako Vave ne tautali mai ia Taupo. Mai ki Nukulaelae fai te mavaega a Valoa i te mea ka galo, muna Valoa kia Tepuku, ka vau Vave ke tuku te filifili kia Vave. Ko Vave mo Taupo ne tofi ne laua te fenua nei. E 28 tagata ne vaevae ei te laukele[.-torn]

Vave [was] a Funafuti man[,] together with Taupo. Taupo was set adrift [as punishment], and Vave followed Taupo here. They came to Nukulaelae[.] Vaaloa was making his will because he was about to die, and [he] told Tepuku to let Vave partition [the land]. Vave and Taupo partitioned this atoll. The land was partitioned among 28 men.

What this document suggests is that the raid left the atoll's authority structure so weakened that land redistribution had to be performed by strangers. These strangers, however, do not appear to have established themselves in a hegemonic position *vis-à-vis* the rest of the population, despite the fact that the situation lent itself to such a scenario.

Planters

After the raid, Nukulaelae was in great need of extra hands to continue performing the traditional exploitation of land and sea, and to ensure that the population could regain its numerary momentum. The opportunity to do so arose in 1865, on the very same ship that dropped off the first Samoan teacher. Nukulaelae people agreed to lease part of their atoll to the captain of the ship, who was acting as an agent for the Hamburg-based firm J.C. Godeffroy und Sohn, later reconstituted as the Deutsche Handels- und Plantagen-Gesellschaft der Südsee-Inseln (DHPG). Godeffroys was the first promoter of corporate capital in the Pacific. Operating from its Samoa headquarters, the company had altered the economic landscape of the region by the mid-1860s through its investments in a lowly commodity, coconut oil, which contributed to the disappearance of the whaling industry (Campbell 1989:97–8, S. Firth 1973:11–15, Munro and Firth 1990). The lease concerned Nukulaelae's largest islet, then known simply as Nukulaelae, and since renamed Niuioka or Niuoku (phonemically, *Niuooku*), i.e., "New York" (see Map 2), where the firm established a coconut plantation, whose twenty-five-year presence on the atoll became a mixed blessing.

Between 1865 and 1890, the largest islet of the atoll was off-limits to Nukulaelae Islanders, a prospect that they had not anticipated when they agreed to its lease, because of their lack of familiarity with European views of land tenure. Since it represents a fourth of the atoll's total area, the community was deprived of substantial food-gathering grounds, and a food crisis ensued. The resulting periodic famines were further exacerbated by factors directly related to the difficulties involved in maintaining a stable system of production. In particular, the atoll was devastated by major hurricanes in 1883 and 1886 (McLean and Munro 1991) that alternated with recurrent droughts. Furthermore, Godeffroys actively discouraged competition, and consequently ships other than those associated with the firm stopped calling at Nukulaelae. As is typical of plantation economies, the planters established a monopoly on the islanders' outgoing copra trade as well as on imports, and they most certainly ensured that this state of affairs worked to their advantage. Before long, disagreements arose between planters and islanders about the terms of the lease, in a classic example of cross-cultural misunderstanding aggravated by the planters' opportunistic duplicity: when the lease was agreed upon for twenty-five years, the islanders thought they were committing the islet for twenty-five lunar months. The Godeffroy representatives stopped paying rent after a few years anyway, while at the same time attempting to expand their operations to other islets. These trying times are vividly remembered in oral traditions, although oral history attributes them principally to the planters' fraudulence and secondarily to their ancestors' naïveté.

Nevertheless, the plantation provided the community with much-needed new blood. As was customary in nineteenth-century plantation economies around the colonial world (Wolf 1982:368–70), the planters did not rely on locally available labor, which in this case might not have been available anyway; rather, they imported contractual laborers from other Pacific islands, including the Gilbert Islands, Kosrae, Niue, Rotuma, Samoa, Hawaii, and the Marshall Islands. Many of these men opted to stay on Nukulaelae at the end of their contracts, establishing affinal ties with the inhabitants who had been spared by the Peruvian raid, amongst which, conveniently, women were in a majority. It is probably the case that the diminutive Nukulaelae community aggressively sought out exogamous ties with the plantation workers. Within a year of the establishment of the plantation, the visiting LMS missionary made the following note in his journal:

One sad blank strikes one painfully in looking upon the community. There are no young men. These were all carried off so that one important link is missing. It is in the way however of being replaced. Several of the widows of those who have gone have all been married since my first visit to young men from different islands who have been in the employ of M[r] Weber of Apia who has an establishment on Nukulaelae. Their term of service has now expired, and five of them have resolved to make Nukulaelae their home. They are a valuable addition to the community.

(Murray 1866:8)

Indirectly, the plantation thus left an indelible mark on the atoll, whose contemporary inhabitants have numerous kinship ties with a large array of island communities scattered throughout the Pacific (for further details on the Niuoku plantation, see Iosefa, Munro and Besnier 1991, Munro and Besnier 1990).

The practice of readily integrating outsiders into the community, which marriage helps to seal, was not new. Even before the raid, the small size of the population, coupled with the strong avoidance taboos between cousins of opposite gender, probably made *aavaga ki tai* "seaward marriages" as desirable in the mid-nineteenth century as it is today. Thus, according to both oral history and European records (Graeffe 1867:1162, Murray 1866:6–7), one finds a man from Tokelau, Luisama, on Nukulaelae at the time of the raid (he was the only person to escape the blackbirders' ship by swimming ashore). Oral history and official records mention a Tongan man, Lutelu (phonemically, *Luutelu*, i.e., Luther), who reached Nukulaelae in a canoe, allegedly after having been driven away from his home island for murder. Lutelu became the first "Nukulaelae Islander" to be sent to Mālua in 1872 for theological training; but he and part of his family were deported back to Tonga in 1890 after he stirred up political trouble on Nukulaelae (Munro 1986). Many of these individuals have direct descendants on Nukulaelae, and, in some cases, elsewhere in the Pacific. Some islanders' ascendants even hail from beyond the boundaries of the Pacific. A Jamaican named Charles Barnard, remembered as *Sale Panaata* or *Te Kuki* (an archaic form meaning "the cook") lived on the atoll at the turn of the century, got married, and now has many descendants.[15]

The situation in which the atoll community found itself at the end of the nineteenth century is thus an interesting one: virtually every inhabitant of the atoll could claim ancestry elsewhere. Missionary reports illustrate the heterogeneity of the community: for example, a plantation worker from Kosrae known as Sione on Nukulaelae (his Kosrae name was Nena Sruhsra) married a Nukulaelae woman with whom he had a son, Alefaio, whose first wife, Ulima, was from Atafu Atoll, Tokelau. How a common culture was reconstructed despite this social heterogeneity is not known. All one can say today is that it was achieved with a great deal of efficiency, as contemporary Nukulaelae society and culture retain no trace of their eclectic origins other than in the genealogical records. However, one is tempted to speculate that the heterogeneity of Nukulaelae's population at the turn of the century must have had some structural consequences, as I have discussed elsewhere (Besnier 1991).

Most relevant for the purposes of this study, Nukulaelae Islanders frequently maintain kinship ties over vast geographical and temporal distances. The assumption that most contemporary islanders make is that they can *ssala olotou kaaiga* "look for their relatives" in various corners of the Pacific and be welcome amongst them. Indeed, many have spent significant periods of time in such places as the Marshall Islands and Kosrae, living with people with whom they share ancestors who were alive back in the 1860s. In return, one of Lutelu's Tongan descendants, a young man named Tangata, spent an extended period of time on Nukulaelae in the 1970s. There is every indication that the concern for keeping kinship networks alive is not a recent phenomenon. As I will suggest in Chapter 4, letter writing has played a crucial role in this process ever since the introduction of literacy to the atoll.

Colonizers

In 1892, Nukulaelae, along with dozens of other islands scattered over several million square miles of ocean, became part of the Gilbert and Ellice Islands Protectorates. The protectorates were declared without much enthusiasm on the part of British authorities: strategically unimportant, the islands and atolls had very little to offer, and there was concern about their becoming a financial drain. The Ellice Islands, even smaller than the Micronesian Gilberts to the north, were swept into the process almost as an afterthought. However, Britain felt some pressure to formalize its domination over the islands to ensure that its share of a sphere-of-influence agreement it had signed with Germany in 1886 was respected (Munro and Firth 1986). On Nukulaelae, the protectorate declaration was ratified by the then chief, Lapana (phonemically, *Laapana*), and his four "councillors" when Captain H.W.M. Gibson called on the HMS *Curaçoa* in September

1892. Significantly, Lapana and one of the five councillors signed the document with a cross, while the other four councillors signed their names in full. In 1916, the protectorate was amalgamated with the Gilbert Islands and the Union Islands (i.e., Tokelau) into a single colony, from which Tokelau was separated in 1926.

The colonial period was characterized by the double influence of the Gilbert Islands and Great Britain. The Ellice Islands lived under the shadow of the much more populated Gilbert Islands, where the colonial administration was based (on Tarawa until 1908, then on Ocean Island, and again on Tarawa after World War II). However, in many respects, the effects of this double influence on atoll life never compared in magnitude to the fundamental changes that Nukulaelae had already undergone during the second half of the nineteenth century. The geographical isolation, the governmental rather than religious nature of the colonial authority, and the local invisibility of colonial agents all contributed to minimizing the impact of colonial rule on the atoll (Brady 1975). Nukulaelae and the rest of Tuvalu remained the backwaters of a colonial entity which itself was considered to be the "Cinderella of the Empire" (Macdonald 1982). The colonial authorities, whose main concern was to ensure that the colony did not become a burden on Britain, administered Nukulaelae and the rest of the Colony with a painfully meager understanding of and interest in their sociopolitical circumstances.

During the seven decades of colonial administration, many changes took place in Tuvalu (Brady 1974, Macdonald 1982, Munro 1982:293–312), the most consequential of which was arguably the establishment of contract-labor migration to Ocean Island and Nauru. However, many changes that the colonial administration brought about were simply codifications of what was already in existence. For example, the *Native Laws*, first issued in 1894 (Ellice Islands Protectorate 1894) and periodically revised, regulated details of daily life, from sour-toddy drinking and breaking the Sabbath to murder, in progressively more detail with each edition. In essence, these laws were merely a systematized version of the regulations that the Samoan pastors had already imposed (the fact that these laws were printed in Samoan is a telling metaphor). A local government structure was established in the form of a five-person body called the *kau pule* (a word which in colonial papers appears as *kaubure* or *kaupuli*, mistranscriptions by administrators unfamiliar with the Tuvaluan language), or "magistrates": three elders, a Colony appointed magistrate (*faamasino*), and an elected "chief" (*aliisili*), seconded by a "native scribe" (*failautusi*). It is not clear that this structure was any different from what it professed to replace. That the names of these various entities are all borrowings from Samoan is indicative of the considerable influence that the Samoan mission was already exerting by the turn of the century.

In 1975, invoking the important cultural differences that separated the Polynesian Ellice Islands from the Micronesian Gilbert Islands, Ellice Islanders asked to separate from the rest of the colony, which Britain consented to reluctantly and only after heavily penalizing the group. At separation, the islands were renamed Tuvalu, the name under which they gained independence in 1978.

Defining an ethnographic context

At first glance (both figuratively and literally), Nukulaelae emerges as a perfect example of the anthropological idealization of a small-scale, geographically isolated and bounded, socioculturally discrete, and internally homogeneous entity, which experiences the turmoil of world-scale historical change as a removed bystander. However, as recent critical works from various anthropological quarters have shown (e.g., Fabian 1983, Fardon 1990, Kuper 1988, Wilmsen 1989, Wolf 1982), the self-contained society unaffected by global processes of social, economic, and political change is but a figment of the anthropological, or at least of the Western, imagination. More and more, anthropologists are finding that what they first described as internally motivated structures and processes in particular societies are responses to world-scale events, and that small isolated communities are as deeply involved in global trends as large-scale urbanized societies. Nugent's (1982) reanalysis of Leach's (1956) classic analysis of the Kachin political system is a case in point. Leach had described a regular oscillation between hierarchy and egalitarianism among the Kachin, which he presented as systematically embedded in the very character of Kachin society; but Nugent convincingly demonstrated that these oscillations were political responses to changing economic conditions created by external events, particularly in the trade of opium (see Nugent 1983 and Leach 1983 for an ensuing debate). Such cases suggest that one should exert caution when defining the outer boundaries of one's ethnographic scrutiny, even in instances that seem as obviously unproblematic as the case of Nukulaelae.

I have chosen to present the analysis that follows as an ethnography of *Nukulaelae* literacy, rather than as an ethnography of *Tuvaluan* literacy. The alternative would have found precedents in sociolinguistic tradition: sociolinguists often take the boundaries of a speech community to be coterminous with language boundaries, despite early cautions by Hymes (1968) and Gumperz (1968). This stance enables them, for instance, to present their work as studies of literacy "in English." However, there are reasons why I will be careful in this book not to make any claims about *Tuvaluan* literacy. First, there is a great deal more complexity to literacy in Tuvalu than I am about to describe. On Funafuti in particular, the literacy experiences of certain segments of the population are much more varied than those of the average Nukulaelae Islander. Funafuti has a public library and an extension branch of the regional University of the South Pacific, and many of its residents have considerably more formal education than Nukulaelae residents. (Most educated Nukulaelae Islanders in fact live on Funafuti or abroad.) A national government is headquartered there, whose literacy output looks formidable when compared to the tokens of literacy produced and consumed on Nukulaelae. In the capital, documents, circulars, educational pamphlets, and public notices are written and read in both English and Tuvaluan. Some residents of Funafuti have published their autobiographies and other works of non-fiction.

Similarly, Vaitupu Island is in many ways the educational center of the Tuvalu group, since it hosts the only secondary school in the country. This school has always defined an intellectual élite for the country, in that only a small percentage of primary school graduates from each island ever make it into secondary school, as discussed in Chapter 3. The question of secondary school literacy opens up a host of questions above and beyond the questions I address here. In particular, the relationship of secondary school literacy practices to literacy practices in other settings must be examined carefully.[16] Obviously, secondary school literacy filters back to Nukulaelae, in the form of letters from school children away on Vaitupu to Nukulaelae relatives and friends, and in the form of literacy practices that secondary school children engage in after their return home. While I will address the relevance of school literacy for Nukulaelae in Chapters 3 and 4, I will not present my discussion as an analysis of *Tuvaluan* literacy, because such an analysis must take into account a much broader variety of literacy practices than is possible within the scope of this book.

At the same time, I remain keenly aware of the inherent and unresolvable problems associated with the definition of this study as an ethnography of Nukulaelae literacy. Broadening the scope of this discussion to issues beyond literacy, one is faced with the delicate question of the extent to which each atoll or island community in the Tuvalu group forms an individual unit of ethnographic analysis, or whether one can speak of "Tuvaluan society" as a meaningful category. Two anthropologists, Chambers (1983), who conducted field work on Nanumea, and Noricks (1981), whose focus was Niutao, have emphasized the unique features of their two field sites, criticizing their predecessors (notably Brady 1970), for glossing over significant inter-island differences of history, social organization, political structure, and economic life. At first glance, these criticisms appear to be backed by local ideologies and ethnographic evidence. Indeed, a very distinctive "spirit" emanates from each island community, and this distinctiveness, which Tuvaluans are keenly attuned to, is obviously grounded in differences in historical trajectories and contemporary socioeconomic conditions. It is also significant that each island of Tuvalu was a separate political entity prior to colonial amalgamation at the end of the nineteenth century. At the same time, very important patterns of commonality emerge between the eight islands of the group, and these commonalities are locally emphasized in appropriate contexts, as Goldsmith (1989a:180–205) skillfully demonstrates in reference to religion. Clearly, one is faced with a dialectic relationship between individualities and commonalities, distinctiveness and uniformity, which informs the problem of how to define ethnographic scope in ambiguous terms at best.

The solution, if there is one, must centralize the dialectic nature of ethnographic categories. As should be already evident from the sketch of Nukulaelae social life I presented in this chapter, the atoll community is very much embedded in a national entity (Tuvalu), a regional entity (the insular Pacific), and a complex array of social and political ties between First World and Third World, microstates and world powers, neo-colonial settings and former metropoles. The importance of these ties is particularly striking when viewed in light of the historical processes that gave rise to them: sustained contacts with the outside world brought about fundamental changes in Nukulaelae society and culture very early on. While this work focuses on one aspect of Nukulaelae social life, I will pay particular attention to the ways in which the atoll community is embedded in a broader world context, and will demonstrate that literacy figures prominently in Nukulaelae Islanders' negotiation of their relationship to this broader context, from both historical and contemporary perspectives.

3

THE DOMAINS OF READING AND WRITING

Continuing in the historical vein of the previous chapter, I now turn to what can be termed loosely the "domains" of literacy on Nukulaelae. I first identify the languages with which literacy is associated. I then discuss the social history of schooling since the 1860s; while the rest of this book is primarily concerned with literacy outside of schools, a brief description of school literacy is nevertheless relevant. I then attend to the historical context of literacy, insofar as it can be distinguished from the historical evolution of schooling and religious conversion. The last section is an overview of the range of social settings in which reading and writing take place on the atoll. In this overview, I pay particular attention to "non-textual" literacy practices, i.e., the production and consumption of lists, slogans, notices, and other written materials of lesser substance and importance than letters, to which I devote Chapters 4 and 5, and sermons, the topic of Chapters 6 and 7.

Languages

Nukulaelae Islanders speak, write, and read a dialect of Tuvaluan. Other dialects of this language are spoken on seven of the eight other islands of the Tuvalu group (the inhabitant of Nui speak a dialect of Gilbertese, a Micronesian language). Its closest relatives are members of the Samoic-Outlier subgroup of Polynesian, which includes Samoan, Tokelauan, Futunan, Uvean (Wallisian), and the languages of all Polynesian Outlier societies enclaved in Melanesia and Micronesia (Pawley 1966, 1967). Within Samoic-Outlier, Tuvaluan may form a lower-order Ellicean subgroup with a number of Outlier languages (I. Howard 1981), although the supporting evidence is inconclusive. Each Tuvaluan-speaking island of Tuvalu has its own easily recognizable dialect, and all dialects are mutually intelligible. The three northern dialects (Nanumea, Nanumaga, and Niutao) form a loosely knit subgroup, while the four southern dialects (Funafuti, Vaitupu, Nukufetau, and Nukulaelae) form another, with less pronounced differences among dialects than in the north. Furthermore, in the south, it is difficult to identify precisely the structural characteristics of each dialect beyond a finite list of shibboleths, many of which concern intonation contours, tempo, and pitch variation, because so much dialect mixing has taken place.

The Nukulaelae dialect is most notably characterized by the presence of /h/ in its phonemic inventory, which appears only in initial position in a dozen high-frequency morphemes where /s/ or /f/ appears in the other three southern dialects (e.g., Nukulaelae *hano* "go" vs. Funafuti *fano, heeai* "negative existential verb" vs. *seeai*). Speakers often switch from h-forms to s/f-forms in mid-utterance, although these and other miscellaneous dialect forms are loosely polarized in terms of their sociolinguistic distribution: Nukulaelae features are typically of family contexts, oral communication, and talk about non-religious and non-public subject matters, and they are more common in the speech of older speakers than younger speakers, and in the speech of women than men. Nukulaelae Islanders generally revert to a register closer to the Funafuti dialect in writing, in political or religious contexts, and in interactions with outsiders. However, in many instances, code-switching seems to carry little or no sociolinguistic meaning. Dialectal variation is only of minor importance in the relationship between literacy and orality. There is some evidence that the dialectal features are being lost, as certain lexemes specific to Nukulaelae in the last generations have now fallen into disuse.[1]

Gilbertese

Over the years, members of the Nukulaelae community have encountered a broad range of other languages. Foreign languages that have had the most impact on their lives are Gilbertese, Samoan, and English, of which only the last two are of relevance to literacy. Many atoll residents are proficient in Gilbertese, a Micronesian language, which they describe as easy to learn. Until the separation of the Gilbert and Ellice Islands, Nukulaelae Islanders and other Tuvaluans who traveled within the Colony encountered opportunities and incentives to learn that language, which was the dominant "vernacular" (as colonial authorities referred to it) of the Colony. In addition, it functioned as the working language of the Colony's capital, Tarawa, where a substantial number of Nukulaelae Islanders migrated more or less temporarily for the same reasons that they now migrate or travel to Funafuti. The children of Nukulaelae and other Tuvaluan people residing on Tarawa sometimes acquired Gilbertese before they learned Tuvaluan. However, Gilbertese never acquired much importance as a language of literacy; save for the occasional government pamphlets that the Colony translated into Gilbertese (and sometimes into Tuvaluan, sometimes not), there were few occasions for Nukulaelae

Islanders to read it, and yet fewer to write it. Even as a spoken language, its use is now dwindling, and will probably disappear within a generation on the atoll.[2]

Samoan

Samoan was introduced by the religious teachers and pastors, many of whom were firmly convinced that Samoan was an essential tool for anyone's survival in the world. As mentioned in Chapter 2, it was the Nukulaelae community that accommodated linguistically to the pastors, rather than the reverse, although it is also probable that most pastors acquired some proficiency in Nukulaelae Tuvaluan during their years of tenure on the atoll. Samoan was for many decades the language of school and church, the language used in interactions with visiting missionaries, and the *de facto* language of law and government. As the language of literacy production (principally for letter writing), it was only gradually replaced by Tuvaluan in the course of the twentieth century. Letters written in the 1960s still bore the imprint of Samoan influence, as I illustrate in Chapter 4. Even the presumably secular government of the Protectorate and later the Colony had its *Native Laws* translated into Samoan, rather than Tuvaluan, until the 1930s, and it required that island magistrates (*kau pule*) be literate in Samoan. The Samoan Bible was in use until it was superseded by a Tuvaluan translation in 1987, and since the Bible is the only readily available reading material, there was until recently a strong symbolic link between literacy and the Samoan language. Samoan and Tuvaluan were in a typical diglossic relationship, with the former serving as the "high" code. Even though younger generations today no longer have any motivation to learn Samoan, most middle-aged or older Nukulaelae Islanders still speak it competently, albeit in a rather stilted, formal manner and with a strong Tuvaluan accent (e.g., dropping all glottal stops). Today, however, Samoan is very rarely used, having been completely replaced by Tuvaluan. It is only heard regularly in church singing: many hymns introduced from Samoa are still sung alongside the substantial corpus of hymns in Tuvaluan that Nukulaelae people have composed since Samoan ceased to be the language of church contexts.

While Samoan–Tuvaluan diglossia has disappeared, Samoan has left a strong imprint on the Tuvaluan lexicon. Borrowings from Samoan are deeply ingrained in the vocabulary, so much so that many speakers of Tuvaluan, particularly younger ones, have difficulty distinguishing borrowings from native words. The only salient phonological change that Samoan borrowings undergo is the deletion of glottal stops, which are phonemic in Samoan but do not exist in Tuvaluan (e.g., Samoan *tāunu'u* "to fulfill" becomes Tuvaluan *taaunuu*). Samoan borrowings are most numerous in the religious vocabulary (e.g., *vii* "song of praise" from

Samoan *vi'i* "to praise," *faifeau* "pastor" from Samoan *faife'au*, literally, "message bearer," *maamoe* "sheep" from Samoan *māmoe*) and among terms relating to schooling and school knowledge (*aaoga* "schooling, school-related" from Samoan *ā'oga*, *mataimanu* "letter [of the alphabet]" from Samoan *matai manu*, *nuumela* "number, arithmetics" from Samoan *nūmera*). Certain technologies and objects introduced in the early days of contacts bear names borrowed from Samoan (e.g., *laulaavalava* "skirt" from Samoan *lau lāvalava* "yardage of material," *apa* "tin can, corrugated iron" from Samoan *'apa*, *seevae* "shoe" from Samoan *se'e vae*), and words relating to government officialdom are often of Samoan origin (e.g., *faamasino* "judge" from *fa'amasino*, *fua* "flag" from Samoan *fu'a*).[3] Finally, a number of grammatical morphemes are of Samoan origin (e.g., *faatoaa* "telic aspect marker" from Samoan *fa'ato'ā*, *ona* "because of" from *'ona* "conjunction," *vaaganaa* "unless" from Samoan *vāganā*). Because of their semantic and contextual associations, borrowings from Samoan are overall more frequent in religious discourse than in secular discourse, in oratory than in casual conversation, and in writing than in speaking.

English

English had a slow beginning on Nukulaelae and elsewhere in Tuvalu. Compared to the inhabitants of Pacific islands that housed mission stations and provided anchorage for whalers in the mid-1800s (e.g., Samoa, Wallis, and Rotuma), Nukulaelae Islanders had relatively few occasions to interact with English-speaking Westerners, and hence few opportunities and little motivation to learn their language (Munro 1985). They did interact with people from many other parts of the Pacific, although nothing is known about how these interactions were conducted. However, the role of English today is rapidly changing. English now occupies several functional slots formerly occupied by Samoan: it is the language of secondary education, government, and communication with the outside world. Even though few atoll residents are fluent in English, there is strong pressure to learn it for academic and economic success. Most inhabitants have some passive knowledge of spoken and written English. I will describe in Chapter 4 that most Nukulaelae letter writers are familiar with English letter-writing conventions, which sprinkle many letters. Materials written in English that reach Nukulaelae are for the most part Bibles in English and Bible concordances and commentaries, but also include occasional letters from past visitors, occasional magazines, some children's books and other pedagogical materials, and tracts put out by various religious organizations. Only token remnants of the grip that Samoan formerly had on Nululaelae literacy practices remain; the language that looms in the background of reading and writing activities is now English.

However, as I will argue in this study, literacy in Tuvaluan is firmly established in the life of the atoll, and, despite evidence of English "leakages" into Tuvaluan literacy practices (e.g., the salutations in letters and headings in sermons are often written in English), literacy in Tuvaluan and literacy in English are not really in competition. There are important quantitative and qualitative differences between the two. First, literacy is rarely conducted entirely in English. For example, only a handful of people are proficient enough in English to write a letter or to read a magazine, and indeed the opportunities to do so are few and far between. Literacy in English is only systematically relevant to the work activities of the handful of government workers in residence (i.e., the primary-school teachers, the Island Executive Officer, and the telegraph operator). Second, when they do use English for literacy, Nukulaelae Islanders are almost entirely consumers of it, while they are both producers and consumers of Tuvaluan literacy. If they learn to write English at school, they typically move to Funafuti or elsewhere to seek salaried employment. However, from that vantage point, English literates do not establish themselves in a hegemonic position *vis-à-vis* the rest of the community, because there are too many social deterrents to ensure that this does not take place.

Other languages

Besides Gilbertese, Samoan, and English, mention should also be made of Cook Island Maori, the Eastern Polynesian language in which Elekana conducted the first literacy instruction and "official" church services on the atoll.[4] It is unlikely that, in the course of the two months that he spent there, anyone was able to acquire any of that language thoroughly enough to read and write it, but older Nukulaelae Islanders today still know a handful of hymns in Cook Island Maori, which presumably have been transmitted from one generation to the other since 1861. In addition, individual members of the contemporary community have gained competence in other languages for a variety of reasons, although they do not use them actively. In this category fall Tokelauan (a Polynesian language closely related to Tuvaluan), Kosraean and Marshallese (both Micronesian languages), Toaripi (a Non-Austronesian language of Papua New Guinea), Nauruan (probably in Pidginized form), Pidgin Fijian, Nauru Cantonese Pidgin, and Pidginized German.

Schooling

The introduction of literacy in the second half of the nineteenth century is intimately linked to the introduction of schools on the one hand and to conversion to Christianity on the other. The three processes were simultaneous and the same agents were responsible for all three. According to his own published testimony, Elekana made schooling a priority upon his landfall:

We then began schools; we met four times every day. I first taught them the names of the letters, and afterwards to form these letters into words. All were anxious to learn; they left off all work, and would do nothing but learn to read. I did nothing but teach them; we had a singing class in the evenings. The various classes brought me an abundance of food in turn as payment for my labour.

(1872:149)

(Goldsmith and Munro 1992a:27–31 provide a detailed exegesis of this and other excerpts of Elekana's text concerning literacy and schooling.) Through these activities, Elekana was pre-figuring the pedagogical activities that would occupy a substantial portion of the Samoan teachers' time after their arrival in 1865. For many decades, the practices of which he had given islanders a glimpse remained essentially unchanged in their basic priorities and content (although the audience of school instruction appears to have quickly become confined to children). In addition to reading and writing, which centered exclusively on the Christian Scriptures, the Samoan pastors taught Nukulaelae children biblical history and Christian doctrine, simple arithmetics, a smattering of English words, and, later, such subjects as basic geography (of the biblical Middle East and, of course, Samoa). The success of their efforts greatly impressed visiting missionaries and other occasional callers, who continued to marvel at the educational accomplishments of atoll dwellers. Missionary journals and reports are replete with remarks like the following:

Not the least interesting part of the day's engagements was the Sabbath-school. There were twenty-nine children present. The progress they had made was surprising. Little boys and girls not only read the Samoan Bible with fluency, but turned up readily chapter and verse as well as hymns in the Samoan hymn-book.

(Murray 1876:399, in reference to his 1866 visit).

At the children's meeting 11 boys and 9 girls read well.

(G. Turner 1876:5)

[A]ll the inhabitants of the island, with the exception of five or six very old people, and young children, can read [the Samoan Scriptures] intelligently.

(S.J. Whitmee on his 1870 visit, quoted in Murray 1876:413)

The practices of traditional instruction, which can be reconstructed on the basis of respondents' recollections and observations of modern-day practices, were comparable to patterns found in contemporary rural Samoa (Duranti and Ochs 1986), as well as many other parts of the Pacific. The emphasis was on rote learning, first of letters and words, then of whole Bible passages recited aloud in unison. While we have no report of early reading instruction on Nukulaelae, a turn-of-the-century Australian visitor to Funafuti, Mrs. David, describes reading classes in the Funafuti school as follows: "The reading throughout the school was fluent, but all read as if they were intoning, and stopped with a curious jerk after each phrase" (1899:85). On Nukulaelae, small children would chant (and still do) the following from Samoan syllabary charts:

> *aa, aa, ato*
> *ee, ee, elefane*
> *ii, ii, ipu*
> *oo, oo, ofu*
> *uu, uu, uati*
> a is for basket
> e is for elephant
> i is for cup
> o is for dress
> u is for watch

Duranti and Ochs (1986) comment on the fact that the illustrated syllabaries used in Samoa mostly depict objects that are not indigenous to Samoan culture. The same remark can be made about Nukulaelae; indeed, four of the five items mentioned in the above recitation are "non-traditional" (in the case of the elephant, the item is something that people only have a very vague concept of). These syllabaries are even more complexly removed from everyday life than in Samoan villages, as they betray a Western orientation mediated by Samoan culture.

Today, many of the same practices linger in pedagogical contexts. In Sunday school, the direct descendant of Samoan pastors' schools, and in the informal pedagogical routines that old women perform with their younger grandchildren (*fai te aakoga* "do school"), instruction consists of highly ritualized rounds of questions and answers, conducted today as it probably was a hundred years ago. Children generally sit in a circle around the adult and answer in unison:

> Q: *Kooi te tagata muamua?*
> A: *Ko Aatamu!*
> Q: *Kooi te fafine muamua?*
> A: *Ko Eva!*
> Q: *Kooi te tagata mafi?*
> A: *Ko Saamasone!*
> Q: *Kooi tou faaola?*
> A: *Ko Ieesuu!*
> Q: Who was the first man?
> A: Adam!
> Q: Who was the first woman?
> A: Eve!

Q: Who was the strong man?
A: Sampson!
Q: Who is your Savior?
A: Jesus!

In these routines, children sometimes confuse biblical characters with real-life individuals of the same name, to the great hilarity of all overhearers. In Sunday school, children are read Biblical passages, which they must listen to quietly. They are sometimes expected to repeat sentences together. Accuracy in repetition is the most important criterion for a successful performance.

Colonial and post-colonial primary schooling

Throughout Tuvalu, schooling remained under the exclusive authority of the Samoan pastors until the 1950s, when the colonial government established primary schools on all Outer Islands of the Colony. From that point on, education appears to have become the site of a subdued territorial struggle between the church and the colonial government, although the historical evidence is fragmentary. Even after the establishment of government schools, pastors continued their pedagogical activities, which became more and more confined to the teaching of reading and writing to pre-school children, and to religious instruction. Today, children attend a secular Western-style primary school controlled by the Ministry of Social Services. More and more primary school teachers are trained at regional institutions (e.g., the University of the South Pacific in Fiji) and sometimes in Australia and New Zealand. While primary schooling is based on contemporary Western educational practices, one encounters there patterns of interaction and instruction reminiscent of the Samoan pastors' school. With respect to literacy in particular, the island primary school places as much emphasis as the pastor school on repetition in group, on copying rather than innovating, and on the acquisition of a few basic notions judged to be essential to one's life.

Yet these practices are effective in imparting basic skills that meet the literacy needs of everyday life on the atoll: reading religious texts, writing letters and notes, taking minutes during meetings, and composing, copying, and reading sermons. Because nearly every child attends primary school, virtually everyone in the community has the literacy skills relevant to these practices. This state of affairs already characterized this society in the very early days of literacy, judging from reports of early visitors.[5] On the atoll, everyone has access to basic schooling, and hence to basic literacy skills. Here basic schooling (frequently symbolized as the ability to read, write, and count) is a marker of basic socialization, and the only unschooled adults are mentally handicapped individuals. Nululaelae Islanders react with shocked disbelief to reports that occasionally come their way of the low rates of literacy and schooling elsewhere in the world. Basic literacy skills, together with the knowledge that one acquires alongside literacy (e.g., lists of biblical protagonists and accounts of their deeds), are necessary conditions for being considered a social entity in this community.[6]

Secondary schooling

Because of the small size of the population and the lack of resources, there has never been a secondary school on the atoll. The only secondary school in the country, Motufoua School, is located on Vaitupu, 125 nautical miles to the north, which today caters to about 250 students. The first secondary school was established by the LMS in 1900, and was first intended for boys only and located on Funafuti (in 1905 it was transferred to Vaitupu).[7] In 1922, the colonial government established a competing school on Vaitupu, Elise Fou School (phonemically *Eelise Foou*, literally "New Ellice [Islands]"). Here again, a pattern of hushed but intense competition between church and state underscores the evolution of secondary education in Tuvalu, forms of which still survive even though secondary schooling today is nominally under the control of the government. Elise Fou's first principal was a New Zealander named Donald Gilbert Kennedy, who remained in the group until 1940 (as a colonial District Officer after 1932). During his long tenure he became an important though controversial figure. Strongly anti-clerical, he deplored the political, cultural, and linguistic hegemony of Samoan pastors and exalted Tuvalu's "traditional" identity. He published two monographs on the culture and language of Vaitupu (Kennedy 1931 and 1946 respectively), compiled with the (unacknowledged) assistance of Elise Fou schoolboys. Kennedy cut a charismatic figure, who trained virtually all Tuvaluans of that generation who went on to be in the employ of the colonial administration and later to found the independent nation of Tuvalu. Today he is vividly remembered amongst his surviving students for the high expectations he had of them, his philandering, his brutality as a disciplinarian, his skills as a hypnotist, his influential role in establishing the first cooperative stores that eventually replaced traders' stores, and his having introduced the first telegraphic unit to the islands (Kelese Simona, personal communication; see also Garrett 1992:411, Teo 1983:136–9).

In contrast to the near universality of primary schooling, very few Nukulaelae Islanders make it to secondary school: at the 1979 census, all 319 inhabitants of the atoll over 10 years of age reported having gone to primary school for at least five years, but only 13 (i.e., 4 percent) had attended secondary school.[8] The transition from primary to secondary schools is characterized by major discontinuities, not only in terms of the

elementary but not primary schooling.

numbers of individuals who have access to each, but in many other respects. First, secondary school students are selected with an entrance examination in English and mathematics, which very few atoll children ever pass. Clearly, the nature of what is tested in this gate-keeping event is at variance with what children learn in primary school, a topic that deserves further scrutiny. On Funafuti, where a national élite principally in the employ of the government has been forming since Independence, the rate of success is much higher, as one would expect. Second, secondary school is taught in English (hence the prominence of English in the entrance exam), whereas children do not have the opportunity to learn much of that language in their early years (primary school is taught principally in Tuvaluan). Third, in contrast to primary schooling, secondary school attendance is not free, and the fees (A$144 a year in 1985) can quickly become prohibitive for families with several school-age children. Finally, attending secondary school requires children to be separated from their families and island homes for many months at a time because of infrequent shipping. The high rate of attrition at Motufoua bears witness to the personal difficulties that result from this separation. For many members of the community, these factors converge to close the door of educational opportunities and subsequent wage-earning employment, hence hindering upward mobility in a broader economic framework in which money plays an increasingly important role. Nevertheless, primary schooling and the basic literacy and numeracy skills it imparts continue to be well adapted to locally grounded needs associated with atoll politics and kinship-based socioeconomic life.

Literacy

It is very difficult to disentangle literacy from the development of education and religious conversion in the nineteenth-century historical records. The introducing agents considered reading, schooling, and Christianity to be three facets of the same evolutionary process towards modernity. This ideology did not go unnoticed on the atoll: one finds in contemporary Nukulaelae representations clear echoes of nineteenth-century European views. LMS missionaries often invoked the metaphor of "darkness" for paganism, illiteracy, and lack of schooling, in contrast to "light," associated with the contrasting categories. For example, these metaphors emerge repeatedly in a missionary's description of Nukulaelae as "[an] island, a few years ago under the undisputed reign of the prince of darkness, now enlightened with the true light, with the visible Church of Christ established as a witness to the light" (Whitmee 1871:12). Similarly, A.W. Murray relates that in Elekana's canoe was a Rarotongan New Testament and hymnal, and that Nukulaelae Islanders asked him to tear out leaves and distribute them before he left:[9]

So eager were the people to learn to read the Word of God that nothing would serve them but the New Testament must be approportioned out amongst them. Elekana yielded to their importunity, and gave two or three leaves to each; the portion that fell to the share of the chief I have now in my possession: he has carefully preserved it, and gave it to me at my request.

(Murray 1865:337–8)

Significantly, Murray entitles this parable "Rays of Light in the Midst of Darkness."

Contemporary Nukulaelae Islanders could easily have thought up this title. One of the pervasive symbols in their social theory is the contrast between *pouliuli* "darkness" (or *poouliga*) and *maalamalama* "light" (cf. Goldsmith 1989b, Koch 1962). These terms are embedded in complex conceptual linkages and have many metaphorical associations. *Maalamalama* refers to the adherence to what Nukulaelae Islanders perceive to be Christian standards of living, i.e., being clothed, clean, schooled, and literate, having knowledge of certain types (excluding, for example, knowledge of sorcery), and maintaining certain standards of social order, in which *fiileemuu* "peace, tranquility, placidity" and *feaalofani* "mutual empathy, interpersonal harmony" play key roles (both these terms are borrowings from Samoan). *Maalamalama* (which also translates as "to understand") is associated to socioeconomic development and modernity, although this relationship is an ambivalent one because modernity is also known to lead one away from Christianity and tradition (see Arno 1993:134–8 for a discussion of this issue in reference to Fiji). In contrast, *pouliuli* denotes non- or pre-Christian values and practices: nakedness, dirt, disorder, lack of social control, warfare, infanticide, and heathenism. The polarity between *maalamalama* and *pouliuli*, versions of which are found elsewhere in the Pacific, is so thoroughly enmeshed with other cardinal symbols in Nukulaelae Islanders' representations of their own culture, where it has an almost Lévi-Straussian quality, that it appears at first glance to be descended from an aboriginal symbolic structure remolded to fit Christian categories. Nevertheless, it is so similar to nineteenth-century missionary discourse that it undoubtedly originated there. The fact that the terms *maalamalama* and *pouliuli* are borrowed from Samoan further suggests that Samoan pastors played a crucial mediating role in giving the concepts the prominence they have in contemporary Nukulaelae ideology.

Literacy is a symbolic cornerstone in the opposition between *maalamalama* and *pouliuli*. Illiterate persons or groups are commonly described as *pouliuli*. The historical introduction of literacy to the atoll is often presented as one aspect of the passage from the *pouliuli* of pre-Christian days to the *maalamalama* of today; however, in these representations, literacy is a co-occurring event, rather than a causal or "enabling" factor.

It is in the context of these ideological constructs that historical accounts of the introduction of literacy to Nukulaelae must be interpreted. Nineteenth-century European visitors (predominantly LMS missionaries) and contemporary Nukulaelae oral history invariably centralize the great curiosity and immense enthusiasm with which Nukulaelae Islanders are said to have greeted the new technology. I have already noted several anecdotal tokens of this imputed enthusiasm: the islanders' purchase of a Bible from a passing ship prior to Elekana's landfall, the substantial amount of precious cash they spent on buying Bibles from visiting mission ships, the success of literacy instruction after the Samoan teacher Ioane's arrival, and the tale of Elekana distributing pages of his books to the islanders upon his departure. There are other anecdotes in which mid-nineteenth-century Nukulaelae Islanders emerge as nearly obsessed with the printed word. Copies of the Bible, for example, were in great demand:

Ten copies of the Samoan Bible had been sent to [Funafuti], and an equal number to Nukulaelae, some time before my visit, and they had all been bought up, and the people were longing for a further supply. Hymn-books also, and other books, were purchased readily. School-books and detached portions of Scriptures were *given* to those who were able to turn them to account.

(Murray 1876:401–2, emphasis in original)

Comparable eagerness to obtain books and literacy skills in the early days of contact have been noted in New Zealand (Cleave 1979, Jackson 1975, McKenzie 1985), Samoa (Crawford 1977), Micronesia (Topping 1983), and Polynesia in general (Koskinen 1957, 1965, Parsonson 1967). Early reports from many parts of the Pacific further emphasize "the sheer magic of the written word in primitive eyes" (Parsonson 1967:44) and the awe of native peoples before the power of the written word. For example, Will Mariner, a beachcomber who spent four years as the captive and then adoptive son of King Fīnau 'Ulukālala II of Vava'u, Tonga, during the first decade of the nineteenth century, reports that at the beginning of his captivity Tongans deprived him of his books and papers, which they feared were instruments of witchcraft (Martin 1817[1981]:65).

However, it is telling that nineteenth-century Europeans imputed this view of literacy to the "Other" everywhere they went in the world, not just the Pacific, and that these projections are still alive today (Harbsmeier 1988). Walter Ong, for example, claims to have "never encountered or heard of an oral culture that does not want to achieve literacy as soon as possible" (1982:175), despite much evidence to the contrary, I should add. As McKenzie (1985) argues pertinently in reference to the New Zealand Maori, the missionaries were anxious to find eagerness for literacy among the missionized populations, and imputed this eagerness to them whether it existed or not: "victims of their own myths, the missionaries found what they wanted to find, and reported what they knew their London committee wished to hear" (1985:16). In the case of Nukulaelae, it is difficult to know much about the attitude of nineteenth-century islanders towards literacy, because their voice cannot be heard today. The only accounts available are those of LMS missionaries of the time, as well as modern Nukulaelae voices, which were essentially shaped by missionary voices. This one-sided silence is not simply the result of nineteenth-century Nukulaelae Islanders' illiteracy, but, more crucially, it ensues from their lack of access to the resources that would have enabled them to make their voices heard. Furthermore, unlike LMS missionaries, they did not belong to a society whose power structure is obsessed with records, yearly reports, accounts, and the like.[10]

Several remarks can nevertheless be made interpretively. First, even if Nukulaelae Islanders were indeed as enthusiastic about literacy as missionaries claim, one should seriously question the extent to which Europeans themselves did not *create* this enthusiasm. Visiting missionaries, for example, placed overwhelming emphasis on literacy skills and concomitant religious knowledge as prerequisites for church membership, and hence for access to the desirable material and symbolic capital that accompanied conversion. In 1870, S.J. Whitmee reports that on his visit, "I found all could read and understand the Samoan Scriptures, copies of which they possessed; but 13 were not as satisfactory in their knowledge as the others, I thought, therefore, it was advisable to allow them to stand over for another year [before admitting them to the Church]" (Whitmee [n.d.]:82). It is not difficult to envisage how these practices resulted directly in playing up the importance of literacy as highly desirable in the minds of those who were thus tested. Later, the Protectorate authorities engaged in similar gate-keeping practices by requiring island magistrates to be literate. In addition, the very first page of the Samoan-language 1894 *Native Laws* stipulates the following:

1. *Ia iai i Nuu sili taitasi, se Failautusi nate tusia **uma** faamasinoga sa fai e le Faamasino, i le Tusi Tulafono . . .*
2. *O le failautusi na te tusia **uma** tusi a le Alii sili, poo Faipule.*
1. On each Island there shall be a Scribe who records in writing *all* judgments rendered by the Judge in the Court Book . . .
2. The Scribe shall write *all* letters for the Chief or Magistrates.
(Ellice Islands Protectorate 1894:6, in original orthography, emphasis added, my translation)

British authorities thus contributed to give literacy great significance in the eyes of the inhabitants of the Protectorate.

Second, LMS missionaries exerted a great deal of authority over the already despotic Samoan teachers, and must have appeared to nineteenth-century islanders to be endowed with superhuman authority and power, whose elusiveness added to the mystique. Thus the names of some LMS missionaries are still remembered more than a century later, in contrast to most other outsiders, who are quickly forgotten unless they leave descendants on the atoll: for example, A.W. Murray is embedded in the community's historical canon as *Misi Male* (a phonological adaptation of "Mister Murray"). If Nukulaelae Islanders resisted the encroachment of literacy, one can well imagine that acts of resistance would not have taken place in full view of the missionaries on their day-long yearly visits, and that they would have escaped completely the attention of the missionaries. Whatever may be the case, if covert resistance to literacy, schooling, and conversion did take place at the time of their introduction, it is entirely absent in modern times.

Finally, the potential role of the Samoan pastor in generating the expected enthusiasm for literacy cannot be overemphasized. The Samoan pastors who descended on Tuvalu were intimately acquainted with English missionaries' values and priorities. Furthermore, visiting LMS missionaries used the islanders' literacy skills, along with such factors as the cleanliness of the village and church attendance, as a yardstick to evaluate the Samoan pastors' work competence, and demoted them if these fell short of expectations (Goldsmith and Munro 1992b). In other words, the Samoan pastors depended for their very livelihood on their flock putting on an impressive show for the yearly visitors. The pressure that they exerted on the community for it to perform well is not difficult to envision.[11] Using the rich body of documentation on nineteenth-century Maori responses to literacy, McKenzie (1985:17) demonstrates that the Maori recited memorized texts while masquerading their performances as reading for the benefit of English missionaries. Although we have no evidence that Nukulaelae employed the same subterfuge, the likelihood that they did is high.

The scope of literacy

Once the technology became established, the enthusiasm for it among islanders is unequivocal. However, their interest in literacy was hardly confined to reading the Bible: by the 1880s, they were constantly in the market for writing implements and paper for letter writing. The atoll's limited natural resources do not include a local source of paper, paper-like material, and writing implements, and the community has always had to rely on an outside supply. Barely twenty years after the initial introduction of literacy to the atoll, a visitor to the atoll expressed his surprise at the islanders' eagerness for letter writing:[12] "The Nukulailai [*sic*] people . . . are well educated, can all read, and are most persistent letter writers. No present is more acceptable to them than a few sheets of paper and some pens . . . We nearly ran out of ink before we got clear of the group" (Bridge 1886:554). Twenty-five years later, after a postal service was inaugurated, the Resident Commissioner of the Protectorate remarked: "[I]t is pleasing to note how the natives have taken advantage of the same, and how quickly they have grasped what is required of them" (Gilbert and Ellice Islands Protectorate 1913:8). By that time, letter writing was firmly established in the lives of people. Evidence of the demand for writing implements and stationery can be gleaned from other circumstantial records, such as trade-store inventories. By the fourth quarter of the nineteenth century, resident traders had become established on every island of Tuvalu, although until 1890 the Godeffroy plantation maintained a monopoly on the import of trade goods to Nukulaelae, as mentioned in Chapter 2. No trade-store inventory for Nukulaelae survives; but writing tools account for a substantial portion of the inventory of the trade store on Nukufetau from around 1884 (cited in Munro 1982:215): it lists pens (at the cost of 6 coconuts), lead pencils (20 coconuts, 9lbs of copra, or 16½¢ each), lead pencils with tops (30 nuts or 18¢), lead pencils with Indian rubber tops (16¢), foolscap copy books (25 nuts, 10lbs of copra, or 25¢), foolscap paper (12 nuts or 6lbs of copra), and small account books (7lbs of copra or 10¢). The interest in literacy above and beyond Bible reading was keen, and the demand for writing tools went hand-in-hand with the popularity of such items as cloth and clothing, metal fish-hooks and fishing line, tobacco, knives and scissors, matches, needles, and mirrors.

Nukulaelae Islanders are unlikely to ever have received instruction in letter writing, since literacy was brought to them for the sole purpose of reading the Bible. Yet they were clearly able to apply their newly acquired literacy skills to suit their own purposes and social designs, thus *empowering the technology* and giving it, from the beginning, a meaning that was related only remotely to the meaning that the agents of introduction intended it to have. Two important remarks can be made on the basis of the albeit scant historical testimony. Nukulaelae experienced an efflorescence of literacy practices in the years following the introduction of the technology; and this efflorescence was the direct result of Nukulaelae people's successful efforts to redefine literacy for their own benefit. Thus, contrary to the impression conveyed by missionary representations, where literacy is equated with Bible reading, a heterogeneous set of literacy practices emerged very early, and islanders were hardly passive recipients of the new technology once it was introduced.

To a certain extent, Bible reading does occupy today a central place in the range of literacy activities that Nukulaelae people engage in. According to the "cover story" that they present of their own society, the motivation for learning how to read is to read the Bible. Despite vastly improved communications in contrast to the late nineteenth century, few printed items ever make it to the other islands of Tuvalu other than Bibles and Church-related ephemera. However, members of the community consume and produce literacy in many different social contexts. Personal letters and written sermons are the most salient literacy items generated on the atoll, and I describe the practices surrounding the production and consumption of these items in the next four chapters. I analyze these two practices in detail because they are the most important "textually" literate products generally composed directly in writing, i.e., the only products that exhibit continuous discourse. However, letters and sermons are not the only items that Nukulaelae Islanders read and write, and a broad variety of written materials is integral to their everyday experience: lists of many types, compilations of traditional skills and genealogies, telegrams, lyrics of songs, minutes of meetings, invitations to feasts, names and slogans woven on mats as decoration, tee-shirt illustrations, and graffiti. A brief description of these materials is part and parcel of an ethnographic description of literacy on the atoll, and I focus here on the more salient among them.

Perhaps the most frequent use to which atoll dwellers put their literacy skills is to establish and keep records of many types, many in list form. Examples include lists of dues for organizations and clubs (e.g., boys' brigade, girl guides, church choir, dance groups), records of various monetary transactions (e.g., fish sales, store purchases), and records of contributions to the community (e.g., thatching for community buildings). Keeping such lists is the responsibility of a broad spectrum of individuals, from household heads to adolescents. The following illustration (in which the original orthography has been preserved) is a record of fish sales. The mixture of English and Tuvaluan is typical of such lists (the left-hand column displays people's names, the word *atu* means "bonito," and the last line means "money borrowed by Luisa: $1.00"):

22nd August, 1981

Saturday

Taataa	*1 atu*	*6½ lbs*	=	*$3.25.*	
Mataua	*1 "*	*5⅓lbs*	=	*2.75.*	*.20 left.*
Esita	*1 "*	*5¼ lbs*	=	*2.65.*	
Kapua		*5¾ lbs*	=	*2.85.*	
Tali		*5 lbs*	=	*2.50.*	*paid*
Kaitalafu a Luisa $1.00.					

Other notable literacy products are written invitations to family feasts (*kkaiga*). Families may give feasts on a variety of occasions: a child's first birthday, a wedding, or the return of a family member from overseas. When such events are held, the hosting household invites the "distinguished" members of the community (*tino fai tofi*, literally "people with responsibilities"). This includes first and foremost the pastor, an invariable fixture at such events (whose girth generally bears witness to this fact), the island chief, and the president of the Island Council. The pastor's presence in particular is *de rigueur* because it sanctifies the gathering and brings *manuia* "good fortune" to the event and to the person being celebrated in the event. Also invited are strangers (*tino fakaallofa*, literally "empathy-worthy people"), i.e., people whom the community tacitly takes the responsibility of feeding: government employees (e.g., the telegraph operator, the Island Executive Officer, the resident nurse and constable) and any visitor to the atoll. Of course, members of the "greater" kin group, including people with whom one is not on very good terms, also attend the feast.

Since the mid-1970s, it has become the custom to notify invited guests on slips of paper referred to as *pepa*, literally "paper." These invitations, which are thought to be patterned on a "Western custom" (*tuu Ppaalagi*), are distributed to their recipients ahead of time (but frequently only a few hours before the feast) by a child or an adolescent, and have become so essential that Nukulaelae people no longer show up to a family feast if they have only been informed by word of mouth.[13] Following is a representative sample of *pepa*, all of which were addressed to me during my 1985 field sojourn (the text is identical to all other invitations that were distributed at the same time):

Niko:
E fakamolemole atu mo te aava lasi kee fakatasi mai ki te kkaiga fiafia a Saakaio & Douglas & Amoe.
Koga: Fale o Fuatia
Taimi: 6:30 p.m.
Fakamolemole pukepuke mai tifa/ipu/sipunu.
Niko:
You are very respectfully asked to join the family feast for Saakaio & Douglas & Amoe.
Place: Fuatia's house
Time: 6.30 p.m. [in English]
Please bring plate/cup/spoon.

Koo manakogina koe kee fakatasi mai ki te kkaiga fiafia o te aso faanau o te mokopuna pele ko Tinilau Salanoa, teelaa ko te kaatoaga o tena tausaga muamua, teelaa ko te aso nei. Fakafetai mai ia Tinilau Elekana mo te kaaiga.
Time: 4.30 p.m.
Koga: fale Tinilau.
You are asked to join the family feast for the birthday of the beloved grand-child Tinilau Salanoa, which is the completion of his first year, which is today. Tinilau, Elekana and the kin group thank you.
Time: 4.30 p.m. [in English]
Place: Tinilau's house.

Niko:
E fiafia lasi maaua o kkami mai koe ki te kkaiga fooliki o te fakaipoipoga a Siata mo Mailagi i te aso nei poo 1/11/85.

Time: 12.00 onward.
Place: Mapusaga's residence.
Niko:
We are very happy to invite you to a small meal for Siata's and Mailagi's wedding today the 1/11/85.
Time: 12:00 onward. [in English]
Place: Mapusaga's residence. [in English]

Note again the conspicuous presence of English, particularly in specifications of times and venues.

Some members of the community keep private written records of recipes, formulae, and instructions associated with traditional expert knowledge, including techniques of deep-sea fishing, swamp-taro gardening, coconut-toddy tapping, house building, and martial arts. The knowledge and mastery of these skills is referred to as *logo* (etymologically related to a word meaning "understanding"), and notebooks in which the techniques are written down are referred to as *api logo* "notebook of traditional knowledge." Alternatively, terms denoting the area of knowledge they describe can also be applied to these notebooks: a book about fishing techniques, for example, is a *muli vaka*, and a book about coconut tending is an *ao*. Also found in *api logo* are genealogies, copies of wills, historical narratives, and family land-tenure records. Comparable uses of literacy are found in other Pacific societies, such as the Austral Islands (Babadzan 1985) and Kiribati (Latouche 1984).

The skills and information that are recorded in these books are the jealously guarded property of particular kin groups, and are transmitted by older men to selected members of younger generations. Nukulaelae Islanders believe that the practice began very early in the history of literacy, when knowledgeable individuals began writing down descriptions of the techniques that they were familiar with, for the purpose, according to respondents, of preventing their disappearance as Western technology was encroaching on the atoll's technological repertoire. Today, owners of these books sometimes recopy them, but it is unlikely that any new book of this type is being compiled nowadays. Because traditional technologies belong to specific descent lines, and because they frequently involve magic, much secrecy typically surrounds the exercise books in which these skills are recorded. Their owners rarely talked about them (although other people often speculate about who owns such books) and they are never shown to anyone outside the kin group. Genealogical records are treated with less secrecy, although they are not commonly shared with members of other kin groups. In Chapter 6, I will return to the topic of *api logo*, and will demonstrate that they bear striking similarities to sermon notebooks.

Literacy emerges in one traditional art form, namely mat waving. Mats are woven exclusively by women, usually with specially treated pandanus leaves. There are several types of mats, each of which is associated with various utilitarian purposes and qualities (see Koch 1961:128–35 for a general description of Tuvaluan mats). Finer mats, i.e., those used as bedding or customary gifts, are frequently decorated with various geometric patterns as well as proper names, sometimes in the elegant Gothic lettering learned in the early days from the wives of Samoan pastors, who themselves learned it from European missionary spouses. Conceptually, writing adorns Nukulaelae mats in the same way that it emerges on nineteenth-century American embroidered samplers (Bilaniuk 1989, Ring 1983, 1993). However, the amount of writing that can fit on a mat is more restricted than on samplers: usually there is only room for a few names at most. Typically, a mat displays the word "Nukulaelae" or the name of a person, usually the recipient of the mat if it is intended as a gift. I have not collected information on sociocognitive aspects of the process of weaving words on mats, although the issue raises interesting questions (cf. Khan 1993 on this topic in relation to Kashmiri carpet weaving). In contrast to other Polynesian societies (e.g., Tonga), Nukulaelae does not have a lively tradition of embroidered writing on such items as pillow cases.

Finally, Nukulaelae Islanders engage in miscellaneous literacy activities in a variety of settings. Singing and dancing are serious business in this community, and songs, dances, and hymns are composed in writing and laboriously copied and recopied. Atoll dwellers often send telegrams to relatives on Funafuti and elsewhere, although the radio telephone is rapidly superseding telegrams. Telegrams are also sent to the Government's Broadcasting Services on Funafuti to request "dedications" (*manako*, literally "requests"), i.e., that a song be played for a particular individual or group. Who dedicates what song to whom and on what occasion is a topic of great interest to everyone, and has clearly emerged as a means of disseminating information about one's activities to the rest of the country without giving the appearance of engaging in self-promotion.

A handful of individuals spend a great deal of time recording inventories, keeping written accounts, writing reports, drawing order forms, taking minutes of meetings, and issuing receipts: in this category fall the employees of the cooperative store, the Island Executive Officer (IEO), the telegraph operator, the resident nurse, and the constable. Some of these activities are conducted in Tuvaluan, others in English. (One of the requirements for employment on Funafuti is the ability to write English; prospective government employees must thus write a letter of application in English.) However, most other community members are the recipients of these bureaucratic literacy practices, and apparently have been for many decades: the 1916 *Revised Native Laws* for the Colony stipulate that the Scribe of every island "shall give a numbered receipt for [all fines collected] in every case" (Gilbert & Ellice Islands Colony 1916:1). Many adults have a savings account with the Bank of Tuvalu, and they take their passbook to the IEO to be updated and stamped when the occasion arises. In this rule-conscious society, everyone appears in the local court as a defendant at some stage, for offenses ranging from failing to sweep one's house-porch to owning a pig that escaped from its pen; the court is a setting in which literacy looms conspicuously, in the form of law manuals and minutes, for example. Everyone is occasionally called upon to sign forms. "Signing" (*saina*) is an important metaphor with a broad range of meaning in this community: for example, it can mean entering into a contractual agreement (e.g., to work on Nauru) or adopting a child. Everyone wears tee-shirts displaying slogans in English, brought back or sent by relatives from Funafuti and beyond, although no one pays particular notice to these slogans or tries to make much sense of them. As a result, it is not uncommon to see respectable elderly women wearing tee-shirts displaying obscene captions, which their seaman sons or grandsons have brought back from overseas. Everyone passes by notice boards near the store or the Island Council office, although again no one pays much attention to the notices posted on them. In short, although not all forms of literacy are given equal prominence, literacy is omnipresent in the Nukulaelae social environment.

4
LETTER WRITING AND READING

Papauta, Sept. 13, 1897

To Mrs. David, the lady,–
My love to you! alas my mother! The thought weeps when I think of you, together with the others, because of your kindness to me. Alas for my love! Dear, oh dear, my heart is full of love, but it is difficult because I cannot speak; but I thought I would try and send this small piece of paper to make known to you my love. Alas my mother! my love is very great, and it is difficult and hard because we shall be so soon parted. Grief continues to grow in my heart when I think of the days we were together in Funafuti. Alas! I do not forget them and you all. I feel I want to be still with you. It is hard that we have been so soon parted on shore. May you return with blessing to your home. This love of mine has nothing with which to make itself known, but I have striven to make appear before you that which was hidden, namely, my love to you. Alas, my parents, love is difficult.
This letter is hurriedly written. May Jehovah remain with us both when we are separated. Good bye.
May you live!

VITOLIA.
(David 1899:88–9)

At the end of the nineteenth century, Lady Caroline David accompanied a geological research team led by her husband to Funafuti, then a remote outpost. After her return to Australia, she received the above letter from a young woman who had been studying at the LMS's Papā'uta School on Upolu, Samoa, and subsequently quoted it in the narrative of her three-month sojourn on the atoll, a treasure of Victorian perceptions of Funafuti society at the turn of the century. By the time this "wailing letter" (David 1899:89) was written, thirty years had elapsed since the introduction of literacy to Funafuti. This letter, the original of which was written in Samoan, thus represents one of the earliest recorded samples of writing by a Tuvaluan.[1]

The historical records are too scanty to enable us to judge the extent to which Vitolia's letter is representative of the written output of nineteenth-century Funafuti Islanders; yet the letter bears much resemblance to the written texts that both Funafuti and Nukulaelae Islanders produce today. In this chapter, I describe what is probably the most salient motivation for writing in the lives of most Nukulaelae Islanders, namely corresponding

72

with people in residence away from the atoll. Evidently, the Nukulaelae community is not unique in its interest in letter writing: letters are a common and valued use of literacy in societies as diverse as the Fore of Papua New Guinea (Rubinstein and Gajdušek 1970), the Vai in East Africa (Scribner and Cole 1981), and the Diyari of Central Australia (Ferguson 1987), and among inner-city American schoolchildren (Shuman 1986) and in the ancient Greco-Roman world (Stowers 1986). Letters probably represent a major percentage of the written output of members of many societies.

Despite its importance, letter writing has not been a major topic of anthropological or sociolinguistic research. The few studies that have focused on the topic have used data from middle-class Western settings, and have commonly treated context as unproblematic (e.g., De Rycker 1991, Mulkay 1985). With a few exceptions, social scientists who have studied letter writing from a cross-cultural perspective have been satisfied with paraphrases and narrative descriptions of what the letters are like (e.g., Berry and Bennett 1991, Bennett and Berry 1991 on the Cree of Northern Ontario, Bloch 1993:103–4 on the Zafimaniry of Madagascar), or, if they present the actual texts of letters, they are usually translated and edited. In these accounts, the voice of letter writers are either stifled completely or are altered through translation and reworking (in a manner that the ethnographer often fails to specify). This stance is based on two underlying assumptions: that meaning resides solely in content, rather than form; and that meaning can be read off, translated, and paraphrased unproblematically across languages and communities. The inescapably interpretive nature of the very act of collecting and analyzing textual data (cf. Tedlock 1983) should not give ethnographers license to take over the voices of their informants and ventriloquize them at will, particularly when these voices can be heard as tangibly as in letters.

In this and the following chapter, I focus on various aspects of Nukulaelae letter writing. I first describe who writes and reads letters, and in what circumstances letters are received and sent. I then turn to the question of the formal characteristics of letters, demonstrating the dialectic relationship between textual form and the historical and contemporary associations of letter writing as a social activity. In Chapter 5, I characterize the purpose and social functions of letters, focusing in particular on a conspicuous facet of letter writing, namely the salience of affect, which I contextualize in terms of the sociocultural backdrop of letter writing on the atoll.

The analysis that follows is based in part on a large corpus of letters gathered during field work. Many Nukulaelae Islanders make it a habit to save the letters they receive, and stacks of letters are frequently found among the personal possessions that every individual keeps in his or her trunk (*pausi*) stored in one corner of the house. Thanks to this practice and to the generosity and trust of many individual members of the community, I was able to collect 327 letters during two sojourns on the atoll (1985 and 1991). I offered a small sum of money (10¢) for any letter that anyone was willing to part with, and advertised this offer in a posting on the Island Council notice board, as well as through word of mouth (the latter method proved to be considerably more effective). I also offered to return the original of letters to anyone who wished to have them back, although no one took up this offer, to my surprise.[2] Judging by the texts of these letters, there is little evidence that any censoring took place before the letters were handed over to me. (Needless to say, I have exercised caution in citing texts in what follows.) The corpus I gathered is probably representative of the mail that residents of the atoll receive. Because Nukulaelae people in temporary residence off-island commonly return to the atoll with the letters they have received during their sojourn abroad, my sample includes letters written from Nukulaelae to off-island addressees, in addition to letters addressed to Nukulaelae residents. This corpus is supplemented by sixty-six letters that have been addressed to me over the years. Although I have kept these letters separate from the rest, most are identical in form and content to other letters in the corpus, particularly letters I began receiving a few years after initial field work from people who had gotten to know me well. In the following discussion, I cite a few excerpts from letters addressed to me, which I mark with an asterisk after the text reference.[3]

Letter writers and readers

Letters (*tusi*, which also means "to write" and "book") are the primary link between Nukulaelae and the rest of the world, and reading and writing letters are the literacy practices that contemporary Nukulaelae Islanders engage in most frequently after reading in church. Almost every adult and adolescent writes and receives letters, although some more frequently than others, and the inhabitants of the atoll have been great letter writers for a surprisingly long time, as discussed in Chapter 3.

Letters and shipping

Letters are received and sent when the government vessel calls at the atoll, once a month on average. By Pacific standards, the frequency of shipping service to Nukulaelae is typical. However, elsewhere in the region, many geographically isolated islands now have airstrips that facilitate communications with the outside world, while Nukulaelae is too small for the construction of a runway, the cost of which would also be above and beyond what Tuvalu could afford in any case.[4] Within Tuvalu, Nukulaelae is visited by the nation's ship less often than other islands and atolls of the

Figure 4   *Government officials arriving on shore on a ship day. Because of the extreme shallowness of the boat passage over the outer reef, passengers and cargo must first be transferred onto the ship's flat-bottom launch visible here, while the ship anchors in deep water outside the reef.*

group despite its relative closeness to the ship's home port, Funafuti. The reason for this pattern is the small size of Nukulaelae's population, which means that passenger and cargo traffic is also small. In addition, Funafuti is the geographical reference point for shipping purposes; Nukulaelae (and Niulakita, which is considered less problematic because it is not an autonomous political entity), located due south of this reference point, is isolated from the other islands of the group, which are strung along a northwestward chain and can all be served by a single trip of the ship.

The shipping schedule is often erratic, and the country's only ship sometimes calls at very short notice. People on the atoll often stay up all night gathering and preparing food for visitors and for relatives on Funafuti and elsewhere clamoring for traditional atoll food (which is particularly difficult to obtain on Funafuti, which has come to depend entirely on imported food of poor quality and often in short supply). While a certain lack of planning may be responsible in part for these last-minute bursts of activity, Nukulaelae people are reminded periodically that planning does not always pay, as they sometimes have to throw away perishables (and waste much food-preparation labor) when scheduled ship visits are cancelled. Among the frantic activities that precede ship visits figures letter writing: people straining with pen and paper in the dim light of kerosene lamps are familiar sights on the eve of ship visits. Similarly, their relatives on Funafuti often have to scribble messages at the wharf as the ship is about to depart, and letters often describe the hurried state they are in:

[brief letter from a young woman on Funafuti to relatives on Nukulaelae]
Ia, te tusi koo fai o gata fua, me ne tusi fakavaavvave fua i te vaka kaa ttala atu.
[letters 1991:728]

So, [this] letter is about to end already, because I wrote it in a hurry, since the ship is about to leave for where you are.

Two to three months sometimes elapse between ship visits, particularly when the ship goes to its annual slippage in Fiji. The ship occasionally calls on its way to Fiji, which makes it difficult to send letters since the next port-of-call is outside the country. In addition, the captain of the ship occasionally forgets to pick up the mail bag before leaving Funafuti, and thus incoming mail can take many months to reach its destination. References to how these communication difficulties affect the frequency of letter writing are not unusual in the text of the letters:[5]

[from a man on Nukulaelae to his teenage daughter studying in Australia]
Ia, E, au koo tusi fakavave iaa koe e faittali mai ki se tusi mai iaa maatou i konei. Kiloke, ona loa ko te auala o te vaka, koo tolu nei taimi e afe mai faeloa i konei i tena auala ki Fiiti. Kae teenei eiloa te taimi muamua ne faatoaa vau ei o foki ki Funaafuti.
[letters 1991:696]

E. I am writing in a rush, because you have been waiting for a letter from us here. You see, it is because of the shipping routes, three times the ship called here on its way to Fiji. This is the very first time [in a long time] that it has called here and then returned to Funafuti.

Some letters describe in a dramatic fashion the anguish that erratic communication can cause:

[from a young woman studying in New Zealand to her mother on Nukulaelae]
Moi mafai laa kee lavea nee koe ko toku nofo pologa mo te mmae teenei e tau ave nee au, ona eeloa ko te seeai o neaku tusi mai iaa koe. See iloa nee au me ko koe e ita, io me ko te seeai o se vaka.
[letters 1991:752]

If you could only see how enslaved I am by the pain I constantly carry with me, on account of the fact that there has been no letter from you. I don't know whether you are angry with me, or whether it is because there has not been any ship [visits].

Some letters, particularly to and from relatives abroad, are sent and received through the mail, although depending on the mail often poses problems, because many people on Nukulaelae cannot afford stamps on a regular basis. If at all possible, letters are entrusted to travelers, who leave the atoll loaded with letters, along with food baskets, frangipani garlands, and other packages to be delivered to a vast array of individuals at all ports-of-call. Indeed, a person planning to leave the atoll is often a major motivation for writing letters. The regularity of epistolary communications with the outside world depends in large part on people's movements to and from the atoll, and on their destinations. Whether letters are sent through the mail or given to travellers, there is a certain degree of uncertainty as to whether they ever reach their destination, a fact that Nukulaelae Islanders are very much aware of. References are often made in letters to concerns about previous letters having been lost:

Kae ko au e fia iloa nee au mai iaa koe me e isi neoutou tusi ne maua i au i te oloatuuga a saa L. Fakamolemole, fakailoa mai. [. . .] Kae ko au e tai faanoanoa maalosi eiloa, auaa maafai seki oko atu aku tusi i te oloatuuga a saa L. Kaafai laa ne oko atu, faafetai. Kae ko au e masalo loa seki oko atu, auaa me seki ai loa se tali o saku tusi i se tasi o koutou konaa ne avatu outou tusi.

[letters 1985:512]

And I want to find out from you whether you got any letters from me when L's party went [to Nukulaelae]. Please let me know. [. . .] And I am going to be very unhappy if the letters I sent along with L's party did not reach you. If they did reach you, thank you. But I suspect that they did not reach you, because I have not received an answer from any of you whom I sent letters to.

Indeed, in the midst of welcoming feasts, visits, late-night conversations (and sour-toddy parties for those who can take part in them when prohibition is not on), travelers often lose letters that are entrusted to them at the last minute amidst sorrowful farewells and the hectic atmosphere that invariably characterizes ship departures in Tuvalu.

Letters and oral messages

Letter writers often entrust travelers with oral messages identical to or elaborating on the content of letters to be delivered. Nukulaelae people have explained this practice as "helping" (*fesoasoani*) the recipient to understand the message of the letter. This explanation finds some justification in my observations of letter reading as a social practice: Nukulaelae Islanders often give evidence of having difficulties reading the letters they receive. It is thus not surprising that the verb referring to letter reading is *ttala* "to decipher," a term also used to refer to chiromantic divination and other interpretive acts involving magic.

When further questioned on the motivations for what appears from a Western perspective to be a duplication of labor, Nukulaelae respondents provide several explanations. They cite problems associated with the poor handwriting of many writers. Respondents who know of my research concerns invoke the lack of a unified orthography. Indeed, as most other

Figure 5 *Ship day: waiting for letters, gossip, and new faces around a kitchen hut near the launch landing.*

written texts, letters exhibit many orthographic idiosyncrasies (see the notes on orthography at the beginning of this book), which clearly impair the efficient decoding of written Tuvaluan. More importantly, a general "lack of practice" (*see maasani* "not familiar with, not adept at") with reading is commonly blamed: like other literacy practices, reading and writing letters are activities that require a cognitive effort unlike the cognitive requirements of everyday routines.

However, reading in other contexts presents no difficulty for many people, and the motivation for supplementing written messages with oral ones lies elsewhere. Underlying local ideologies of literacy is the view that certain forms of oral communication are more reliable than writing. At best, letters are seen as a complement to oral messages: unlike letters, which can be and often are misplaced among the innumerable plastic bags, buckets, boxes, and woven coconut-frond baskets that many Nukulaelae Islanders travel with, oral messages will not slip between the woven fronds of baskets, fall into the ocean during reef-crossings in rough weather, and get soiled to the point of illegibility in contact with cooked swamp taro.

Thus, rather than leading an autonomous existence from oral communication in the local communicative ideology, letters are closely associated with orality. In essence, the oral message that duplicates or elaborates upon the letter provides a social and communicative context for the letter. Kulick and Stroud (1990[1993]:54) describe strikingly similar patterns among the Gapun of Papua New Guinea. The Gapun, in contrast to Nukulaelae Islanders, go to extremes: they pay no attention to letters if they are not accompanied by an oral message. Nukulaelae Islanders simply find letters without messages more difficult to decipher (*ttala*), socially less fulfilling, and potentially less effective, particularly if the writer wants the addressee to do something for him or her. These views probably constitute yet another motivation for bypassing the postal system whenever possible.[6]

Nukulaelae Islanders thus provide a clear counter-example to the autonomous model of literacy which maintains that written communication is *intrinsically* more reliable than oral communication. This view has already been challenged by historians like Clanchy (1993), who shows that oral oaths carried more weight than written contracts in assessing the legitimacy of charters in thirteenth-century England. As Street points out, the "literate mentality" that regards writing as more reliable, trustworthy, and autonomous than oral communication is in large part "*constructed*; it is not something imposed by the form of literacy itself as though the 'technology of the intellect', as Goody terms it, were determinate" (1984:47, emphasis in original). The Nukulaelae data further suggest that attributes like "message permanence" are not only constructed, but they may be constructed differently across literacy practices. Indeed, in Chapter 7, I will show that Nukulaelae Islanders do view certain literacy practices, like the hypothetical "standardized" written recording of oral history, as more trustworthy than oral communication. They thus attribute divergent qualities to literacy in different contexts. The extent to which the messages conveyed in any communicative act are permanent and reliable, or ephemeral and untrustworthy, does not depend on whether the communication takes place in the spoken or written mode. Rather, relative message permanence is a function of cultural evaluations of the communicative act and of such factors as the nature of the technological environment in which communication takes place, and hence the economic resources that communicators have access to.

Correspondents

Nukulaelae Islanders generally correspond with people they know, namely relatives and friends, and rarely write to strangers. During my sojourns among them, people on the atoll would express their surprise when I received letters from people I had never met. (They would also complain, only half-jokingly, that most of the mailbag's content was for me.) Among the several hundred letters I gathered, only one letter was written to a near-

Table 4.1 *Origins of letters in the corpus*

origin	number of letters
Funafuti	80
other islands of Tuvalu	20
Nauru	42
Fiji	20
Kiribati	18
other Pacific island countries	6
Australia & New Zealand	36
other metropolitan countries	6
seamen working overseas	9
unidentifiable	10
Nukulaelae	80
Total	327

stranger: written by a Tuvaluan Jehovah's Witness missionary to a Nukulaelae Islander whom he had met only once, this letter was clearly designed to proselytize, and is highly marked in both form and content. Furthermore, except in special cases about which more will be said presently, Nukulaelae people generally do not write letters to other inhabitants of the atoll.

Who are the recipients of letters written on Nukulaelae and the writers of letters that the atoll's residents receive? I was able to trace both the origin and destination of most letters in my corpus, thanks to the fact that Tuvaluan letter writers often write their own and the recipient's names and addresses on the letters themselves. When letters are hand-carried, envelopes, which are costly and often not available, are commonly dispensed with, and the addressee's address is simply written on the folded letter. Table 4.1 provides a breakdown of the origin of letters in my corpus. (Letters in the sample that originated on Nukulaelae were addressed to people in temporary residence away from the atoll who brought them back when they returned home.) Assuming that this sample is representative, a pattern emerges: a significant proportion of letters (32 percent of the 247 incoming letters) originate on Funafuti; many letters (17 percent) originate on Nauru; and the rest of the mail comes from a variety of locations, among which figure prominently Fiji, Kiribati, Australia, and New Zealand, four countries where Tuvaluans commonly go to study and work.

These patterns are easily explained when one takes a qualitative look at the corpus. Most letters are exchanged between relatives, particularly between children and their natural or adoptive parents, and between siblings. Because young unmarried people are considerably more likely to leave the atoll than older people, they are more likely to write to both older and younger relatives and to friends. Indeed, younger people appear to be the most prolific writers and the most likely recipients of letters. Of the 301 letters whose writer is identifiable, 139 (i.e., 46 percent) are written by islanders generally characterized as *tamaafine* "young [unmarried] woman" or *tamataene* "young [unmarried] man," and 113 (i.e., 38 percent) are addressed to members of these two groups. Among younger people, women appear to write and receive many more letters than men (97 women writers vs. 42 men writers, 83 women recipients vs. 29 men recipients). I observe no comparable gender imbalance among older letter writers and recipients.[7]

Funafuti is the most likely destination of migrations and visits away from the atoll. As described in Chapter 2, Nukulaelae Islanders migrate to Funafuti to seek employment opportunities, which are virtually non-existent on the atoll. However, individuals who are not involved in any cash-generating occupation also visit Funafuti to "take care" of their relatives who have migrated, particularly during pregnancies, illnesses, or at other times when extra hands and moral support are needed. Nauru also hosted until very recently a large contingent of Nukulaelae Islanders employed in the phosphate and service industries. Both Funafuti and Nauru figure prominently among the originating points of incoming letters because they are also where most imported cash and commodities come from. As I will discuss further in Chapter 5, letters are commonly written to monitor economic transactions, which explains the large volume of mail from Funafuti and Nauru. Finally, a noteworthy source of letters is the handful of Nukulaelae children attending Motufoua Secondary School on Vaitupu, who correspond with their parents and age-mates when shipping schedules enable them to do so.

As noted in Chapter 2, in historical times at least, Nukulaelae people have always been inclined to travel widely and to establish kinship ties with the outside world. In this respect, modern-day islanders are no different from their ancestors. These patterns explain why letter writing became so popular so early in the history of literacy on the atoll. One can surmise that the motivations for writing letters in the fourth quarter of the nineteenth century were essentially the same as they are today: to maintain contacts with relatives traveling away from the atoll and off-island relatives acquired through marriage (recall that exogamous alliances were aggressively sought out in the years following the 1863 blackbirding raid). For well over a century, atoll residents have had strong affective and economic motivations to keep communication links alive with their relatives scattered around the world, and letter writing has long been the primary method of doing so.

Most letters written on Nukulaelae fall into a category called *tusi alofa*, literally "letters of empathy," that can be roughly described as personal letters. Personal letters and other forms of written messages are almost never exchanged within the confines of the atoll. The islet on which the bulk of the atoll's population resides is very small (0.5 mile long), and messages (*fekau*) from one household to the other can easily be conveyed verbally, a task which usually falls on children and adolescents.[8] However, there are other types of letters, which are much rarer and can be sent either to off-island destinations or to other Nukulaelae residents. In this category fall job-application letters, legal letters of various types, threatening letters, and business correspondence, all of which are only written in very unusual circumstances for most people. One example is the letter that a Nukulaelae middle-aged man wrote in 1991 to a woman on Funafuti who had accused him during a spirit-mediumship session of engaging in sorcery. In his letter, the writer threatened to take the spirit medium to court for defamation. Another example dates back to my 1985 field sojourn, when another Nukulaelae man led a schismatic movement in the island community following a political dispute with the rest of the community. This man and his followers refused to partake in community events, including meetings of the Council of Elders. Negotiations between the Council and the schismatic group took place through letters, even though the breakaway group remained on the atoll. The schismatic group's letters were read aloud in meetings of the Council, and responses were drafted during those meetings. Such letter-writing practices are very rare and are considered to be indicative of grave interfactional or interpersonal crises.

Letters are rarely truly "personal" in this society, in the sense of being protected from the scrutiny of third parties. Even though writers generally do not address letters to more than two people, all adult members of households usually get to read incoming mail in turn, and do so silently or in low voice. Reading letters is an event in which everyone (or at least every adult) partakes, a pattern that characterizes many other activities in this society. Like letter writers elsewhere (De Rycker 1991:618), Nukulaelae people do not overtly ratify secondary audiences in the texts they produce. Yet the eventuality of a secondary audience, which can also include snoopers, becomes a concern when the text includes sensitive material, such as damaging gossip or risqué jokes. Teenagers, who are particularly prone to include such material in their writings, sometimes append a postscript urging the recipient to burn the letter:

[A teenage girl to another teenage girl]
Kaafai koe e oti, koo ssunu aka nee koe te tusi teenaa, i te mea maa maua nee se tino.
[letters 1985:529]

When you are done [reading it], please burn this letter, otherwise someone might get ahold of it.

(In this particular case, the recipient obviously did not follow the writer's directive.)

There is ample evidence that what one writes in letters can have serious consequences. In 1990, a seventeen-year-old woman sent a letter to a friend on another island in which she made fun of other Nukulaelae girls, accusing them, among other things, of being afflicted with ringworm, and in which she boasted of having provoked the recent divorce of a young couple on the atoll. Word of the content of this letter reached Nukulaelae, and the culprit was dragged to the monthly meeting of the Council of Women, during which she was thoroughly chastised. The Council made her apologize formally, and both her mother and an affinal aunt (FBW) also contributed emotional apologies. Thus the consequences of a seemingly inconsequential letter from one teenager to the other can suddenly reach dramatic proportions.[9] However, the importance of this young woman's letter does not derive from the fact that her insults and boasts were in writing, since no member of the Women's Council saw the letter. In a separate case, a man publicly threatened to take key members of the community to court for having allegedly disparaged him during a phone call to Nauru. This situation bears some similarities to the young woman's, and demonstrates that confrontations can arise whether defamation takes place in writing or orally.

The radio-telephone

There is another way to communicate with the outside world, which has become an increasingly important alternative to letter writing. A short-wave radio-telephone links Nukulaelae to Funafuti, and its use has increased dramatically in recent years. This increasing popularity is aided in part by the greater sophistication and reliability of the technology available to Tuvalu's Telecommunications Division for radio-telephone communications with the Outer Islands. In the early 1980s, solar-powered equipment was installed on all the Outer Islands including Nukulaelae, which proved considerably more dependable than the earlier outfits, which depended on diesel generators that periodically broke down or ran out of fuel. The radio-telephone link between Nukulaelae and Funafuti is active daily for one hour in the morning and one hour in the afternoon. At these times, a crowd of people always gathers to listen, and what is said during telephone conversations feeds the gossip network within seconds. Problems with privacy are widely recognized, and have given rise to a number of serious incidents. In recent years, the Telecommunications Division has installed a telephone booth. When the receiver in the booth is out of order, which happens frequently, callers revert back to the old system, speaking into a microphone and listening to the incoming voice over the receiver's loudspeaker, in full hearing range of everyone. Thus there is a sense in which letters afford more privacy than the radio-telephone. However, people do not always view the lack of privacy associated with telephone calls as a "problem": in many instances, callers clearly savor the presence of over-hearers (e.g., by cracking jokes for the benefit of all present) and exploit it to enhance their own prestige, knowing full well that what they say over the radio-telephone will be repeated within moments in many atoll households.

The social function of the radio-telephone resembles that of letters: for example, phone calls are placed to monitor and activate gift-giving between atoll residents and their off-island networks. In terms of their formal characteristics, they share some features with letters and others with formal speeches. (Because of the sensitivity of the issue of privacy in radio-telephone calls, I did not attempt to tape-record any such calls, although I recognize that their formal and social characteristics raise very interesting questions.) The radio-telephone has the advantage of being available on a daily basis, in contrast to letters, which can only be sent and received once a month at most. Thus Nukulaelae people often place calls to relatives on Funafuti just before a ship visit has been announced to request items that cannot be purchased on the atoll; by letter, several months can elapse between the request and its fulfillment. It is also more difficult to dodge requests made over the radio telephone, in contrast to letters, which can be studiously left unanswered (see below). However, telephone communications are considerably more expensive than letters: in 1990, the base cost of a three-minute conversation was A$1.50. Yet, because many calls are directed to salaried relatives on Funafuti and are made collect, the cost of the technology is not much of a deterrent. This pattern further contributed to the extremely severe financial pressures placed on employed Nukulaelae people on Funafuti, about which more will be said presently. (Indeed, a large percentage of calls are placed to request store-bought items of various sorts.) Since 1991, international calls can also be made from Nukulaelae, although the Telecommunications Division has wisely forbidden international collect calls. In true Polynesian fashion, Nukulaelae people have integrated the telephone into their lives with a vengeance.[10]

The form of letters

This section presents a brief analysis of the formal characteristics of letters written by and to members of the atoll community. I focus in particular on the "peripheral" aspects of letters such as salutations, introductory paragraphs, and forms of address, which are often neglected in descriptions of letter writing because of their non-textual nature. Yet non-textual aspects of letters deserve close scrutiny, since they provide a "frame" (cf.

Goffman 1974) to the text, i.e., "guidelines" for its interpretation. In particular, a number of features frame the letter in a literal sense.

Opening frames

As mentioned earlier, letter writers often inscribe their address at the top of the letter. This act is frequently superfluous, because recipients normally know where the letter is being written from, and because addresses in Tuvalu can be as streamlined as one wishes them to be: a first name and the name of an island is theoretically all a letter needs to finds its addressee. Yet Nukulaelae correspondents frequently specify their own address in great detail and make it look like a street address in a Western country (e.g., *Nukualofa Side, Nukulaelae Island, Tuvalu Group*). The address is not the only attribute of the frames of letters to betray some influence from English letter-writing norms: the date often appears in English, and so does the salutation. The latter often consists of the word *dear* followed by a name, or a vocative kin term like *Sis* or *Mummy*. Although these English words are widely known on Nukulaelae, even by people who do not speak English, they are very rarely used in spoken Tuvaluan. Sometimes, the salutation is in a mixture of English and Tuvaluan (e.g., *Dearest K mo te kaaiga kaatoa* "Dearest K and the entire family"). Occasionally, the salutation is written entirely in Tuvaluan. Frequently, both the first and last names of the addressee are included, although again last names are virtually never used in face-to-face interactions.[11] Salutations in letters that have been addressed to me offer a good representative sample that can be cited here without betraying the identity of recipients of letters in my corpus ("Faiva" is my alternative name on the atoll):

Dear Niko Faiva B	
Dearest Niko F B	
To Faiva	
To Faiva Besnier	
Dear Bro Niko	
Kiaa Niko F. Besnier	"To NFB"
Kiaa Niko F.B.	"To NFB"
Kiaa Niko taku tama	"To N, my child"
Ki te tama pele ko Niko Faiva	"To the beloved child, NF"
Moo taku tama ko Faiva	"For my child F"
Moo koe Niko	"For you N"
Ia Niko	"To N" (in Samoan)

In letters written before the sixties or by older people, very little or no English appears. This fact indicates that the English used in contemporary letters is a recent innovation, possibly introduced by children who have attended secondary school at Motufoua. Older letters usually begin with a

heading and salutation in Samoan, even when the rest of the letter is in
Tuvaluan. Here is an example, in the original orthography (the date does
not specify a year, but the events referred to in the letter indicate that it was
written in the fifties):

Setema 30
Ia F
*Si omatou alofa ua ou taui atu. Lenei tusi e fai ma mea tatou feiloai. E muamua pea ona
tatou via pea le alofa o le Atua i lana tausiga ia itatou.*

[letters 1985:624]

[all the following in Samoan]
September 30
To F
We are sending our love to you. The purpose of this letter is for us all to meet. We
first praise the Lord for the love through which he looks after us.
[continues in Tuvaluan]

The main body of letters usually begins with a greeting identical to the
greeting used in face-to-face interactions (*taalofa* "hello," a Samoan
borrowing). This is followed by references to the health of everyone at the
writer's and the recipient's ends, and a sometimes very long series of
invocations to God's grace and kindness. Many introductory paragraphs,
of which the following examples are typical, observe a standard pattern:

[from a woman on Funafuti to her father on Nukulaelae]
*Taalofa koutou katoa! Fakafetai, e maalosi katoa loa maatou i konei, kae koo ne maua
foki nee maatou outou tusi, ne logo foli maatou ia S mo A, me e maalosi fua koutou. Ko
te viikiga mo te taavaega o ttou Tamana ki te see gata mai.*

[letter 1985:552]

Greetings to all of you! Thanks, we are all in good health at this end, and we also
have learned from your letters, and have also heard from S and A, that you are in
good health. We praise and glorify our Father for ever and ever.

[from a 75-year-old woman on Nukulaelae to her grand-daughter in Australia]
*Fakafetai koo maua nee au se avanoa gali peenei o tusi atu ei nee au te tusi teenei moo
feiloai aka ei taaua. Ia, a kaafai e oko atu te tusi teenei kae ttusa taaua i te alofa o te
Atua. E avatu ei nee taaua te fakafetai ki te Atua, auaa tena tausiiga alofa kia taaua te
faanau see llei i ana mua. Ia, kae avaka nee taaua taavaega ki te see gata mai, e see gata
mai eiloa. Aamenc.*
Ia, a maatou nei e maalosi fua. Ia, kaati laa koutou foki i konaa, kaati e maalosi katoa.

[letters 1985:521]

Thanks are due for the fact that I have this beautiful opportunity to write you this
letter so that we can both meet through it. And if this letter reaches you, we are both
equally under the protection of God's love. We both send out thanks to God
because he is taking care of us, his sinful children before him. And we praise him for
ever and ever, for ever and ever. Amen.
So we are all in good health here. And perhaps the same applies to all of you over
there, perhaps you are all in good health.

Variations in the form and order of these introductory elements do occur, and sometimes can take on a poetic tone reminiscent of the opening flourishes that speech-makers produce in the maneapa:

Fakafetai ki te poto mo te malaga o te Atua o te lagi mo te lalolagi ki tena fakatokaga moo ttou olaga i aso taki tasi o taatou, ka koi oola taatou i tena lalolagi gali teenei. Ko ana mea alofa kesekkese kolaa e maua faeloa nee taatou mai tona alofa tauaanoa, ko te ola, ko te maalosi e mafai ei nee taatou o fai a niisi mea kolaa e tau mo ttou olaga. Teenei foki koo maua ei nee au te ola, te manuia o puke ki te peeni teenei, kae maise ko te lau pepa, o sauttala maalie atu kiaa koe, taku tama. Me koo gali te pula mai o te laa, mo laakau pula ggali, ko te gali teenaa o tena alofa, kae maise mo tamaa manu kolaa e gaaseessee i luga o pula, kae agi mai ki ei te matagi. Taapaa! Ko ana fakasalalauuga maalosi ei te manonogi mai o pula laakau, koo fakasauga ei nee taatou te manogi llei o te alofa mai o te Atua kia taatou, ona tagata teelaa e tau ei i taagata faatauvaa, o tuku faeloa ki te Atua ona viikiga mo ona taavaega i te ola nei, kee oko ki te see gata mai eiloa.

[letters 1993:872*]

Thanks be given to the cleverness and inventiveness of the Lord of heaven and earth for what he has prepared for our lives each day that we are alive in this beautiful world of his. The various gifts he has bestowed on us from his bountiful compassion are our being alive, our being healthy so that we can accomplish the various tasks that we must accomplish to live. It is also because of it that I am alive and healthy enough to pick up a pen as well as a sheet of paper to chat with you for a while, my child. Because the sunshine is beautiful, and so are trees with beautiful flowers, and these are beauties of his compassion, even the birds that fly about the flowers, and the wind blows hither because of it. Oh! He spreads the fragrance of flowers, through which we sense the aroma of God's compassion for us, the people that can be described as his worthless people in this world, and thence until eternity.

Like orators in the maneapa, letter writers always adhere to a religious reference scheme in opening frames, Christian for the majority, or Baha'i, etc., for the handful of religious converts. In letters written by younger people, the introduction is usually much shorter and more predictable in content than that of letters written by older individuals. These introductions bear many similarities to the beginning of formal speeches.

The opening of letters frequently includes self-deprecating expressions of various types. For example, some writers express that it is their "weak conjecture" (*fakattau vaaivai*) or their "silly opinion" (*manatu valea*) that the recipients are in good health:

*E tuumau faeloa te ola mo te maalosi i luga i au i konei, mo te **fakattau vaaivai** me e peenaa foki koulua i konaa.*

[letters 1985:560]

I am well and alive here [lit.: life and good health are constant upon me here], and my **weak conjecture** is that you two are the same at your end.

*Au nei e maalosi fua, kae kaati e see taumate ko taaua fakatasi i te laina e tasi. Kaafai laa e tonu te **manatu valea** teenei mai konei, [. . .]*

[letters 1985:561]

I am just in good health, and perhaps it is possible that both you and me are along the same line in this respect. If this **silly opinion** from this end is correct, [let us thank the Lord].

Self-deprecating statements can refer to the writer as the above examples do, or, if they are couched in religious terms, they can be more generic:

Fakafetai moo te alofa o ttou Tamana ki Tena tausiiga ki luga ia taatou, te faanau ssee mo te nofo sala i Ona mua.
[letters 1985:515]

Thanks [are due] to our Father for protecting us, **His wrong-doing children who live in sin before Him**.

Following these introductory remarks, writers usually present the motivation for the letter. Most of the time, this motivation is described as a phatic one. It is in this context that they often refer to their letters as conversations (*sauttala*), in which the writer and the addressee "meet" (*fetaui*):

*Ia, a ko te ala o te tusi ko te fia **sauttala** atu mo koe.*
[letters 1985:636]

So, the reason for the letter is that I want to **chat** with you.

*Fakafetai mo koo **fetaui** taatou i te lau pepa teenei. Ia, see ko mata, ka ko lau pepa.*
[letters 1985: 542]

Thanks for the fact that we can **meet** through this piece of paper. **It is not a face-to-face [encounter], but [one that takes place] through a piece of paper**.

Letters are thus presented as surrogates for face-to-face encounters, a feature that Nukulaelae letters probably share with letters in many other societies (e.g., Stowers 1986:62 on Greco-Roman letters). It is also in the opening paragraphs that writers may acknowledge having received earlier letters, which they invariably have read with great happiness (*mo te fiafia lasi*):

*Ia, P, fakafetai, me koo oti ne maua nee maatou au tusi kolaa ne aumai, mo tau uaeelesi foki koo oti ne maua nee au; ne faitau nee au **mo te fiafia lasi**.*
[letters 1985:138]

So, P, thank you, because we have received the letters that you sent, along with your telegram, which we have also received; I read them **with great happiness**.

Alternatively, writers express their great unhappiness (*faanoanoa maalosi eiloa*) about not having heard from the addressee, as illustrated in the previous section. Many letters then refer to the fact that there is nothing new to report at the writer's end:

Ia, tala o te koga teenei ko tala mau loa, ia, kae kaati e peenaa foki te fenua o taatou mai konaa.
[letters 1985:644]

So, news from this location are the usual news, and perhaps it is the same over there on our atoll.

Ia, tala o te fenua nei seeai, ko tala mau eiloa ki mea tau fiafiaga.
[letters 1991:734]

So, these are no news from this atoll, other than the usual news about feasts and dances.

Such statements sometimes precede narratives of eventful happenings; for example, the second excerpt above is immediately followed by a detailed retelling of how the chief of Nukulaelae was nearly lost at sea while fishing, an event which monopolized the attention of the entire community for long and tense hours as search parties were sent out to find him. It is thus clear that remarks such as these are part of the ritual infrastructure of the letter.

The text of Nukulaelae letters is sometimes paragraphed, particularly if the writer has had formal schooling. Older individuals tend to write continuous texts with no paragraphing and little punctuation. Topic changes are usually announced with the abundant use of the topic-transition particle *ia*, which is elsewhere particularly associated with styles of secular oratory. The addressee's first name is often invoked in paragraph-initial position, sometimes following *ia*, and sometimes with a vocative particle (*ee* in preposed or postposed position, or *oo* in postposed position).

Closing frames

At the end of letters, there is often evidence of strain in the handwriting, confirming Nukulaelae Islanders' description of letter writing as physically and mentally strenuous work. This strain is often further aggravated by the threatening pressure of the ship's impending departure. Letters sometimes refer to the writer being sleepy at the end of the letter, either because solitary activities like reading and writing are generally described by Nukulaelae people as having a soporific effect on them, or because the letter is written in the middle of the night, after the completion of preparations for the ship's visit:

Ia, kaati koo gata atu i konaa te sauttalaaga, ia au koo fia moe.
[letters 1985:639]

So, perhaps the conversation will stop here, because I am sleepy.

Writers commonly announce that the letter has reached its conclusion, as the above example illustrates. This announcement sometimes follows the following formulaic parallelism or a variant of it:

*Ia, ttusi **kaa fai o gata** atu moo koulua, maatua pele i te loto, a ko te fia sauttala atu mo koulua **seki taaitai o gata**.*
[letters 1985:591]

So [this] letter to the two of you, my beloved parents in [my] heart, is **about to come to an end**, but [my] desire to chat with you **is not about to come to an end**.

Letters end with a long list of people sending their *alofa* "love, empathy, compassion." This list commonly includes the names of all members of the immediate kin group, including children, and is followed by a parting salutation identical to that used in face-to-face encounters, usually *toofaa* "goodbye" (another Samoan borrowing):

*Koo gata i konei ttou sauttalaaga, kae **fakamoemoe** taatou ko te **alofa** o te Atua e maua ei te **manuia** mo te **fiafia** kee toe fetaui fakamuli. Alofa atu Oolepa, Vave, mo Tausegia, Saavali, Aaifoou, Luisa, Uiki, Vaefoou, Fagaua, Aalieta, kae sili ei maaua ou maatua see aogaa moo koe. Toofaa laa.*

[letters 1985:605*]

Our conversation will stop here, but let us **hope** that we shall obtain **luck and happiness** from God's **love** for us to meet again in the future. Oolepa, Vave, and Tausegia, Saavali, Aaifoou, Luisa, Uiki, Vaefoou, Fagaua, Aalieta all send their love, but, above all, we two, your parents who are useless to you. Goodbye.

The parting salutation *toofaa* is sometimes written twice, a feature that echoes the common practice in face-to-face parting contexts of exchanging two sets of salutations, the second one being usually abbreviated to *faa* (A: "*Toofaa!*" B: "*Toofaa!*" A: "*Faa!*" B: "*Faa!*"); of course, in letters, only one "side" of the interaction is heard. A religious formula sometimes closes the letter, usually of the form *Ko Ieesuu Keriso e maavae kae toe fetaui ei taatou* "it is in Jesus Christ that we part and will meet again," or a variant thereof. Letters are signed, often with the writer's first and last names, echoing the pattern found in the opening salutation. In letters addressed to parents, grandparents, children, or grandchildren (i.e., between members of different generations), an affect-laden self-descriptor often precedes the signature, in which the writer may characterize him- or herself in self-abasing or pitiable terms. Examples include *ko tou maatua alofa tonu moo koe* "[I am] your mother who truly loves you" (letter 1991:700), *ko au ko te tama liakina* "I am [your] abandoned child" (letter 1991:768), *te tama see fakalogo pati* "[your] disobedient child" (letter 1985:586). In addition, an affectively loaded statement frequently appears at the end of letters, in which the letter writer asks the recipient to forgive anything that he or she may have found offensive in the letter or the writer's behavior in general, or to "correct" (*fakasao*) anything in the letter or the writer's behavior that might be "wrong" (*ssee*):

[from a young man on Nukulaelae to a friend on Funafuti]
Ia, au e fakamolemole atu kiaa koe, kaafai seaku mea koo ssee, fakamolemole mai.
[letters 1985:511]

So, I am asking you, if I have done (or said) anything wrong, I ask for your forgiveness.

These statements are often found in letters that follow the writer's or the recipient's departure from the atoll. The only other context in which statements of the kind are found is during farewells prior to the departure of a family member or house-guest, when the departing person and an older person representing the family ask for each other's forgiveness for any offense that might have been committed.

Letter writing and reading

To summarize, several significant points have emerged in the foregoing discussion. First, even though letter writing is a common activity that has penetrated the lives of nearly every member of the community, it bears the imprint of outside influences: the Samoan language is conspicuous in older letters, while contemporary letters rarely lack at least one or two English words. The role that English plays in letters is particularly interesting because English phrases appear even in letters written by people who know very little English, and who would be extremely reluctant to use any English in face-to-face interaction, out of *maa* "shame, shyness, embarrassment." Clearly, letter writing and reading are outward-oriented activities for Nukulaelae Islanders, i.e., activities that connect them to the outside world (and hence the world of English and, in former days, Samoan), and activities that were historically inherited from the outside, despite the degree to which they have become integrated into the society.

Second, letter writing is intimately connected with face-to-face communication. Letters are ideally accompanied by an oral message replicating and elaborating the content of the written text. Writers present their letters as a medium through which they can chat (*sauttala*) or meet (*fetaui*) their interlocutors, and they sometimes deplore the fact that the conversation can only take place through the medium of writing. These characterizations bear witness to the fact that oral communication frequently acts as a frame for letters, in the sense of providing a context in which they can be properly interpreted and evaluated. The relationship can also be reversed: letter writing can become an integral part of face-to-face interactions, a point that is strikingly demonstrated in gossip contexts, which I describe in Chapter 5.

Third, while letters resemble and are embedded in oral communication, they do not align themselves with any particular oral genre, but instead evoke the characteristics of various genres of oral interaction. For instance, letters share formal and metaphorical characteristics with everyday casual conversations: the same greeting and parting salutations are found in both genres, and letter writers refer to their letters as conversations. However, letters also resemble oratory: the poetic opening tirades, religious allusions, apologies, and topic-transition particles encountered in letters also characterize oratorical genres. Yet it would be a mistake to think of letters as a "mixed" genre, i.e., as a less than fully established genre in contrast to more "canonical" genres of oral communication. Nukulaelae letters are neither more nor less cohesive and homogeneous as a genre than any other genre. They simply share characteristics with several other genres, and are embedded in the communicative repertoires of the members of the community in a complex manner, which cannot be described as merely "in between" more canonical genres.

Fourth, the formal features of letters are saturated with a particular type of affect. The formulas used in the openings and closings of letters require the use of emotion verbs like *alofa* "to feel empathy, to love." In opening sequences, writers express their happiness (*fiafia*) about meeting the addressee through the letter and about having received and read his or her previous letter. If the writer has not heard from the addressee, he or she may describe the pain (*mmae*) and great unhappiness (*faanoanoa maalosi eiloa*) that this silence has caused. Writers also express their regrets that their meeting with the addressee takes place through writing, and not in person. At the end of a letter, the writer must leave, but does so regretfully, because "[the] desire to chat with [the addressee] is not about to come to an end" (letter 1985:591). And letters close with a list of people to whom *alofa* is to be conveyed. Utterances describing the writer's inadequacy or worthlessness are common in both openings and closings. Thus affective experiences like love, longing, and regretting, and powerlessness, uselessness, and being at the mercy of circumstances are salient components of the framing conventions of letters. These very same experiences will be encountered in other aspects of letter writing.

5

LETTERS, ECONOMICS, AND EMOTIONALITY

Letter writing and reading are of relevance to several aspects of Nukulaelae social life. First, letters play an important role in monitoring economic exchanges between members of the community and the outside world. Second, letters are embedded in information-sharing networks, which weave in and out of orality and literacy and connect Nukulaelae people over large distances. Third, letters can carry moral messages that resemble in some respects the moral content of certain genres of face-to-face communication, but differ from them in other respects. Fourth, letters emerge as emotionally cathartic communicative events, a characteristic that colors all the other functions of letter writing. The social role that a particular letter plays depends in large part on the relationship of the writer and the addressee, and on whether the letter is sent to or from Nukulaelae. Furthermore, all letters, other than brief notes scribbled as the ship departs, straddle several functional categories: moral, economic, informational, and affective dimensions of letters are often inextricably interwoven with one another.

Letters and economic life

By far the most salient motive for writing letters is to monitor, record, stimulate, and control economic transactions associated with the exchange of gifts between Nukulaelae residents and their off-island relatives. As such, letter writing has become thoroughly incorporated into the socioeconomic life of the community and in the economic ties between the community and the rest of the world. Hand-delivered letters frequently accompany food baskets, packages, or gifts of money. A substantial number of letters, particularly shorter letters written in a hurry on the Nukulaelae beach or the Funafuti wharf, list the contents of packages:[1]

[from a teenage woman schooling in Samoa to her parents]
N & S, e fia fakailoa atu kia koulua me koa oti ne avatu nee au te afiifii fooliki mo te toeaina ko S. Mea i loto, e tasi te t-shirt lanu moana, tasi te sulu solosolo, tasi te suipi, mo fusi ei e lua. Kiloke, ee S, tou fusi brown teenaa, koo see fakattau mei eiloa i te ttogi

mmafa. Te suaa fusi uli, see iloa nee au me e saisi tonu mo koe me koo too fooliki. [...]
Tou sulu solosolo, ne fili nee au, kae i taku fakattau, me e fiafia tou loto ki ei.

[letters 1985:588]

N and S, I want to let you know that I have sent along a small package with the old man S. Its contents are one blue tee-shirt, one striped loin-cloth, one deck of cards, and two belts. Look, S, the brown belt [I am sending] you is extremely expensive. The other belt, the black one, I don't know whether it will fit you. [...] I chose the striped loin-cloth for you, [and] I surmise that your heart will be happy with it.

Letters are written to request (*aakai*) such items as food, money, and trade goods. Nukulaelae Islanders living on Funafuti often ask for staples like swamp taro, coconuts, caramelized coconut toddy, and salt fish, because these items are in short supply in the capital, particularly for resident Outer Islanders who have no access to local land. They sometimes also request delicacies like coconut crabs and birds, for which Nukulaelae is famous. In return, Nukulaelae Islanders write to their relatives on Funafuti and abroad for money, clothes, fishing gear, and construction materials, as well as edible items, like rice, flour, and sugar, which frequently run out at the island store:

[from a 40-year-old woman on Nukulaelae to her 40-year-old cousin abroad]
Muna a P [...] kee ttogi mai se vvele moo vvele aka tena talafa. Kiloke, a te tuaatina o
S teenei e fai foki kee ttogi mai ana tteuga ki te kuata, kae kiloke, kaafai koutou e
mmai, kee ttogi mai nee koe ne papa moo S. Kaati ttausaga foou koo fakaogaa nee ia a
papa. Kaati laa koo too uke a mea a maatou e fai atu kiaa koe.

[letters 1985:549]

P asks [...] that you buy him a razor so he can shave his beard. Look, S's mother's brother also asks that you buy him clothes for the [forthcoming] celebrations, and look, when you come here, buy some wooden planks for S. [Because] maybe next year he will need to have wooden planks. Perhaps we keep asking for too many things from you.

Gifts also need to be acknowledged, in part because baskets of food and other gifts sometimes get lost, stolen, or misplaced during transportation; this motivates further correspondence:

[from a 60-year-old woman on Funafuti to a 35-year-old nephew on Nukulaelae]
Ia, a ko au e fakafetai lasi atu moo pulaka a maatou ne aumai. Ne maallie maatou i te
ggali o pulaka. [...] Ia, kae saa toe taa mai nee koe ne mea llasi iaa koe e fiittaa.

[letters 1985:590]

So, as for me, I want to thank you very much for the swamp taro you sent us. We were very pleased because the swamp taro was very nice. [...] But don't dig up any more big [swamp taro] for us, because it tires you out.

In some cases, people write letters to try to track down items that have gone astray:

[from a young woman on Nukulaelae to her adolescent brother on Funafuti]
Ia, A, a M nei teenei e maalooloo i konei. Ka ne fai mai kiaa T mo F me isi se $5 a koe ne

tuku atu nee ia kia T kee tuku atu kiaa koe maa foki ifo koe ki te fakkai. Kae see iloa atu nee maatou me tonu me ikaai. A, au ne fano o ssili kia T me ne tuku nee ia kiaa ai au meakkai, kae fai mai me ne tuku nee ia kia L, iaa koe laa seki fanaifo ki te fakkai i te taimi teenaa. Kae kaafai e mea, koo ssili tonu aka koe kiaa L me isi ne meakkai ne oko atu me ikaai.

[letters 1985:543]

So, A, M is here on holiday. And he said to T and F that he gave T $5 to give to you when you come to the village [i.e., the main settlement on Funafuti]. But [we] don't know whether it is true or not. A, I went to ask T who he gave the food [we sent] for you to, and he said that he gave it to L, because you never showed up in the village that time. So if you get a chance, ask L once and for all whether she received any food for you or not.

Predictably, economic matters are most salient in letters exchanged by people between whom reciprocity ties exist. The most common type of relationships that meet this description are between parents in residence on the atoll and salaried adult children residing on Funafuti, on Nauru, or in industrialized countries. Indeed, letters from older Nukulaelae residents to their off-island children are the prime locus of *aakai* "requests" for cash and store-bought items. Because the only tangible items with which Nukulaelae Islanders can reciprocate are perishable produce (e.g., swamp-taro pudding, caramelized coconut toddy, dried tuna) and goods whose transport across borders is restricted (e.g., mats), only letters from Funafuti include requests for atoll products with any frequency. Nukulaelae people working abroad have to content themselves with the symbolic capital they are accumulating in exchange for the unreciprocated flow of goods and cash.

The texts of both inbound and outbound letters bear witness to the enormous pressure that Nukulaelae Islanders employed in the cash economies of the capital and overseas countries are under to produce the fruit of their labor and hand it over to relatives and the community. Outbound letters are full of requests that exceed by far what most employed islanders can afford, given the very modest salaries that they receive:

[from a middle-aged Nukulaelae man to a nephew employed on another island]
A te fenua nei, koo seeai loa se vaka e matea, naa eiloa ko paopao koi matea, a ko vaka loa koo seeai eiloa e matea, koo fai katoa loa ki mooto mo pooti. Te faaika mo mea aumai motu, koo fai katoa ki pooti mo mooto. Teenei laa, au e fakamolemole atu loa kiaa koe kee aumai fua laa te pooti mo te mooto kia maaua i konei moo aumai saale aka aku popo io me ko te faaika. Au e fai ttonu atu loa kiaa koe, au nei koo see fakattau mai loa toku maa i taeao katoa, koo nofo faeloa au o kilokilo ki pooti o tino koo ttele ki motu, kae aatea e olo o ttaki. Kae ttoe ifo ko maaua faeloa mo A, a maatou nei, i leaa aso ma leaa aso, e nnofo fakaaallofa faeloa o kilokkilo ki ika a tino mo popo foki a tino e laku mai.

[letters 1985:577]

On this atoll, one sees no more large canoes, all that's left are small canoes, while large canoes are not seen any longer, everything is done with outboard motors and dinghies. Fishing and the transportation of things from the islets are all done with dinghies and outboard motors. Thus I am asking you to please send me a dinghy and outboard motor for us here, so as to enable me to transport the copra I make or to go fishing. I am saying this straight to you, I am extremely ashamed every morning, I stay and watch some people navigating their dinghies to the islets, while others go trawling. All that's left [without a dinghy] are A [the writer's son] and I, we just stay pitifully day in and day out, watching the fish that some people and the copra that other people haul in.

Living on Nukulaelae, it is very difficult to acquire much of a sense of the hardships associated with life as a menial worker in a capitalist economy. Since it is still possible to live reasonably comfortably on the atoll with access to minimal amounts of money, Nukulaelae people with little or no experience of cash labor rarely pay much attention to the outflow of money that life in cash economies requires. A few letters in my corpus express the writer's belief that their relatives living overseas are living in extreme comfort. Witness this young woman writing to her mother on Nukulaelae about her older sister F who, perhaps unbeknownst to the younger sister, is living on welfare as a single mother in an industrialized country:

Au see faameo, kae ko au fua e ofo i te mafai nee F o puli mai koe i tena maumea i mea tau sene.

[letters 1991:751]

I don't [mean to] criticize, but, as far as I'm concerned, I am just amazed by the way F has completely forgotten you [i.e., failed to send you money] even though she is very rich in way of money.

It is probably the Nukulaelae community on Nauru that feels the most pressure to supply cash and goods to people back home. As described in Chapter 2, Nukulaelae workers on Nauru are crucially important to the economic viability of the atoll, and this responsibility places them in a vulnerable position from which they are easy targets for their relatives' demands. Letters to Nauru frequently consist of long shopping lists; in return, Nukulaelae people on Nauru often write back to express the discouragement they experience upon receiving these lists, and to explain, often in eloquently despairing terms, their inability to meet the unreasonable requests that come their way:

[from a young man on Nauru to his parents]
N, fai atu kia A me ko ia naa e alofa mai i toku fiittaa i te maafaufau kee naa oti te fale o taatou. E aatea a sene a laaua e ave atu, kae aatea foki e taulagi mai kee ttogi atu ne mea i konei. Kofea laa sene kaa ave atu? Kofea foki sene kaa ttogi atu ki mea e manako a ia ki ei?

[letters 1985:572]

N, ask A whether she has any compassion for me, whose mind is constantly preoccupied so that our house [on Nukulaelae] be completed. I already send them money, but then on top of it they keep asking me to buy things for them here. Where will I get the money to send to them? And, in turn, where will I get the money to buy what she wants?

Koo maagalo toku tautino, kae toe nei ko te faigaa meaa alofa, mo te taaulaga a aku seki fai. Kae fai i te fakaotiiga o Mee. [. . .] Teelaa laa, koo see iloa nee au te uke o mea tau tupe. Konei e fakammae ki toku maafaufau. Koo uke atu foki a tupe o tautino o maatou i te peeofuga o oku. Teelaa laa, au koo naa fai kee naa tele atu au mai konei. Teelaa laa, e ui loa i te feituu tenaa, kae teenei loa au e taumafai maalosi ki luga i taku gaaluega. Kaafai e tai tuai atu a te pela o te pooti mo ulu ttaki, kaati ko te mea seki lava i oku lima a tupe moo ttogi.

[letters 1985:558]

My contribution to the atoll community is done, [and] now what's left is the gift [to the pastor], and I have not made my contribution to the church yet. I'll do that at the end of May. [. . .] I can't even keep up with money matters any more. My mind is hurting just to think about it all. The contribution we [each] have to make is greater than my own salary. So I wish I could just run away from here and return home. But despite that, here I am, applying myself to my work. If I don't send you soon the dinghy propeller and the fishing lures [that you've requested], it's probably because I don't have enough money in my hands to buy them.

Letters from Nauru also frequently voice the writer's displeasure with the dearth of gratitude they receive in return for what they have managed to send. The tone of letters when they touch on this issue is often pleading and sometimes bitter:

Naa laa, niisi tino o ttou fenua e oola fiileemuu faeloa, kae konei niisi faanau e mmate fua i te faiga o mea a te fenua. Koo see mafai loa nee taatou o fai aka peelaa faanau kolaa i Nauru. [. . .] Kae teelaa laa kaa maannava atu a maatou ki uta i ttou fenua, seeai loa se tino o te fenua e fia saga mai. E saga loa ki tena faanau too tino.

[letters 1985:537]

So some members of our atoll community go on living in peace, while here are the rest of us [on Nauru] killing ourselves providing for the atoll community's projects. We should not be called [Nukulaelae's] sons on Nauru. [. . .] And then when we reach land on our atoll for holidays, no one wants to pay any attention to us. They pay attention only to their own children.

Clearly, island workers abroad often feel that the affective credit they accumulate is not commensurate with what they provide.

One option that Nukulaelae people working off-island have in dealing with these demands is to leave letters and telegrams unanswered. Later, they always can attribute their silence to the vagaries of inter-island communications. Many letters refer to unanswered requests:

A te uaeelesi a N teenaa ne avatu kia koulua, see iloa nee ia ma kai maua nee koulua te uaeelesi teenaa. Kaafai laa seki maua nee koulua, au laa teenei koo fakailoa atu kiaa koe, fano laa o fai kia F te fekau a N ne fai atu loa kia koulua, ne fai atu kee fia maua fakavave mai se tupe mai iaa koulua moo fai tena fakalavelave o te aavaga a A e fai i te maasina foou.

[letters 1985:577]

N is uncertain whether you have received the cable that she sent you. If you did not receive it, I will inform you now here of the message that N [tried to] convey to you, which you should also inform F of, she said that she wants you to send some money to her quickly to pay for the expenses of A's wedding next month.

There are cases in which Nukulaelae people, having severed all contacts with the atoll for extended periods of time, reappear when they are again financially able to meet their relatives' demands, or when everyone else has understood the message in all its subtlety. In a couple of instances, individuals appear to have permanently cut all ties with their relatives. As I will discuss at the end of this chapter, the voluntary or involuntary disappearance of a loved one into the vast unknown world is a possibility of which everyone is acutely aware, particularly at farewell time. However, voluntary disappearance assumes that one has access to an economic and affective safety net in one's host country. I also surmise that it is an act of desperation that carries an enormous affective price, in light of the fact that Tuvaluans are extremely attached to their kindred and their home island (even more so than many other Pacific Islanders).

While emotionality in general figures prominently in both the ideology and praxis of economic life, certain emotions play a particularly important role: for example, *alofa*, which can be roughly translated as "empathy, love, pity, generosity" depending on the context, is the primary means through which economic reciprocity and gift giving are socially controlled. It is because of *alofa* that one gives, and *alofa* is meaningless if it is not accompanied by a gift. This view is articulated explicitly by a middle-aged man in the course of a good-natured spontaneous argument with his sister, during which he made the following pronouncement (his sister was trying to coax him into making a gift of food to a relative, which he was reluctant to do):

Kaa alofa koe, te mea teelaa e igoa ki te alofa, ko te mea e isi te mea teelaa i tou lima e manako koe ki ei, "Aa!, fakaasi toku alofa." Teelaa. A kaafai see- e fai mai peelaa, "alofa, alofa!" kae seei se mea e puke i te lima, mea naa see tau ki vaegaa alofa teenaa, me e seeai. Kee fai foi tino o te alofa, ko te mea kee puke ou lima ki ei, tuku, "Ia!," koo nofo tuu mai te alofa. A kaafai taatou e fai peelaa ttou pati, "aallofa," kae seeai se foi tino o te mea e fakaasi i ei te- te- kee matea, tena uiga kia au seeai se foi tino, alofa loi.

[conversations 1985:3:B:165–175]

If you have *alofa* [for someone], [if you have] what's called "*alofa*," you should have something desirable in your hand, "There, I'm showing my *alofa*!" Like that. But if you keep saying, "*alofa, alofa!*" and you have nothing [to give] in [your] hand, that doesn't count as *alofa*, because there's nothing [to give]. For *alofa* to have a substance [lit., body], you have to have something in your hand, give it, "There, take it!," you're giving *alofa*. But if your *alofa* does not have a- a- a substance that can be seen, then it has no substance, [it's just] false *alofa*.

It is *alofa*, for example, that makes Nukulaelae people take care of the needs of outsiders living in their midst (e.g., the pastor, government workers, visiting relatives, and the ethnographer), who are referred to euphemistically as *fakaalofa*, literally, "objects of *alofa*, cause for *alofa*."[2] Similarly, it is another emotion, *maa* "shame, shyness, embarrassment," that controls excessive or socially inappropriate *aakai* "requesting." For example, feeling *maa* prevents people from making demands of people they are not related to or whom they do not know well. Emotionality (or perhaps certain important emotions) is conceptualized as intimately linked to systems of reciprocity and gift-giving: emotions can be converted into economic action, which in turn can generate other emotions (e.g., gratitude, longing, more *alofa*), they can be foregrounded in particular contexts and in particular relationships for economic purposes, and they can be allotted to monitor the flow of commodities. In short, one can speak of an *economy of affect*, i.e., the flow and exchangeability of affectivity on the one hand and economic resources on the other, which is in turn linked, as in all other societies, to such categories as power, prestige, knowledge, and other symbolic commodities (Bourdieu 1984, 1991).

As should be evident from the excerpts already cited in this section, affect is given particular prominence in letters that deal with economic matters. In letters that accompany or announce the imminent arrival of gifts, writers often express their hope that the recipient will be satisfied (*malie*) or happy (*fiafia*) with the gifts:

*V, kiloko, a te afiifii teenaa e ave atu, **malie mai oulua loto** i mea konaa koo maua atu i ttaimi. Kae llei me e uke taimi konei e mmai mai mua nei. Konei laa mea: [. . .]. Konaa mea i loto i te afiifii, kae **malie mai eiloa oulua loto**.*

[letters 1985:522]

V, see, the parcel I am sending to the two of you, **your hearts be satisfied** with what I am sending you at this time. There will be other opportunities [to send more] later on. This is what I am sending you: [lists contents]. This is what is inside the parcel, **your hearts be satisfied**.

*Kaati taku fakattau koo **fiaffia** loa koulua ki te aofaki tupe teelaa ne maua atu nee au, e peelaa mo taulua uaeelesi.*

[letters 1985:558]

I surmise that perhaps you are happy with the sum of money that I sent you, as per the cable you sent me.

The prominence of affectivity is particularly striking in letters that do not accompany gifts. For example, in letters in which the writer acknowledges having received a gift from the address, *alofa* is a recurrent theme:

[from an adult man on Funafuti to an older male relative on Nukulaelae]
*Peelaa mo mea koo oti ne oko mai ki omotou lima, e toe ttao atu loa te fia fakafetai, ona eiloa **ko tootou aallofa mai** ki mea kolaa ne manako ei maatou.*

[letters 1985:534]

As for the things that have reached our hands, I want to express again my thanks **for your *alofa* toward us** [expressed in the form of] the things that we had requested.

Occasionally, letter writers invoke affective categories as they offer to send gifts to their correspondent, as in the following excerpt, in which the writer is attempting to establish reciprocity with the addressee:

[from a young woman on Nanumaga to her bond brother on Nukulaelae]
*Tuagaane, kaafai e isi se mea (e) fia fai mai, fai mai. Io me ko ou kaaiga i konaa, fai mai, **kee saa maagina laa, ia au nei foki maa maa iaa koe**. [. . .] Kae alofa mai kia au.*
[letters 1985:517]

Brother, if there is something you want, tell me. Or if one of your relatives over there [wants something], tell me, **don't be ashamed, otherwise I am also going to be too ashamed to ask you.** [. . .] And feel *alofa* towards me [and send me things].

In letters that are motivated by the writer's inability to fulfill his or her economic obligations, the affective component of economic transactions is even more salient. Such letters are written with "a great deal of *alofa*," and ask the addressees to "appease their heart" and to forgive the writer for being unable to meet the addressee's requests:

[from a teenage daughter on Funafuti to her parents on Nukulaelae]
*Ia, [. . .] koo tusi atu ttusi mo te **alofa** lasi kia koulua maatua, auaa e seeai se mea e maua atu. Kae kiloke, maatua, onosai maalie kee foki mai au i Saamoa, koo maua atu taulua sene i au io me se aa.*
[letters 1985:587]

So, [. . .] I am writing the letter with a great deal of *alofa* toward you, my parents, because nothing is being sent to you. But look, my parents, be patient, when I return from Samoa, I shall send you some money or whatever else.

[from a young man on Nauru to his parents on Nukulaelae]
*N, kae peelaa mo te mea teelaa e manako koe moo fai tou tautino ki te aso o faafine. Kiloke, **malie tou loto**, te tusi ne maua nee au i te poo 17. Ko tena uiga, kaafai e ffao atu nee au i taku tusi, e taumuli atu. Koo oti te aso o faafine. Teelaa, **malie tou loto ki ei**.*
[letters 1985:536]

N, regarding what you wanted for your contribution to the woman's day festivities. Look, **appease your heart**, but I received your letter on the 17th. This means that, had I enclosed [the money you wanted] in my letter, it would have reached you too late. **So do appease your heart.**

[from a woman in her 60s on Nukufetau to her 40-year-old daughter on Nukulaelae]
*S, te afiifii o A teenaa e fanatu mo K. Kae **faanoanoa** me seeai se sulu o F e maua atu. A G nei e tasi loa tena sulu mai ia T. **Fakamoemoe** ki se taimi mai mua, maafai e maua soku sulu.*
[letters 1985:584]

S, K is bringing you a package for A. **But I feel sadness** about the fact that there is no loin-cloth for F. G here got only one loin-cloth from T. **Let us hope** for another time, when I get another loin-cloth.

Letters thus offer a striking illustration of how affect can be exchanged for commodities: emotions are saliently expressed when gifts are absent or inadequate, or when gifts are acknowledged. That letters should be a prime locus for the "conversion" of affect into commodities and vice versa is a reflection of the monitoring role that letters play in economic transactions: since letters are used to control and stimulate the flow of goods, they are an obvious tool for the manipulation of the principles underpinning the links of reciprocity between the community and the outside world.

Letters, gossip, and news

Another important motivation for writing letters is to narrate recent personal and social events. Letters provide news about the writer, the writer's family, people known to the writer and the addressee, and the atoll community in general. Weddings, births, illnesses and deaths are eminently reportable events:

Kae kee fai atu taku tala kia F, teelaa ki te fekau a L. A F nei koo ita i pati a K ne fai kia F. Ana pati i te laveaaga nee ia F, "Taapaa ee! au see taaitai loa o loto kia F." Teelaa laa, F koo oko loa i ana kaitaua. Fai loa kia T kee naa fakafoki te fekau a L.

[letters 1985:565]

And let me tell you my story about F, the one about L's marriage proposal. F is angry at K for what she told F. When she saw F, she said, "Hey! I have absolutely no intention to [accept] F [as a father-in-law]." So F is absolutely furious. He told T to withdraw L's marriage proposal.

A L koo oti ne faaipoipo mo T i te vaaiaso teelaa koo teka, te fakaotiga o Mee. Koo oko loa te toko uke olotou kaaiga ne ommai, ko K faatoaa vau mo ttaina o S ko S mo tena aavaga se fafine Maasela. E ttusa loa mo te vaaiaso e tasi te nnofooga maatou i te aavaga, kae nei koo oti maatou ne fakamaavae. [. . .] e isi semaa tusi ne aumai ia M, kae fai mai i te fekau a F koo oti ne ave ki te tamaafine Nuui e neesi i Naaluu, kae koi ttali nei laatou ki te tali.

[letters 1991:688]

L has gotten married to T last week, at the end of May. Numerous relations of their's came [for the wedding], K came here for the first time ever, accompanied by S's brother, S, and his wife, a Marshallese woman, we all celebrated for one week, and we've just ended the celebrations. [. . .] M wrote us a letter telling us that F has proposed to a young Nui woman who works as a nurse on Nauru, and they're still waiting to see if the proposal is accepted.

Feasts and other celebrations, games, arrivals and departures, the visit of a ship other than the usual inter-island vessel are other frequent themes. The often convoluted political life of the community is the topic of frequent commentaries:

[from a 50-year-old woman on Nukulaelae to her daughter abroad]
Ia, kae iloa nee koe, a te paalota teenei ne fai, koo oko loa te gali a te kaaiga o taatou. Ko M mo T koo see olo i loto i mea a te fenua. [. . .], konaa fale koo see olo i mea a te

fenua. E iita loa ia T seki maaloo i te paalota, kae iita. Koo see llei te kaaiga o taatou.
[letters 1985:548]

And, you know, in the elections that took place, our kin group behaved beautifully [facetious]. M and T don't want to take part in island affairs any more. [list of names], these are the households that don't take part in island affairs any more. They are angry because T did not win the elections, and they are angry. Our kin group is in disarray.

Nukulaelae people take an extreme interest in the lives of others, particularly in breaches of social norms, such as interpersonal disputes, factional strife, divorces, illegitimate pregnancies, and allegations of sorcery. Islanders in residence elsewhere clearly relish receiving such news from the atoll in letters, as witnessed by the common requests for news that incoming letters contain:

[from a middle-aged woman on Nauru to relatives on Nukulaelae, asking about allegations of sorcery levelled at X]
E tonu laa tala kia X? Maaua nei mo U see iloa atu me e tonu tala konaa, me seeai nemaa tusi. A kaafai e tonu, au e ofo ma kaiaa e maua ei nee S o fai peelaa i ana tama koo maattua, i ttoko lua e fakaaallofa. Teenaa ko tena [tautali] kia Y.
[letters 1991:801]

Are the stories about X true? U and I don't know whether the stories are true, because we haven't received any letters [from Nukulaelae]. But if they are true, I am outraged, how can X behave like this, her children are now older, the poor things. That's the result of her hanging around with Y [a notorious sorceress].

In many letters exchanged between close relatives or friends, newsworthy stories often take on a tone comparable to face-to-face gossip:

A te mea a F mo I ki te olo saale ki Funaafuti koo see fakattau loa, kae konei koo oti ne ffoki mai. A ko te professor ko L teenei loa e mmoe maatou, e pule loa i te taimi e vau ei o moe. [. . .] Te fakafaafine o L koo fai me se gatu pei tolu.
[letters 1991:661]

F and I are constantly going to Funafuti, it's incredible, and they've just now come back [yet once again]. As for the "professor," L, she has been sleeping at our house, she just comes to sleep when she pleases. [. . .] L's flirting is like a triple-layered piece of clothing [i.e., she spends all her time flirting].

The colloquialisms, innuendos, and sarcastic characterizations in this excerpt bear a striking resemblance to gossip, an activity for which Nukulaelae Islanders are famous in the eyes of the rest of Tuvalu. Letters easily become a medium through which writers disseminate gossip that originates in face-to-face contexts. One thus encounters in letters many belittling remarks about third parties, disparaging allusions, and damaging stories that fuel gossip in one way or another. Writers also use letters to deny allegations made about them through the oral grapevine:

A ko au nei ne logo i tala ne fai i konaa me ia aku te pati teenaa ne fai iaa koe e vau fua o aasi fakaloiloi kia A, kae vau koe kee faanau a S. Au e tautoo loa ki mata o V mo A, seeai loa saku mea e iloa iaa koe e vau. [. . .] Teelaa, au koo oko loa toku faanoanoa ki te tala teenaa me ne aumai mai fea me ia ai foki te pati.

[letters 1991:727]

I heard that stories are being told over there that it was me who said that you were not really coming to visit A, but [were using this as a pretext] to come and see S through her child delivery. I swear on V's and A's heads that I knew nothing about your coming over. [. . .] So I am extremely saddened by those tales: where did they emerge? Who accused me the first place?

Letters can carry gossip over great distances, and letter writing and reading are interwoven with face-to-face arguments and confidential conversations. In one typical case, gossipy letters were exchanged between Nukulaelae and Funafuti, Funafuti and New Zealand, and from New Zealand back to Nukulaelae. In these various locations, recipients showed some of these letters to their author's rivals, creating a *dramatis personae* so complex that retelling the ensuing events would take up several pages of text (and would probably betray the identity of those involved). Following is the brief extract of a gossipy interview during which the story was told to me, which gives an idea of the complex manner in which oral and written communications are interwoven, and how conflicts are aggravated by snitching and the unsanctioned sharing of letters:[3]

[The story concerns two compromising letters that Z previously received from another party]

Naa laa i ei, tusi ei taku tusi kia X peenei, aku muna, "X, a mea katoa konaa koo oti ne tuku atu nee au kiaa koe, a tusi kolaa e lua, heei loo he tusi ne faitau i ei i tusi kolaa, i tusi kolaa ne faitau eeloo nee koe, hee iloa foki nee au a pati i loto i tusi, a ko pati konaa ne mai eeloo mo tino iaa koe koo oti ne fakalaulau i Funaafuti [. . .]. A pati i loto i ttusi naa, ne iloa mai loo nee- nee tino konaa ne fakalaulau ei koe i Funaafuti. A kiloko, ee X, au e heei he fafine e maasei kae paugutu," aku muna ki ei. [. . .] "Ee Y, au ne logo tusi konaa e lua ne ave kia X kee faitau nee E." Teenaa, taku faipatiiga loo teenaa, mea loo koo tagi Y. Muna a-, "Ee, ee Z, ne iloa nee koe iaa ai i au tusi ne faitau nee E?" Muna a- aku muna, "Tino loo konaa ne nnofo i loto i haa P, ne fakamatala mai ki aku, i aku tusi konaa e lua ne ave nee X kee faitau nee E."

[interviews:Z 1991:1:B:039–064]

So then I write a letter to X like this, and I say [i.e., write to her], "X, I handed over both [letters] immediately to you, I did not read anything from them, you were the one who read them. I don't know anything of what was written in those letters, people you gossiped to on Funafuti brought back here what was written in those letters [. . .]. I learned about what those letters said from people you gossiped to on Funafuti. Because you see, X, I'm not a bad gossipy woman," I said [i.e., wrote] to her. [. . .] [I then say to Y,] "Y, I heard that X gave the two letters to E to read." As soon as I said that, Y started crying. [She] says, "Oh, Z, who told you that E read your two letters?" I say- I then say, "People who were staying at P's explained to me that X gave the two letters to E to read."

The intricate communication networks that such exchanges create and sustain span great distances between several islands and countries, and straddle several modes of communication, including letters, face-to-face conversations, and radio-telephone calls. This interactional web enables individuals to negotiate, manipulate, distort, and destroy personal reputations, interpersonal relationships, and the truth.

As with the economic components of letter writing, emotions and affect play an important role in the news reporting and gossipy aspects of letters. Letter writers make many overt references to the feelings of the participants in the events that they are reporting. Several excerpts provided in this section illustrate the importance of emotions in news and gossip (cf. discussions of *faanoanoa* "[disapproving] sadness" in letter 1985:727, *ita* "displeasure" in letter 1985:548, and *kaitaua* "anger" in letter 1985:565). Narrators pay detailed attention to the emotional reactions to events of all parties involved. In the following excerpt, the *alofa* and *salamoo* "remorse" that the author experienced in the narrated events are given focal prominence:[4]

[from a woman in her 20s on Funafuti to a male relative in his 40s on Nukulaelae, relating her recent boat journey from Nukulaelae to Funafuti]
*Ia, tala o te malaga a maatou koo oko loa i te maasei. Kaati e lavea loa nee koutou te maasei o te tai. Maatou e tolu a galu ne ffati ki loto i temotou pooti. Teelaa laa, temotou pooti kaati e llave loa ia T, mooi seeai a T, kaati taku fakattau e mafuli, taku fakattau loa a aku. Teelaa laa, **toku ate palele loa ne kai i toku alofa ia T**. Teelaa laa, **toku salamoo**, ia koutou ne fai mai kee nnofo maatou, a ko maatou e aummai loa.*
[letters 1985:547]

Now, as for the story of our journey, it was very bad. You probably saw how bad the ocean was. We had three waves crash inside our launch. And our launch was stable thanks to T, had it not been for T, in my opinion, it would probably have capsized, this is just what I think. **So my liver is eaten up by my *alofa* for T**. And **I am full of remorse**, because you advised us to stay, but we left anyway.

The description of affective responses thus plays a major role in the informational component of letters.

Letters and morality

Writers frequently include in their letters advice and admonitions, the form and content of which resemble strikingly exhortations in ancient Greco-Roman letters (Stowers 1986:91–152). Letter writers advise recipients of their letters to "behave properly" and not to engage in reprovable activities, and reprimand them if they have gotten wind of their correspondent's wrongdoings through the gossip grapevine. Exhortations can call for the recipient to change his or her deleterious ways, or to continue leading a moral existence (protreptic and paraenetic exhortations respectively – cf. Stowers 1986:92). However, only negatively sanctioned past behavior is ever mentioned overtly, which gives exhortatory passages a conspicuously admonitory tone; even paraenetic exhortations seem to be triggered by some unmentioned damaging report. Letters addressed to younger women and men are particularly likely to include admonitions. Young men are told not to drink sour toddy or liquor, to refrain from fighting, to attend church regularly, and to be generous toward their kin, while young women are warned against gossiping too much, acting wantonly, and neglecting their studies if they are in school. Exhortation can be tied to a specific occasion, or can be of a more general nature:

Ia, N, masaua nee koe aku pati, e tapu koe i te kava. Kaafai koe e see fakalogo ki aku pati, ko au koo see alofa kiaa koe. I au e logo ia L i te inu o tamataene o taatou koo oko loa, a ko tamaliki foolliki eeloa. Teelaa laa, au e fai atu kiaa koe kee mmao koe mo te koga teenaa. Ma kaa fai nee koe, see toe avatu nee au neau mea.

[letters 1985:564]

So, N, remember my words, [I] forbid you to drink. If you do not obey my words, I will no longer feel *alofa* for you. Because I heard from L that our young men have been drinking a lot, even little children. Thus, I am telling you that you should stay away from this behavior. If you engage [in this behavior], I will not send you any more things.

Kae nofo fakallei koe, ttalo ki te Atua kee manuia koe (kee) toe feiloai taatou i se aso i tena alofa lasi, oti te inu, kae fai fakallei tou 21 i konaa, alofa mai laa kia A maa uke au mea e maua i konaa.

[letters 1985:550]

And behave properly, pray to God so that you may be lucky enough for us to meet again one day, stop drinking, celebrate your 21st birthday properly over there, feel *alofa* toward A [the recipient's brother] here in case you get a lot of things over there.

While letters from older people to younger people are the canonical contexts for such discourse, it is surprisingly common in letters that younger people write to older relatives:

[from an adult man to his elderly mother (S) and his sister (P)]
S, nofo fakallei, au see manako kee oola fiittaa koutou. Gaalue ki mea e kkai ei, koutou koo malooloo. Saa toe fia saga ki gaaluega valevale [. . .] Kae nofo fakallei, saa taua saale, fai fua tou loto kee fiafia. Teenaa te mea gali kae sili. [. . .] S, alofa kia P mo F.

[letters 1991:829]

S, behave properly, I don't want you to lead a tiring life. Work to get just what you need to eat, and then rest. Stop trying to attend to all sorts of tasks. [. . .] And behave properly, don't get into arguments, just do what it takes to make your heart content. That is the best and most beautiful way [to live]. [. . .] S, have compassion for P and F.

Exhortations appear frequently in letters that I receive from Nukulaelae, particularly from older people who know me well, even though the same individuals would rarely or never admonish me in like fashion in face-to-face interactions. Most admonitions I receive in letters exhort me to observe Christian rituals and to adhere to Christian beliefs (which do not play much of a role in my life away from the atoll, as many Nukulaelae people suspect):

Teelaa laa, Faiva, saa puli tou fou kau mosi i soo se koga o te lalolagi e tiu ei koe, tou kau mosi ko te Atua. Kee ppiki mo koe, e tokagamaalie i ei a soo se faigaa malaga e fano koe ki ei i au fekau mo gaaluega. Faiva, ttalo fakatasi taatou katoa kee oola manuia maatou peenaa foki koe mo L i Motufoua, kee toe nnofo tasi taatou fakamuli i ttou tamaa pui kaaiga fakaalofa nei.

[letters 1993:873*]

So, Faiva [i.e., NB], do not forget your crown of laurels wherever in the world you are cast [ashore], your laurels are God. Stick to them always, [because] any journey you undertake for your work and duties will be free of trouble through them. Faiva, let us all pray so that we [be able to] live in good fortune, and that you and L at Motufoua [School] do as well, so that eventually we can live together again in this pitiful little kin group of ours.

As will be evident from the above examples, the primary focus of the language of admonitions is the affective comportment of the recipient. In the following two examples, emotion verbs such as *alofa* and *fakamoemoe* "hope" play a central role in the organization of the admonitory acts:

[from a 75-year-old woman on Nukulaelae to her grand-daughter in Australia]
*Ia, kae fai au kiaa koe, nofo fakallei, **alofa** ki tou maatua, mo koo seeai sou tamana, kae toe fua naa ko tou maatua. Ia, kae saga fakallei ki tau gaaluega, ko te mea kee oola llei ei koulua mo tou maatua, ia koulua koo seeai se isi tino e **fakamoemoe** koe ki ei.*

[letters 1985:521]

So, I am telling you, behave properly, **be kind and generous** to your mother, because you do not have a father any more, only your mother is left. So pay attention to your work, so that you and your mother can live well, because you do not have any other person **to hope for**.

[from a 50-year-old woman on Nukulaelae to her daughter abroad]
*Kae nofo fakallei, **alofa** kia S mo tena aavaga, kae masaua aku pati, tausi tou foitino, kae ttalo ki te Atua kee manuia mea e **fakamoemoe** taatou ki ei.*

[letters 1985:548]

And behave properly, **be kind and generous** to S and her husband, and remember my words, take care of your body, and pray to God so that our **hopes** may be fulfilled.

Even admonitions that do not refer overtly to the emotional comportment of the recipient have a salient affective component. For example, the imperative phrase *nofo fakallei* (literally, "stay in good fashion"), which I have translated as "behave properly," is an extremely common opening to admonitory sequences, as amply illustrated in the above excerpts. It evaluates the social acceptability of the recipient's behavior, and is thus heavily affective.

Admonitions in letters bear a striking resemblance in form and content to an oral genre known as *polopolooki*. This genre is characteristic of occasions such as the more or less formal reprimanding of younger people by older relatives following a reprehensible act on the part of the latter, or conversations in which parents or grandparents give advice to younger family members on consequential life decisions. However, the canonical contexts for *polopolooki* are farewells. At some stage in the preparation for departure, while bags are being packed, feasts held, and provisions for the journey prepared, older family members make brief monologic speeches of a semi-formal nature, during which they may acknowledge the departing person's good deeds, exhort him or her to behave properly while away, and urge him or her not to forget the family. It is in these contexts that people may ask each other's forgiveness for any wrongdoing they may have been responsible for, an act that also surfaces in letters, as described in Chapter 6. What is said during face-to-face *polopolooki*, as well as the way it is said, is identical to admonitions in letters. However, two features of *polopolooki* in letters stand out as particularly significant. First, *polopolooki* in face-to-face interactions only occur on very specific occasions, while the genre can potentially permeate any letter. Second, in letters, younger people can *polopolooki* their older relatives, which is unheard of in face-to-face contexts.

Letters and affect

Whatever their primary motivations may be, the vast majority of letters share one important characteristic: they are a medium in which affect is given considerable prominence. In a previous work (Besnier 1989a), I demonstrated that selected emotion verbs were considerably more frequent in letters than in conversational discourse. Indeed, the content of many letters is first and foremost *about* affect. Letters tell of crying, hoping, regretting, and longing:

[from a young woman on Niutao to her parents on Nukulaelae]
*Taapaa! [. . .] Kaati ko te vaaiaso teenaa ne masaki i ei a L, au i te vaaiaso teenaa koo **tagitagi** faeloa kae **manatu** mai i te taeao kee oko ki te afiafi. Taapaa! [. . .] Te maasei, au e **tagi** faeloa maa kilokilo aka au ki te mataafaga. E pelu laa naa ootou mea, ka ko au teenei loa e **tagitagi** atu.*
[letters 1985:545]

Oh! [. . .] It was perhaps the week that L was sick, that week, I was **crying** constantly and **longing** for you from morning till evening. Oh! [. . .] It is so bad, I always **cry** when I look at the beach. While you are taking care of your daily business, and I am here **crying** for you.

[from a teenage woman schooling in Samoa to her parents]
*N mo S, ne tusi nee au taku tusi, kae **tagi** au. Toku tino e nofo i konei, kae toku maafaufau koo fano mmao. Kae see aafaaina, se taimi koo toe feiloai taatou, maafai e tuumau te ola.*
[letters 1985:588]

N and S, I have been writing this letter while **crying**. My body is here, but my mind is very far. But no matter, we will be together again at some stage, if life continues on its current course.

They express empathy, happiness, and love:

[from a young woman on Nanumaga to her bond brother on Nukulaelae]
*Ia, ee tuagaane, e peelaa loa mo tau muna teelaa ne fai mai ia taaua koo ssai loa ttaa
tuagaane. A aku koo oko loa i toku fiafia, koo see fakattau mai loa. Aku foki koo oti ne
fai ki oku maatua mo oku tuagaane ttonu, koo oko loa i te fiaffia.*
[letters 1985:517]

So, my brother, as for what you told me about our establishing an adoptive brother–
sister relationship. I am absolutely **delighted** about it. I also have told my parents
and my blood brothers, and they are very **happy** about it.

*A maaua i taimi katoa e maua ei nee maaua au tusi, e peelaa loa me se aa te mea tafasili
koo maua nee maaua i temaa fiaffia mo temaa **loto alofa** kiaa koe. Teelaa laa, e faitau
nee maaua au tusi kae **ttagi**, ona ko te maafaufau atu moo koe.*
[letters 1985:650*]

The two of us, every time we get a letter from you, it is like the most **joyous** event for
the two of us and one through which we feel our **love** for you in our hearts. So, we
read your letters and **cry**, because we keep thinking about you.

Positive affect is particularly salient when writers thank the recipient of
their letter for gifts they have received, or for their hospitality while they
were visiting the atoll:

*Teelaa laa, N, au see taaitai o maagalo taku kaitaalafu iaa koe, mai taku
tamaafineega loa, kee oko ki te taimi ne aavaga i ei.*
[letters 1985:565]

So, N, my debt to you is not about to be paid off, [for everything you have done]
from the time I was a teenager until the time I got married.

Many of the norms governing affective displays in other interactional
contexts do not seem to apply to letters.[5] For example, while face-to-face
interactions between young men always have a subtle undertone of negative
competition that leaves little room for positive affect, particularly if the
interactors are brothers, letters exchanged between young men sometimes
display a great deal of positive affect:

[from a man in his early 20s to his friend on Nukulaelae, also a young man in his
early 20s]
*Au manako kee fetaui faeloa taaua, kae see manako kee maavae taaua. Au e tusi atu
nee au mea katoa konei i toku loto, koo see kkafi nee au o fakkii. [. . .] Koo see iloa nee
au me se aa te faiga kaa fai ko te mea kee toe nofo au i konaa.*
[letters 1991:725]

I want to see you at all times, and do not want us to be apart. I am writing to you
everything that's in my heart, because I can no longer endure it. [. . .] I am at a loss
trying to think of a way for me to be over there again.

Letters between cousins of opposite gender who are normally supposed to
avoid each other's presence, let alone exchange any remotely affective
words in face-to-face interaction, display as much affect as any other letter:

[from a man in his 50s on Nukufetau to his female cousin in her 50s on Nukulaelae]
Fakafetai foki moo taimi ne fakatasi ei taatou i konei, fakafetai. **Koo malie katoa te**
loto *i faifaiga ggali.* *Te **fakamoemoe** kee tuumau te **loto feaalofani**.*
[letters 1985:582]
Thanks for the moments that we spent together here, thank you. The heart is
completely satisfied with the beautiful actions [that took place then]. It is hoped that
the spirit of mutual love will remain.

Even when affect is not the primary focus of a letter, it always lurks
immediately beneath the surface of the discourse. As illustrated earlier in
this chapter, affect is conspicuous in discussions of economic transactions
and in news updates. For example, when monitoring economic reciprocity,
letter writers give prominence to *alofa* and *maa*, the principal affective
regulators of the community's economic life in the local economic theory.
When relating news, much emphasis is placed on the emotional aspects of
the narrative: narratives are given, as backbone, the affective reaction of
individuals involved and the writer's emotional evaluations of the narrated
events. Admonitions to younger people are also affectively charged: readers
are told to comport themselves as kind, generous, and responsible adults,
entities whose local definition centralizes affective comportment. Thus,
even when addressing topics that are not essentially affect-oriented, letter
writers bring out the emotional aspects of what they describe. The overtness
of this affect contrasts sharply with the covertness with which affect
permeates everyday discourse in most face-to-face contexts, including
damaging gossip. In letter writing, a license to display affect seems to be
operative that is not found in most face-to-face interactions.

Reading and writing practices demonstrate that affect is not a purely
textual characteristic of letters. Indeed, in the frenzy of preparation for the
ship's visit, as relatives and friends leave and arrive, letter writing is a major
preoccupation, along with food preparation, itself defined as an expression
of *alofa* for travelers and relatives living off the atoll. Late at night, on the
eve of the ship's visit, women and men of all ages can be seen feverishly
filling pages of writing, concentrating on a handwriting which gradually
becomes looser, more disorganized, and more lyrical. Similarly, letters are
carefully and laboriously read, and tears often accompany this decoding
process; when pictures are enclosed, this effect is further increased. Letter
writing and reading are thus defined as affectively charged events. While all
affective categories that surface in the text of letters may also surface in face-
to-face contexts, their intensity and frequency in letters is remarkable. Also
remarkable is the fact that affect in letters is considerably more overt and
explicit than in face-to-face contexts, where affective meaning tends to be
alluded to indirectly. Thus letter writers make little use of punctuation,
underlining, and others ways of "superposing" affective meaning in the
written texts produced by members of other societies (cf. Besnier

1990a:428–30, Ochs and Schieffelin 1989:18–21). Rather, they lexicalize and grammaticalize affect.

The question of whether such affect represents "genuinely felt" emotions to which one feels "committed" needs to be contextualized in Nukulaelae ethnopsychological theory. Like members of many other Pacific societies (Levy 1984, Lutz 1988, Ochs 1988, Rosaldo 1984, Schieffelin 1990, Shore 1982), Nukulaelae Islanders do not disassociate emotion, affect, and social action. Emotions on Nukulaelae are defined behaviorally. In light of this ideological construct, the fact that letters are more affectively charged than other communicative contexts (to the extent that writers over-ride restraints placed on affective displays in other communicative situations) is in and of itself analytically significant.

However, not all emotions are equally prominent in letters. Particularly salient in letters are expressions of the writer's vulnerability to circumstances and strong emotional experiences, and of the writer's positive feelings towards the addressee (cf. the frequent references to *alofa*), a characteristic which I will interpret in the conclusion as being bound to a cultural logic of gender. These emotional categories constitute the common denominator of all letter writing. This is of course not to say that all letters display these emotions and only these emotions emerge in letters: writers of gossipy letters of the type discussed earlier can talk about anger and displeasure. However, these emotions are less commonly expressed in letters, and Nukulaelae people perceive "angry" letters as particularly disturbing, as "problems" that need to be solved. Furthermore, even in "angry" letters, some positive affect and expressions of emotional vulnerability emerge, often to tone down the impact of angry words. For example, in letter 1991:727, the writer attempts to deny rumors about her having said something inappropriate about the addressee; significantly, while the tone of the excerpt I cite above is clearly one of anger, she describes her anger as *faanoanoa* "sadness," which often has disapproving connotations, but it also denotes the intense vulnerability of the experiencer to outside events.

Levy (1984) proposes that particular emotions may be "hypercognized" or "hypocognized" in different cultures. For example, a hypercognized emotion is a frequent topic of conversation, be it as socially sanctioned or disapproved of experience. Finer semantic distinctions are made to refer to hypercognized emotions than to hypocognized ones, and the latter may even be unnamed categories. I propose that these notions can also be used to describe the relative importance of specific affective categories across social contexts, arguing at the same time for a more event-sensitive approach to the culture of emotions. In certain social contexts, individuals may deem it appropriate to express their emotions directly and overtly;

affect in general can be said to be hypercognized in these events. In other contexts, only certain types of affect can appropriately emerge; this affect will thus be selectively hypercognized. Finally, emotional displays, of an overt kind at least, may be disapproved of in a third type of context. Affect in these contexts can be said to be hypocognized. Events like letter writing and reading on Nukulaelae thus hypercognize affect: emotions are referred to more overtly and frequently than in other communicative events. Certain types of affect, however, appear to have a privileged position in the texts of letters: *alofa* and *maa* emerge as considerably more hypercognized than, say, anger. As in the Tahitian language (Levy 1984), many fine distinctions are made in the Nukulaelae Tuvaluan lexicon for different types of anger, an indication of the hypercognized status of anger in this society. In letters, references to anger and "angry talk" are marked: they are unusual, they are seen as problems, and are conveyed indirectly. Anger, thus, is a hypocognized emotion in this social context.

Clearly, Nukulaelae Islanders *define* letter writing and reading as affectively cathartic contexts, in which certain types of emotions are hypercognized. How did letters come to be defined as such? On Nukulaelae, letters are highly "concentrated" communicative events: opportunities to receive and write letters are comparatively few and far between, in sharp contrast with the constant face-to-face socialization that daily life on a tiny crowded islet affords, for better or for worse. The effect that this may have is that, if individuals are going to convey any message in the letters they write, they had better do it in an intensive manner. However, a more compelling explanation materializes when one takes a closer look at other social contexts in which the same emotions as are expressed in letters are conspicuous. Vulnerability and strong positive affect toward one's interlocutor are found with comparable intensity in one highly marked situation, namely parting interactions. Farewells on Nukulaelae and elsewhere in Tuvalu are extremely emotional events.[6] Witness Lady Caroline's nineteenth-century description of the departure from Funafuti of the author of the letter quoted at the beginning of Chapter 4:

But the full meaning of "palenti too moshy cly" [i.e. "plenty too much cry"] did not dawn on me until I saw [Funafuti Islanders] say good-bye to one of their own girls, Vitolia, who was going on the *John Williams* to Apia, to the High School there. All the village assembled on the beach. Vitolia came out with swollen eyes and damp countenance, in a frock just presented to her by another girl. When she was close up to the boat her mother clung round her neck, rubbed noses, and set up the most dismal howl that ever anyone's nerves were thrilled with. Then the mother stood aside, emitting fearful howls at intervals, and raining down a perfect tropical shower of tears; and one after another the girls went up to Vitolia, hung on her neck and wailed, until I feared the girl would be reduced to pulp with the squeezing and the tears. By this time the wailing had become general, and was so dismal and bitter I felt it was approaching the unendurable. Just then Vitolia was hustled into the boat and taken away. The people dried their eyes and left off howling to watch the boat, and in about half an hour were capering about all smiles and high spirits.

(David 1899:277–8)

Nukulaelae Islanders frequently speak of living together in *fiileemuu* "peace" and *feaalofani* "mutual empathy," of "communing together" (*maafuta fakatasi*), and of performing daily routines together, as the epitome of a fulfilling life. When these ideals are disrupted, as during farewells, or when these disruptions are highlighted, as in letters written to loved ones living far away, much sorrow ensues. The sensitivity of members of this community to separation is particularly well illustrated by the case of an elderly woman who spent the last decades of her life in a state of extreme senility, rarely getting up from the ground, totally speechless, and affectively unresponsive. Nukulaelae Islanders universally attributed her state of *fakavalevale* "craziness" to her inability to bear the sorrow of parting with her last born, who left for Samoa to go to school in the 1950s, and never returned to the atoll. Clearly, the fear of never again seeing a loved one when one bids farewell is grounded in vivid first-hand experiences.

I have already made several allusions to the affinity between letters and farewells: it is in the interactions preceding someone's departure from the atoll that one typically hears *polopolooki* "admonitions" akin to what writers include in their letters, and that individuals ask for each other's forgiveness for wrongdoings. The affinity between the two events goes further. For example, letters not infrequently refer to the emotional trauma of farewells, particularly when "proper" farewells have not taken place:

Ia, au nei koo oko loa i te faanoanoa, ia taatou seki fakamaavae. Koo tusa nei mo te lua o aku malaga ki Nukulaelae, kae foki mai au, taaua seki fakamaavae saale. I au, maafai e vau, see iloa nee au me kaiaa. Kaati koe e tai vaaivai maafai e fakamaavae taaua.

[letters 1985:565]

So I am very sad indeed, because we did not get to say goodbye. It is now the second time I travel to Nukulaelae, and when I return, you and I have not said goodbye. When I return, I don't understand why. Perhaps you are emotionally vulnerable at the time of farewells [literally, weak, i.e., you might cry].

[from a young man to another young man]
Au e fakamolemole atu loa moo te see llei o te fakamaavaega a taaua i konaa. J, fakamolemole loa. E iloa nee koe, au see kkafi loa o fakasae atu i te toe taimi. Me e iloa nee koe, toku loto ko ia loa koo vaaivai i taimi peenaa.

[letters 1991:725]

I apologize for the fact that we did not say goodbye to one another over there. J, I am sorry. You know, I was incapable of coming to you at the last moment. Because, you know, my heart is vulnerable at such times.

When farewells are not explicitly referred to, allusions are made to the possibility of never meeting again and the uncertainty of the recipient's whereabouts:

*Te tusi nei e tusi atu eiloa i te vaveao, ka ko te taimi ko aafa te faa. Au ne masaki. Kae ala aka loa i ttaimi koo manatu loa au kiaa koe, tusi loa mo taku tusi, **kae see iloa nei nee au me teefea te kogaa koga o te lalolagi koo nofo nei koe i ei.***

[letters 1993:873*]

I am writing this letter at dawn, it is now half past four. I was sick earlier, but then I woke up thinking about you, so I began writing this letter, **but I do not know where in the vast world you are right now.**

Letters often describe longing for loved ones who are living far away and reminiscing about being together:

*Niko, talu mai te aso ne maavae ei taatou, i te afiafi teenaa, a maatou mo S, O, T, S, mo tamaliki katoa, koo ttagi i te masausau atu kiaa koe. I te paleleega o temotou lotu, a ko O koo fakamasau aka nee ia a tau maasani i taimi o ttou lotu afiafi, a koe e see mafai loa o fano ki se koga fakaaatea, [. . .]. A S i te taimi teenaa koo tagi, a ko au foki koo tagi, a maatou koo ttagi katoa loa i te maafaufau atu ki ou uiga ggali mo ou faifaiga llei ne fai i loto i te kaaiga, peelaa foki ki te fenua. Koo leva kkii eiloa temotou sagasaga, takatokkato foki, kae faatoe fai temotou meakkai. **Maaffaga laa o mea maasei ko te olaga nofo tasi i se maafutaga solosolo llei, kae toe maavae i se taimi.***

[letters 1985:656*]

Niko, on the day that we parted, that evening, all of us, S, O, T, S, and all the children, we cried while reminiscing you. After our evening prayer, O started reminiscing about your habit of not going off somewhere else during prayer, [. . .]. S then started crying at that time, and I cried too, and all of us cried thinking about your nice attitude and the nice things that you did at the heart of the family, and also in the island community. We sat or lay down for a very long time, and then finally had dinner. **There is nothing more painful than living together in harmonious communion, and then another time be parted once again.**

That letters should have come to be defined as cathartic contexts clearly results from their association with farewells and separation, situations in which emotions identical to those that are centralized in letters emerge (compare Pedersen 1990).

Literacy and emotionality

In this chapter, I have shown that affect permeates Nukulaelae letters at several levels. First, as demonstrated in Chapter 4, letters are framed by affectively charged expressions. The opening and closing sequences of letters are indeed statements about the affective state of the writer. Second, as discussed in this chapter, the four topic areas that Nukulaelae writers address in their letters all have clear affective connotations. For example, discourse about economic issues, whether produced in the oral mode or the written mode, always touches on affect, because economic transactions are regulated by emotions like *alofa* and *maa*. Since monitoring economic transactions is one of the main purposes of writing letters, affect surfaces frequently and saliently in letters. Similarly, admonitions, whether oral or written, frequently focus on the affective behavior of younger people, who are told to be kind and loving, generous and peaceful. Since admonitions play an important role in letters, it is not surprising that affect should play such an important role in the text of letters. Another important characteristic of affect displays in letters is that writers do not shy away from employing the most overt affect-communicating strategies like emotion terms and expressions. The result is that letters are defined as emotional outpourings in which affect surfaces at all discourse levels.

While the form of letters bears the imprint of alien origins and influences, there is every evidence that letter writing and reading are part of the very fabric of social life in this community. This is strikingly illustrated by the extent to which letters are integrated in gossip networks and the economic life of the society. However, letter writing has not just been thoroughly integrated into the communicative system of the society, it has been *constructed* in a particular way. Letters are, above all, devices through which affect is communicated, to an extent and of a kind that is rarely found in oral communication.

What this analysis demonstrates is that literacy was not merely "imposed" on Nukulaelae society in the late nineteenth century from the outside as a foreign technology and sociocultural construct. Nukulaelae Islanders were not the powerless recipients of a literacy ideology, the passive witnesses to the introduction of literate technologies, as incipiently literate societies are often portrayed to be in areal (Jackson 1975, Koskinen 1965, Mühlhäusler 1990, Parsonson 1967, Topping 1983, 1992) and theoretical works (Goody 1977, Goody and Watt 1963, Ong 1982). Rather, they took an active role in *empowering* literacy (Kulick and Stroud 1990, McLaughlin 1992) by constructing it and adapting it to their communicative repertoire, and providing it with a culturally specific meaning – a process which may have begun very early in their post-contact history.

The materials I have presented in this chapter and the previous chapter have implications for our general understanding of emotionality and modes of communication. While considerable progress has been made in the last few years toward an understanding of the role and nature of affective meaning in oral discourse (see Besnier 1990a for a comprehensive review), little attention has been paid to the communication of affect in writing within any speech community. The little research that has addressed the question of writing and affect has mostly focused on Western literary genres (e.g., Haviland 1984), and not on the day-to-day written output of ordinary folks. (Social historians have made much more progress than anthropologists or sociolinguists have in this respect, e.g., Frank 1992, Ko 1989, Møller 1990, Sandersen 1990, Smith-Rosenberg 1975.) Yet the sociolinguistic literature on orality and literacy is replete with allusions to affective categories. For example, it is commonly assumed that spoken language is universally more "involved," "emotional," and better suited for the representation of emotions than written language. Textual evidence commonly advanced in support of this is the greater incidence in spoken language of such features as pronouns and questions, which are understood to be markers of personal involvement (e.g., Biber 1988, Chafe 1982, 1986, Chafe and Danielewicz 1987, Tannen 1982, 1985). The assumption is made that the participants in a spoken (particularly face-to-face) interaction are more prone to becoming "emotional' than readers and writers (cf. Linell 1985, 1988). In particular, the immediacy of an audience allows speakers to invoke more personal elements in spoken discourse, while writers cannot afford to do so to the same extent because of the lack of a visible audience. However, most of these claims have been supported with data from contemporary mainstream Western contexts, where writing is viewed as being less "subjective," less "emotional," and generally more "reliable" than speaking. The literacy practices associated with Western, school-oriented, middle-class settings, particular academia and other loci of cultural reproduction, are particularly prone to such characterizations (Brodkey 1987, Gilbert and Mulkay 1984).

The evidence presented in this chapter suggests that these views merely derive from a specific ideological construction of literacy. Affect is related to modality, but this relationship is a particularly complex one. In particular, it is mediated by the social context in which particular forms of literacy are practised: the identity of the participants in the literacy event, the purposes of literacy, and the social environment in which it is produced, consumed, and conveyed not only "influence" the shape of written texts, but *define* literacy as a social practice.

6

BETWEEN LITERACY AND ORALITY:
THE SERMON

No social arena is as suffused with literacy on Nukulaelae as religion. The religious service is the only regular occasion in most Nukulaelae Islanders' weekly routine during which they read from a book, and carrying a Bible to church is a must (a hymnal is optional but desirable). On Sunday mornings, just before the beginning of the service at 9 a.m., a familiar domestic scene takes place in many Nukulaelae homes: as household members adjust their Sunday best and finish combing their hair, much good-natured bantering takes place over who will get to take the family's Bibles to church, since there usually aren't enough copies for every adult and child.[1] Even four-year-old Semi in our household knows the particular relevance of books to church contexts: on many Sundays, to everyone's amusement and feigned indignation, he quietly sneaks away to Sunday School (held at the same time as the service in a thatched building adjacent to the pastor's house) clutching his father's Bible under his shirt, and hoping to be at a safe distance from the house before the disappearance of the Bible is noticed. Some Nukulaelae Islanders also bring to church books that are not generally used there, like an English Bible (a high prestige commodity), copies of religious pamphlets gleaned from various sources, or other printed materials of no obvious religious relevance, which they may or may not open during the service.

Besides the Bible, the most important token of literacy in the church service is the written version of the sermon. Nukulaelae sermons are complex communicative events, in that they are first prepared in writing and then delivered orally to the entire community. One question I address in this chapter is whether sermons are tokens of oral communication, manifestations of the literate mode, or a complex interweaving of both. In contrast to letter writing, an essentially secular practice, sermon writing preserves the strong associations that literacy had with religious matters when it was first introduced. Sermons bear witness to the complex role that religion plays in contemporary Nukulaelae society: at once an institution of foreign origin and a set of practices and beliefs that have penetrated the very core of the culture, Christianity on the atoll is both ideologically constructed by and reflected in sermons. In this chapter and the next, I investigate how this process takes place, and examine the role that literacy plays in it.

The literacy practices associated with religious contexts differ in quality, sometimes considerably so, from literacy practices found in other contexts of social life, such as letter writing. Here we find none of the vulnerability and emotionality that emerge in letters; instead, sermon texts and performances are suffused with authoritative assertiveness, an emphasis on individualism, and a centralization of the truth. One of the purposes of this chapter and the next is to highlight the extent to which sermons diverge from letters. As a result, the categories and processes that I will examine will sometimes be radically different from the categories and processes I discussed in reference to letter writing, and the connection between the different literacy practices that Nukulaelae people engage in may seem a little obscure at first glance. However, I will devote part of the conclusion to bringing together these various strands and demonstrating the importance of understanding literacy as a fundamentally diverse phenomenon, even in small-scale societies like Nukulaelae.

diverse phenom

The following investigation of sermons and their context draws on two research strategies. First, I will analyze the texts of both written and oral sermons, and show that a close examination of selected features of these texts can inform an understanding of what sermons mean for Nukulaelae Islanders. This methodological stance does not differ substantially from the way I approached letter writing and reading in Chapters 4 and 5. However, sermons differ from letters in that the performative dimensions of the former are considerably more important than in the latter. I will thus pay particular attention to the sermon as a performance, i.e., as behavior situated in particular institutional contexts in which a performer *displays* communicative competence to an evaluative audience. As advocates of performance-centered approaches to folklore and verbal arts have argued convincingly (Bauman 1975, 1977, 1986, Bauman and Briggs 1990, Briggs and Bauman 1992, Hymes 1975), viewing texts as emerging within a social context offers a considerably richer framework for understanding their social and communicative meaning than an exclusively text-centered approach does. As a result, my search for the social meaning of sermons will lead me to consider problems that may appear at first glance marginally relevant to the study of literacy; nevertheless, I hope to demonstrate the value that these investigative forays ultimately hold for an understanding of literacy practices on Nukulaelae.

The church service

Three church services a week are regularly held on Nukulaelae: one on Sunday morning, one on Sunday afternoon, and a third in the early morning on Wednesday. Everyone is under very strong social pressure to attend at least the two Sunday services. As they are taking place, a patrol of two or three members of the Church makes the rounds in the village, stopping at the home of anyone not in church, ostensibly to conduct a brief prayer. At the close of the Sunday afternoon service, a member of the patrol reads out the list of absentees along with their respective alibi, which the entire congregation listens to with great interest. As described in Chapter 2, similar patrols also regulate many other aspects of Nukulaelae life. From an orthodoxic standpoint, the practice reinforces community cohesion, an extremely important value in the Nukulaelae normative order, and emphasizes to everyone the value placed on each and every individual's presence in church. From a heterodoxic perspective, which converts to other religions adopt, the practice is highly intrusive and coercive.

The Sunday morning service is normally conducted by the pastor, while the other services are conducted by a deacon (*tiaakono*) or a lay preacher (*fai laauga*) whom the pastor designates at the conclusion of the previous Sunday's afternoon service. The practice of delegating the responsibility of leading religious ceremonies to qualified members of the community is solidly grounded in the self-identified congregationalist orientation of the Nukulaelae Church. (However, I do not know when the practice actually began.) For adult men, becoming a deacon or lay preacher is an intrinsic part of their role as responsible members of society. Younger men are expected to join their ranks many years before they play any role in other arenas of public life. Women are heavily underrepresented in the ranks of deacons and lay preachers; however, they do preach on special occasions, particularly when the occasion is seen as specially relevant to them (e.g., yearly celebrations of Women's Day or Children's Day). Women's involvement in conducting religious services is also changing, and more rapidly so than their involvement in politics. During my last field sojourn, there were considerably more women preachers than during any of my previous sojourns in the field.[2]

When a deacon or lay preacher has just returned from another island or overseas, he becomes a prime candidate to lead the first available Sunday afternoon service. Similarly, deacons and lay preachers visiting from other islands are usually asked to conduct one service during their sojourn on the atoll. This practice has several overtly articulated purposes. One is to add variety to the usual round of preachers and to hear fresh ideas and new preaching styles that newcomers might have picked up off-island (as long as these innovations do not diverge too much from the norm). Another motivation is to acknowledge the guest's or new returnee's presence in a public manner, and hence to pay him the respect due to newcomers. In Chapter 7 I will discuss the fact that the practice has other, less explicit meanings, which shed light on the meaning of sermons in the general context of social life.

Some lay preachers and deacons are thought to do a better job of conducting church services than others, and some individuals have recognizably personal styles of doing so, which are particularly identified with the way they orchestrate sermons. Nukulaelae people talk about this diversity in the same terms as they discuss distinct levels of proficiency in any other activity that women or men engage in (e.g., delivering political speeches, building a canoe, weaving mats): some people are more *maasani* "adept" at certain skills than others, aptitude being the direct result of practice (the word *maasani*, a borrowing from Samoan, also means "familiar with").

Church services are highly formal, organized, and ritualized events, during which a great deal of attention is paid to time (see Goldsmith 1989b for a historical perspective on this preoccupation). A complex cycle of bell ringing is performed before the service, and there are two time-pieces in the church building, a chiming clock facing the congregation and another clock at the other end of the building, for the preacher's benefit. Some Nukulaelae Islanders also wear watches, prized articles whose display is particularly appropriate in church. The service begins right on schedule: 9 a.m. for the Sunday morning service, 3 p.m. on Sunday afternoon, and 7 a.m. on Wednesday morning. If the preacher or pastor runs as little as three or four minutes late, the congregation starts murmuring disapprovingly and there is gossip about it after the service. In no other social context is promptness given so much importance.

A concern for order and consistency permeates every aspect of the church service, many tokens of which will be described later in this chapter. It is this concern that explains why testimonials or witnessing performances occur very rarely. Spontaneous testimonials typical of revivalist and evangelical events in other cultures (e.g., Lawless 1988a, 1988b, Titon 1988) would be totally out of place on Nukulaelae. Testimonials do occur in highly circumscribed occasions, but they are carefully pre-orchestrated and their affective tenor is poised and full of *gravitas.* There is of course no room in the Nukulaelae service for Pentecostal-style glossolalia and other such performances.

Order and unity also figure prominently in local accounts of the historical impact of Christianity on atoll life. For example, contemporary islanders credit the Samoan pastors for having consolidated into one single village the small settlements previously scattered all around the atoll. The precise alignment of dwellings along two parallel paths in the village, which Nukulaelae people find particularly *gali* "beautiful," is also attributed to the Samoan missionaries. The historical validity of these beliefs is ambiguous because colonial administrators were equally obsessed with order and unity (Goldsmith 1989a:82–7, 1989b). Yet this ambiguity matters little; what is important is that they are locally associated with the coming of Christianity and, by direct association, with the practice of Christian life.

The church service is not the only social context in which order and predictability are important. A highly organized approach also characterizes events like feasts and meetings, which are always run according to a specific *polokalame* "program." Even when highly spontaneous activities take place during secular events, they are presented as part of the *polokalame*. This *polokalame* is the responsibility of the master of ceremonies (*tuku muna, tagata fai polokalame*) who always presides over feasts, and whose job it is to devise the most interesting, varied, and enjoyable set of activities.[3] However ingenious and creative they may be, these diversions are always presented as part of the set *polokalame*, which the master of ceremonies announces (*folafola*, literally, "unrolls") at the beginning of the function, and from which no one can escape. This elaborate concern with *polokalame* and the uniformity they enforce is clearly grounded in deeply seated social dynamics in this society (Besnier 1991). However, nowhere are order, predictability, and consistency as elaborated as in the church service.

The various components of the service are ordered in a strict sequence, from which departures are rare. The word for "sequence," *fakasologa*, is a key term that also describes such ordered sets as genealogical sequences, items on the agenda of political meetings, and the words in a sentence. The service always opens with a hymn, which is followed by the communal reading of the Bible passage or passages which will form the *matua* "core" of the sermon. Then comes another hymn, then a prayer performed by the preacher, then another hymn, then the sermon, followed by another hymn and a final prayer. (Once a month, communion follows the final prayer, but even this event is clearly marked as falling outside of the temporal boundaries of the regular service.) Hymns thus punctuate each transition, adding to the sense of regularity and order. When deviations occur, as when a particularly modernity oriented pastor asks more than one person to participate in the production of the performance, there is a strong tendency to minimize departures from the set sequence and also to confine the exceptions to special occasions. Thus the structure of "deviant" services, which are never initiated by anyone other than the pastor, only reinforce the normative pattern.

Predictability and order permeate many microscopic aspects of the church service. The communal Bible reading has a very particularly prosodic structure comparable to British communal prayers and Bible reading performances that Tench (1988:72–9) describes. The lento rhythm is punctuated by regular and lengthy pauses that correspond closely to the punctuation of the written text, and the delivery is very monotone: the phrase-internal pitch is always level, while phrase-final tone is always falling. Following is the transcript of a typical reading performance, with an approximate rendering of the overall intonational contours:

E isi se fai aakoga o te tuulaafono ne vau

kae ne taumafai o tofotofo a Ieesuu

ana muna

te fai aakoga

se aa te mea e ttau o fai nee au

ko te mea kee maua nee au te ola see gata mai

ne tali atu a Ieesuu kiaa ia

ne aa muna e tusi i te tuulaafono

se aa tou iloa i ei

ne tali mai a te tagata teenaa peenei

e ttau mo koe o alofa ki te Aliki tou Atua mo tou loto kaatoa

mo tou agaaga kaatoa

mo tou maalosi kaatoa

mo tou maafaufau kaatoa

kae e ttau foki mo koe o alofa ki tou tuaakoi

e peelaa eiloa mo koe kiaa koe

[sermons: Ti 1991 : 2 : B : 006-014]

The text from which this was read appears as follows (I have preserved the orthography and line breaks of the original):[4]

²⁵ *E isi se faiakoga o te Tulafono*
ne vau, kae ne taumafai o tofotofo
a Iesu, ana muna: "Te Faiakoga, se
aa te mea e 'tau o fai ne au, ko te
mea ke maua ne au te ola se gata
mai?" ²⁶ *Ne tali atu a Ieesuu ki a ia, "Ne*
a muna e tusi i te Tulafono? Se a tou
iloa i ei?" ²⁷ *Ne tali mai a te tagata*
tena penei: "'E 'tau mo koe o alofa ki
te Aliki tou Atua mo tou loto katoa,
mo tou agaga katoa, mo tou malosi
katoa, mo tou mafaufau katoa,' kae
'E 'tau foki mo koe o alofa ki tou
tuakoi, e pela eiloa mo koe ki a koe.'"

²⁵On one occasion an expert in the law stood up to test Jesus. "Teacher," he asked, "what must I do to inherit eternal life?" ²⁶"What is written in the Law?" he replied. "How do you read it?" ²⁷He answered: "'Love the Lord your God with all your heart and with all your soul and with all your mind'; and, 'Love your neighbor as yourself.'"

[Luke 10:25–27]

The overall effect of this reading style is laconic and low in affect; the lengthy pauses and predictable phrase-final falling intonation contours are particularly effective in conveying a sense of order and predictability.[5]

The value associated with orderliness, formality, and predictability in church context is also saliently manifested in hymn singing. Hymns are sometimes sung by the entire congregation, but they are more often sung only by the choir. The choir, referred to as *aaogaa pese* (a borrowing from Samoan) or *kau fai pese* (a Tuvaluan coinage), is a group of women and men of various ages organized like numerous other clubs and groups, i.e., with a president, a secretary, a treasurer, a bank account, and rigid rules of conduct: members must attend all choir-practice sessions and business meetings, pay a fine if they are late to practice or absent without a valid excuse, and so on. A specific sense of order is thus embedded in the social organization of hymn singing in church: one has to meet specific social criteria to be entitled to sing. The choir sings from Nukulaelae's very own hymnal, cyclostated and bound at the Church of Tuvalu office on Funafuti in the early 1980s, as Nukulaelae people considered it a priority that the hymns in the repertoire be recorded on paper, collated, indexed, and numbered, even though many can sing the entire repertoire from memory. During choir-practice sessions and church services, the choir sings in a rigidly formal fashion, never deviating from a set tempo and never adding ornamentation, vibrato, or syncopation to the melody (contrast Titon 1988:213–56 on Appalachian Gospel hymns). There is of course no dancing and no clapping of hands. As in other Polynesian Christian traditions, the singing is vigorous, even vociferous, but it is highly controlled. A conductor chosen from among the few specially trained members of the group generally leads the choir; staring straight ahead, his body rigid, he conducts with automaton-like movements of his baton. He begins the hymn with a commanding gesture, and cuts the hymn off at the end with a decisive sweep of the baton.[6]

To my ear, Nukulaelae hymns lack grace and affect; for a Nukulaelae listener, the beauty of the performance resides precisely in the monotonous regularity of the tempo and the rigidly controlled cadence.[7] Yet syncopated, antiphonal, and affectively charged hymn-singing performances comparable to American Gospel singing are not foreign to Polynesia: they are heard in Wesleyan churches in Tonga and are characteristic of the famous Tahitian *hīmene* tradition. (Interestingly, older Nukulaelae Islanders appear to sing hymns with considerably more "swing" than the younger people, who predominate in the choir.) While the Nukulaelae hymn-singing style is probably not unique in the Pacific, the rigidity, flat affect, and high degree of formality that characterize both the music they produce and the social organization of hymn singing are not fortuitous. I will argue presently that the formal characteristics of activities such as Bible reading and hymn singing give a specific meaning to church-related literacy.

The sermon

The *pièce-de-resistance* of the church service is the sermon, or *laauga* (a term borrowed from Samoan), to which approximately half of the fifty- to sixty-minute service is devoted. That the Nukulaelae term for "sermon" is a borrowing from Samoan bears witness to the fact that its referent is a manifestation of "high culture"; indeed, much of what contemporary Nukulaelae Islanders identify as "tradition" (in which Christianity and its semiotic tokens figure prominently) has been constructed since missionization on the basis of institutions introduced by Samoan missionaries.

Under normal circumstances, preachers receive no formal instruction in sermon composition, and few pedagogical tools are available for this purpose. (There are a few copies of "how-to" manuals on the atoll, but they are in English and their owners usually keep them carefully hidden.) Less experienced preachers learn how to write and deliver their sermons through observation and imitation, the way knowledge is traditionally transmitted in this community. Historically, sermons given by lay people were undoubtedly influenced by sermons delivered by the Samoan pastors who originally missionized the atoll. Nevertheless, since the mid-1980s, pastors who have received more modern schooling occasionally conduct pedagogical workshops for deacons and lay preachers. The island Church also takes advantage of occasional visits by young Nukulaelae pastors with theological training by asking them to give similar workshops. As a result, one may expect sermons to show more and more influence from Western religious traditions. However, formal pedagogical opportunities are very infrequent.

Sermons are typologized into three categories, each identified by a different argumentative structure, *laauga vaevae* "sermon in sections," *laauga fakaoomelia* "sermon in the homiletic style" (*faka-* "in the way of," *oomelia* "homily," a borrowing from Greek via Samoan), and *laauga sikisiki* "sermon with a progressive structure." This typology may have been inherited from Samoan sources, although the lack of comparative work on Samoan sermons does not enable me to investigate this hypothesis further. In all cases, the sermon is based on the Scripture passage that the congregation reads before the sermon. According to Nukulaelae respondents, a major goal of the sermon is to contextualize these readings and relate them to contemporary living. This concern with establishing a link between the Scriptures and the congregation's everyday life is certainly common across Christian traditions. For example, it is at the root of the particularly elaborate tradition of weekday "occasional sermon" in Colonial New England, in which preachers would address issues of secular concern, such as the importance of civic obedience (Stout 1986:27–30). (In contrast to Puritan New England, "secular" and "religious" themes are not carefully separated in Nukulaelae sermonic tradition.) However, linking the secular and the divine is not viewed as necessary or desirable in all forms of Christianity: for example, in Hutterite sermons, the relevance of the Scriptures to day-to-day concerns is of no interest (Hartse 1993:94).

This analysis is based principally on data gathered during Sunday afternoon services, which, as explained earlier, are the responsibility of members of the community rather than that of the pastor. A focus on a more diversified event than the services conducted by the pastor avoids the danger of overgeneralizing from a single individual's discursive production, namely that of the pastor. From a textual standpoint, sermons that pastors deliver are not distinguishable from sermons that lay preachers and deacons deliver. However, the two events differ in terms of the relationship between participants. Goldsmith (1989a:226–76) describes in great detail the complexities of the pastor's relationship with his congregation; how this relationship affects the communicative aspects of church services is an important question that I will not discuss at length, although I will address it briefly in the next chapter. I am particularly concerned here with the way in which religious ideology is articulated in sermons authored by members of the community and addressed to other members of the community.

Sermons and speeches

The word *laauga* "sermon" also refers to a genre of political and recreational oratory associated with secular settings, principally the maneapa.[8] Religious sermons and oratorical speeches share certain characteristics as genres and communicative events. For example, in both, speakers develop logically connected arguments to convince their audiences of the truth, relevance, and validity of certain propositions or points of view. In addition, in both communicative events, a single person addresses a group of listeners. However, there are important differences between the two. Most straightforwardly, they take place in complementary settings: sermons are never delivered outside of church services, while speeches are typically delivered during community feasts, dance performances, political meetings, and family feasts. An equally conspicuous difference is the fact that sermons are topically confined to questions of a religious nature, while speeches can touch on a broad variety of topics, including religious ones.

The two types of events have distinct participant structures. First and foremost, sermons differ from oratorical performances in that a higher authority, namely the pastor, selects who conducts particular church services, while orators self-select. During feasts and other public events, the order in which orators make speeches is loosely regulated by the norm that orators sitting at one end of the maneapa alternate with orators sitting at the other end; when there is a clear binary opposition between two groups of participants (e.g., hosts vs. guests), members of each party take turns at making speeches. These norms are nevertheless not strict, and violations abound. In addition, within each party or side of the house, any qualified person may take a turn at speaking. A secular speech is also commonly "answered" by another speech, whereas the religious sermon is a self-contained event. Thus, in contrast to the multivocality of contexts in which speeches are made, the religious service is very much focused on a single sermon performance and, for that matter, on a single performer.

Sermons may be delivered by a much broader subset of the community than speeches. As mentioned earlier, sermons are the responsibility of deacons or lay preachers, which most adult men are. In contrast, only senior men generally deliver speeches, particularly to public assemblies that include members of more than one kin group. Younger men are entitled and expected to give sermons before they are perceived to be "ready" to engage in secular oratory. Although it is not explicitly presented as such, delivering religious sermons serves as an apprenticeship for secular oratory: the two types of discourse share many formal properties, and the mastery of one essentially implies the mastery of the other. By the time a man has reached the age and stature to take the floor in public, he is likely to have given several sermons. One's first sermon performance is acknowledged as an informal rite of passage (e.g., one may be congratulated by friends and relatives after the performance); one's first speech in the maneapa, in contrast, is not marked in any way.[9] Similarly, women preach on special occasions, but they do not engage in secular oratory in most public contexts. (Again, there are exceptions: women do make speeches at meetings and feasts that are attended predominantly or exclusively by women, or at more "intimate" functions in which only a small subset of the community takes part.) Thus sermon giving involves a broader cross-section of the atoll community than does secular oratory.

Speeches given in public contexts are considerably more variable in length than sermons, whose duration is rigidly set. The range of speech acts and communicative moves allowed during speech making is also much less constrained than it is in sermon delivery: for example, orators frequently crack jokes in speeches, sometimes in a risqué fashion, which would be unthinkable in a sermon: sermons are serious business, and no context for humor. During speeches, members of the audience may express their approval by punctuating the oratorical delivery with interjections (e.g. *auee!* "indeed!," *ko ia!* "that's it!"). Secular speeches are also frequently delivered while audience members are eating, talking among themselves, or attending to practical chores like cleaning up, preparing for a dance performance, or taking care of children. In contrast, the audience's role in the construction of the sermon is more focused and constrained. Here, audiences contribute no back-channel cues, no exclamatory encouragements, and no verbal tokens of approval. The preacher and the audience do not engage in the call-and-response interactions characteristic of Christian ceremonies in many ethnographic settings (e.g., Callender and Cameron 1990, G. Davis 1985, Hartse 1993, Holt 1972, McGinnis 1986, Smitherman 1977, Spencer 1987). Sometimes, particularly at the beginning of the sermon, the preacher may request that an audience member read aloud a Scripture passage, frequently specifying that the reader be a younger person:

Preacher: *A te muna koo filifili nee au i te taeao teenei kee maafaufau fakatasi taatou ki ei, e maua mai i te Feagaiga Mua, Ioosua, i te mataaupu e lua sefulu faa, ka koo filifili nee au te foaiupu e sefulu lima kee maafaufaugina moo te taeao teenei. Fakamolemole se tamaafine o te kau talavou kee faitau mai nee ia te foaiupu e sefulu lima.*

A: *"Kaafai see fia taavini koutou kia ia, e filifili i te aso nei, mo kooi e fia taavini koutou ki ei, ko atua ne taapuaki saale ki ei ootou tupuga i Mesopotaamia, io me ko atua o tino Aamoli, e teenei e nnofo koutou i telotou fenua. Ka ko au mo toku kaaiga, e taavini eiloa maatou ki te Aliki."*

[sermons:Me 1991:2:A:039–058]

Preacher: The passage I have chosen this morning for us to think about together is from the New Testament, Joshua, chapter twenty-four, I have chosen verse fifteen for it to be thought about this morning. Would a young woman from the Youth Group please read verse fifteen.

A: "But if serving the Lord seems undesirable to you, then choose for yourselves this day whom you will serve, whether the gods your forefathers served beyond the River, or the gods of the Amorites, in whose land you are living. But as for me and my household, we will serve the Lord."

Otherwise audience members sit and listen in apparent awe at the power of the sermon and its delivery; their silence is broken only by the ruffling of fans, as they bravely attempt to cope with the oppressive combination of heavy Sunday clothing and the lack of ventilation in the church building.

Nevertheless, audience members do play a role in the construction of sermon events, although their contribution is *delayed*. It takes place after the service, when the relative merit, efficacy, and appropriateness of the performance are discussed either in the intimacy of small groups of kinsfolk and friends, or, in a more public way, in the context of speeches given at feasts when held shortly after the service. Following is an example of these post-hoc evaluations:

A ko ia koo hee fano ttonu i luga i tena matua teelaa ne fai. [. . .] Te faiga o tena laauga, naa laa muamua paa me e tai logo llei eeloo te vauuga, nee? Kae fakamuli peelaa koo ttele fakaaattea loo ana- ana manatu mo tena matua, peelaa koo faaopoopo ua ki luga i mea kolaa i tena maafaufau.
[interviews:Si 1991:1:A:029–042]

But he [i.e., the preacher] did not proceed directly according to the Bible reading he started out with. [. . .] When he gave his sermon, first it sounded pretty good, see? But then later on it's like his thoughts were running away from the reading, it's like he was just ad-libbing on the basis of what was on his mind.

While the audience is not entitled to make an audible contribution during the sermonic performance, it reserves the right to evaluate the sermon critically later on. Generally speaking, sermons are more "formal" communicative events (Irvine 1979), when viewed as bounded events, than secular oratorical performances. Sermons and speeches are distinct genres and events, even though they are given the same label in Nukulaelae Tuvuluan.[10]

The last notable difference between religious sermons and secular oratory stems from the fact that literacy permeates the former, but is completely absent in the latter. Reading and writing are involved in the trajectory and substance of religious sermons in several ways. Sermons take place in a context where reading plays an important role, as described earlier. Most importantly, sermons are written out before oral delivery, in contrast to secular oratorical performances, which are never based on a written document drafted ahead of time. In the next section, I describe written sermons in detail.

Sermons and literacy

According to common practice, preachers write out their sermons ahead of time, generally during the week prior to the sermon delivery. Preachers take this composition process seriously, and some, particularly less proficient ones, agonize over it. Sermon writing is a time for individual reflection and religious introspection, characteristics that leave their mark on the text. The preacher designated to conduct the service the following Sunday is sometimes seen by himself, during the week, poring over the composition task, an uncommon sight at times other than ship days (when letters are written).

Preachers generally write their sermons in a blank notebook reserved for this purpose, typically a school exercise book. These notebooks, called *api* (another borrowing from Samoan), are carefully saved after the sermon. Alternatively, if no exercise book is available, the preacher may use any available sheet of paper, and saves this sheet in a Bible or inside the trunk or suitcase in which every islander stores clothing and other intimate possessions. These written sermons do not form a rigid and consecrated canon in the same way that old-school Hutterite sermons do (cf. Hartse 1993, Stephenson 1990). Nevertheless, sermon notebooks constitute an important corpus of exegetic texts.

An important feature of written sermons is that they are a *gendered* literacy practice. Women generally do not compose their own sermons, but rather ask male relatives to lend them an *api* or to compose a new sermon from scratch for them. Women explain this practice as stemming from their lack of *maasani* "aptitude, familiarity" with the genre. While this may indeed be the case for some, there are women in the Nukulaelae community who are perfectly capable of engaging in extemporaneous oratory in appropriate secular contexts, and do so with great skill. This suggests that the meaning of written sermons and of their relationship to gender is more complex than local accounts make it to be. However, for everyone involved, having a notebook or piece of paper in front of one is an intrinsic aspect of conducting a religious service. While in many Christian traditions sermon performances are similarly based on written drafts that are subsequently saved (e.g., Stout 1986:34 on Colonial New England), the practice is by no means universal. In the Tongan Methodist tradition, for example, sermons cannot be written out ahead of delivery; in eighteenth-century New England, certain itinerant ministers disdained sermons prepared in writing before delivery (Stout 1986:192–211); and in contemporary Baptist Appalachia, "written and read sermons – whether or not produced by

seminary-trained ministers – are understood to violate the rules of Spirit-
leading and to be powerless and ineffective" (Titon 1988:312).

The most striking characteristic of these documents is their highly
organized appearance. They are frequently very neat (much neater than
letters, for example), and their text is organized in sections, each preceded
by a heading clearly set apart from the text and sometimes underlined. In
some older sermon notebooks, these headings are occasionally in English
(in oral delivery, no English is used):

28/10/79
Reading: Luka 14:7–14; faitau 1–14.
*Text ("Matua"): Luka 14:11; "Soo se tino e loto fia sili kaa fakamaalalogina. Ka ko
ia teelaa e loto maalalo, kaa fakamaalugagina."*
Manatu maaluga: Te llei o te loto maalalo.

[sermons:F 1985:427:1]

28/10/79
Reading: Luke 14:7–14; read 1–14.
Text ("Core"): Luke 14:11; "For everyone who exalts himself will be humbled, and
he who humbles himself will be exalted."
Main thought: The value of humility.

Written sermons are commonly given a title, which usually consists of the
word *laauga* "sermon" centered across the page, sometimes followed by a
date. Each segment of the main text of the sermon may also be numbered:

Fakatoomuaga
[. . .]
1. Ko te alofa
[. . .]
2. Ko te fiileemuu
[. . .]
Akoakoga
[. . .]

[sermons:A 1991:4]

Introduction
[. . .]
1. Love
[. . .]
2. Peace
[. . .]
Lesson
[. . .]

Sermon writers use little (and often no) punctuation, or else place periods at
the end of each major sentence constituent. These patterns are not specific
to sermons, as they also characterize the general written style of many
individuals on the atoll.

Many Nukulaelae preachers are already accomplished orators, who could in all likelihood deliver a coherent, well developed sermon without relying on written prompts. Indeed, many preachers regularly engage in impressive extemporaneous oratorical performances in secular contexts that are sometimes comparable to religious sermons in length and rhetorical complexity. Yet having some sort of written document in front of one during sermon delivery is obligatory. So why the need for sermon notebooks? Before tackling this question, I turn to the relationship between sermons as written and oral texts and events.

From written mode to spoken mode

A major juncture in the trajectory of a sermon is the transition from written to spoken mode. While most textual features of the written sermon (e.g., order of the key points, organization into sections, logic of the exposition) remain unaffected, both textual expansions and reductions may take place during this transition. Many of these transformations are clearly the result of the preacher's effort to save time by deleting certain passages from the written outline, or feeling inspired by a particular argument and expanding on it during oral delivery. The extent to which oral and written sermons differ from each other is highly variable across individuals or occasions. Generally speaking, the more experienced the preacher, the more telegraphic his or her written notes, and thus the greater the "distance" between these notes and the oral text (Rosenberg 1970a, 1970b makes similar observations on Southern revivalist sermons in the US). While more insecure preachers do little more than read their written text making few or no changes (some even memorize the text beforehand), more proficient preachers may base elaborate sermons on little more than a few written lines. Hence written sermons vary greatly in length, from half a page to several pages, while the oral delivery of sermons is considerably more uniform: most sermon deliveries last between twenty and twenty-five minutes.

Besides minor changes in the content of the text, structural transformations of several types emerge in a comparison of spoken and written texts. First, oral deliveries are always framed by openings and closings, which consist of metalinguistic statements relating to the sermon or Scriptures, and which are usually absent from the written version. For example, in one of the oral sermons I recorded, the preacher introduces the sermon with the following:

Konaa foaiupu koo filifili nee au kee aumai moo taatou i te afiafi teenei, kae talitonu a te maafaufau me i te taulasiga io mo ko te tokoukega o te kau fai gaaluega, kae maise ko ana taavini koo maasani o lagona ssoko nee taatou a foaiupu konei e akoako mai kia taatou. Teelaa laa, koo toe fusi fakatasi nee au a foaiupu konei e lua, kae kaa maua ei se manatu e takitaki ei a ttou maafaufauga i te afiafi teenei, e fai peenei, "Saa manavasee, kae manavasee." Io me, "Saa manavasee iaa koe, kae manavasee ki te Atua."

[sermons:Ke 1991:2:A:320–330]

These are two verses I have chosen to bring to us all this afternoon, and my mind believes that the majority of the church's workers, and of course its pastors, are used to hearing these verses through which we find our teachings. So I will bring together these two verses, and will get from them a depiction which we can use to lead our thoughts this afternoon, which goes like this, "Do not be afraid, but be afraid." Alternatively, "Do not fear for your [welfare], but fear God."

This paragraph is completely absent from the written version. Similarly, preachers frequently close their sermons with an expression of good wishes, often similar in wording to the final framing utterance of a secular speech:

Kee manuia taatou i te afiafi teenei i te alofa o te Atua.

[sermons:Ke 1991:2:A:456–457]

Let us be blessed in God's grace this afternoon.

These closing devices usually do not appear in the written version of the sermons.

Both written and oral sermons are highly organized, but this organization is marked differently. All Nukulaelae sermons share certain components: a core (*matua*), in which the readings are announced; a main theme (*manatu maaluga* or *manatu silisili*), which the preacher extracts from the core; any number of expansions (*magaaupu*); and a lesson (*akoakoga*). In writing, boundaries between these components are usually marked by headings, as described in the previous section. In the oral performance, these headings are sometimes read out, particularly when the preacher is less experienced. However, more experienced individuals dispense with these headings and rely on their ability to convey the organization of the sermon through the text itself.

Repetitions in oral delivery are frequent, but they are rare in the corresponding written texts; oral repetition also characterizes sermonic performances in many traditions (e.g., Callender and Cameron 1990, G. Davis 1985, Holt 1972, Rosenberg 1970a, 1970b, Smitherman 1977, Spencer 1987:11–15). A frequent target for repetition is the opening of each section of the sermon. Compare the heading of a section of a written sermon in the first of the following excerpts with its oral rendition in the second excerpt:

3. **Ko Ieesuu e toka ei ottou loto manavasee.**

[sermons:Ke 1991:10]

3. **It is in Jesus that our anxious hearts find serenity.**

Ttoe manatu o te laauga, ko Ieesuu e toka ei ottou loto manavasee. Ko Ieesuu e toka ei ottou loto manavasee.

[sermons:Ke 1991:2:A:413–416]

The last reflection of the sermon, **it is in Jesus that our anxious hearts find serenity. It is in Jesus that our anxious hearts find serenity.**

Preachers whom I have questioned maintain that repetitions flag important points and help identify transitions. Repetitions foreground certain elements of the oral sermon against others.

The delivery of an oral sermon is frequently interspersed with vocative references to the audience, which commonly do not appear in the written texts of sermons. Following is a typical example, in which the Congregation is referred to as *Te fenua o te Atua* "God's island community":[11]

Te fenua o te Atua!, kae maise tena Eekaaleesia mmalu i te afiafi teenei!
[sermons:Ke 1991:2:A:427–428]

God's island community!, and particularly his esteemed Congregation this afternoon!

These vocative phrases occur at junctures between different parts of the sermon, particularly at the beginning of the moral "lesson" (*akoakoga*). In the following, the vocative phrase occurs between the conclusion of the sermon and its repetition:

*Filifili laa koe, filifili au, mo kooi te atua kaa taavini koe ki ei. **Te fenua o te Atua i te taeao teenei!** Filifili koe, filifili au mo kooi te atua kaa taavini koe ki ei. Me ko atua kolaa e loto ki ei te Atua, me ko atua kolaa e iifo taatou ki ei.*
[sermons:Me 1991:1:B:114–121]

You [must] then choose, I [must] choose which god you will serve. **God's island community this morning!** You [must] choose, I [must] choose which god you will serve. Whether it is the gods that God wants, or whether it is the gods that we worship.

Significantly, these vocative expressions have a genre-specific form, in that they commonly consist of address terms rarely used in ordinary spheres of social life. For instance, the Samoan borrowing *taugaasoa* "[bond] friend" (which is also one of the terms used to refer to apostolic disciples) is not used outside of church-related contexts as a vocative expression, but appears frequently in sermonic performances:

*E aa taaua, **taugaasoa** fakalogollogo i te afiafi teenei?*
[sermons:Ka 1991:1:B:072–073]

How about the two of us, **friends** who are listening this afternoon?

The same is true of *taina* "classificatory sibling of same gender as ego" and *tuagaene* (or *tuagaane*) "classificatory sibling of opposite gender from ego":

*E mafai peefea nee taaua o oko atu ki te maaloo o te lagi, auaa taaua e oola i te lalolagi? **Taina, tuagaene!** Ne takato i konei ttaeao nei, ne puke tou lima ki ei, ne tuku nee koe i tou gutu mo te muna e fai peenei, "Puke, kai, inu!"*
[sermons:P 1991:1:B:456–459]

How can the two of us go to the heavenly kingdom, since we both live on earth? **Brothers [and] sisters!** [He] lay down here this morning, you reached for Him with your hand, you took Him to your mouth while saying, "Take, eat, and drink!"

Outside of religious sermons, vocative uses of these terms (particularly *tuagaene*) are rare. The marked nature of terms of address found in oral sermons is one of the many characteristics that index Nukulaelae church services as bracketed social events.

I have described the various transformations that sermons undergo in the transition from writing to speaking. Some of these affect the sermon as text: for example, preachers use framing devices, vocative expressions, and repetitions in oral delivery that are not present in written form. These patterns are probably common in many Christian traditions where sermons are written out. However, they are not universal: old-school Hutterites, for example, do not insert vocative expressions, do not use repetitions, and do not deviate from their written sermons when reading them out during church services.

What can be deduced from the above is that many Nukulaelae Islanders are adept handlers of literacy at the pulpit. They tackle the cognitively complex task of transforming a written text into an oral performance, often with great success by both local and Western evaluative criteria. They clearly have a sense of when it is appropriate to deviate from the written version of the sermon, and when to expand on it or reduce it if time is running out. They are able to keep track of the written text while simultaneously performing under the entire community's close scrutiny. The sermon performance demonstrates that Nukulaelae society and culture are steeped in literacy.

The meaning of written sermons

Earlier in this chapter, I introduced the following problem: why are sermons written down ahead of time? This question arises in light of the fact that many preachers are accomplished public speakers, and have no compelling need for a written document. The question becomes particularly puzzling in reference to certain women, who take the oratorical floor in certain secular contexts without blinking an eyelid, but do not have the confidence even to compose their own written sermons. Clearly, the value of written sermons is complex.

When questioned about this topic in ethnographic interviews, Nukulaelae Islanders often have a lot to say. Among my respondents' explanations, several patterns emerge. First, when sermons are stored in notebooks, they can be reused in "emergency" situations. Thus a preacher in the possession of an *api* is never caught off guard:

Teenaa laa, me iloa laa nee koe a te mea naa koo oti ne fakatoka nee koe i ou taimi avanoa, mo soo se taimi, peelaa, e tuku fakavave mai se- se toofiga kiaa koe, nee? Naa laa, koe koo see toe fano o- o sukesuke, peelaa, toe salasala ne maafaufauga, me vau fua koe, kilo ki luga i-, au muna, "Aa! Teenei te laauga e tau tonu eiloo moo aso konei!" Teena te aogaa o te mea teelaa e igoa ki te- te tusi laauga, nee?

[interviews:Ma 1990:3:A:512–521]

So, you know that you've already prepared something during your free time, and if at any time, like, you are unexpectedly given the responsibility [of delivering a sermon], see?, you don't have to go and- and do more research, like, to find new ideas, all you have to do is come along, look at your-, and you say, "Ah! This is the sermon that fits beautifully with these times!" That's why what's referred to as a sermon notebook is useful, see?

Preachers with a store of written sermons are thus always *toka* "ready, prepared," a quality that is given much positive prominence in public forms of discourse, particularly in reference to men: being *toka* means being alert, self-controlled, and ready for any challenge, particularly if these challenges take the form of orders emanating from higher authority, such as the Council of Elders or, in the case of sermons, the pastor.

However, the explanatory power of this account is somewhat mitigated by other factors. While recycling certain ideas is condoned, recycling entire sermons is frowned upon, even though some individuals do it. A recycled sermon, called *laauga api* "sermon from a notebook," never fools the congregation, as Nukulaelae Islanders' memory for the spoken word is sharp:[12]

"Ttapa! Mea nei ko tena laauga foki i ttausaga teelaa?" I tino laa e iloa eiloo nee laatou. Kaafai e tasi ttausaga me lua me tolu, e iloa llei eiloo nee tino kolaa fakalogollogo, a ttagata nei koo ne toe laauga foki i tena laauga i ttaimi teelaa.

[interviews:Ma 1990:3:A:544–548]

[People will say,] "Heavens! Isn't this the same sermon he gave a few years back?" Because people know. Even though one or two or three years have passed, people in the audience know well, this man is using the same sermon as the one he used that other time.

The motivation for writing out sermons is thus more involved.

Another theme that emerges in local accounts is the fact that sermon notebooks have a pedagogical value. As noted earlier, there is no tradition of formal sermon-composition instruction on the atoll. Sermon notebooks thus play an important role in the informal training of novice preachers: older, more experienced individuals selectively lend their *api* to less experienced preachers, who can use particular sermons on a one-time basis, or laboriously copy the entire notebook verbatim for later use. Following is a particularly cogent description of this process:

Teenaa, ia, peenaa laa mo koe, nee? Koe laa koo fia fai seou tofi, nee?, kee fai koe moomoo fai laauga, nee?, i te fale saa. Kae ona laa ko koe siki maasani o fai nee koe ne

*laauga, nee?, naa laa koo vau koe ki au, koo fai ei nee au te aa?, te faoao teelaa, nee? Fai
nee au a te-, peelaa, "Me- me laauga, teelaa te matua e fai ki ei i loto i tTusi Tapu,
teelaa ttagata e tuu i ei. Teelaa, teelaa te manatu muamua e ttau o fai." Ia, koo tusi.
"Te lua, teelaa te mea e ttau te lua e fai ei." Palele, koo tusi ei te laauga, nee? Teelaa
koo tusi. [. . .] Ia, palele te laauga teenaa, toe fai te isi laauga, teelaa tau- tau faoao
teenaa, mea kolaa i loto ne laauga peelaa. Teenaa laa, koo nofo ei mo koe, kaa- kaa
oko ki ttaimi teelaa koo fai mai te- te faifeau, "Ia, koe, Faiva, kaa fai nee koe te lotu o
te vaaiaso teelaa," ia, koo vau koe o onoono ki tau faoao teenaa, filifili nee koe i loto se
aa te laauga kaa taumafai koe o tauloto moo fai tau laauga.*

[interviews:Ma 1990:3:A:401–416]

All right, like you, right? You want to have a position in the church, right?, and to be
a lay preacher, right?, in the church. But the thing is that you are not adept at
delivering sermons, right?, so you come to me, and I bring out that whatchamacallit,
that notebook, right? I say the-, like, [I say], "When you give your sermon, this is the
core reading from the Bible, this is what it says. So this is the first thing [you] should
preach about." So [you] write it down. "Second, this is the thing that comes
second." So [we]'re writing out the sermon, right? So [you] write it down. [. . .] When
that sermon is done, you go to another one, so that your- your notebook, it's full of
sermons like it. So it stays with you, and when- when the time comes when the- the
pastor says, "All right, you, Faiva [i.e., NB], you're going to conduct the service that
week," so you come and look at that notebook, you choose from it the sermon
you're going to try to study to prepare your sermon.

The circulation of sermon notebooks has important consequences. First, it
has the effect of blurring the authorship of sermons, since particular written
sermons can be transmitted from one person to the other sequentially, a
point whose significance I will comment on in Chapter 7. In addition,
lenders of *api* are sometimes from another island, and the texts of the
sermons they have introduced onto the Nukulaelae market have linguistic
features from dialects of Tuvaluan other than the Nukulaelae dialect.[13] It is
also interesting to note that the practice probably originated with the
Samoan pastors, who themselves were emulating a tradition that nineteenth-century English missionaries inaugurated in Samoa. Witness what
George Turner, the founder of Mālua Seminary in Samoa (where all
Samoan missionaries to Nukulaelae were trained), writes on the topic: "For
fifteen years I have continued to give out to the students copies of my notes
and lectures, at an average, during most of that time, of twelve pages per
week . . . At the end of his four years' course, a student took with him about
2000 pages of lectures and notes" (G. Turner 1861:133–5). Despite the
probably foreign origin of the tradition, sermon notebooks circulate from
one person to another in patterns that resemble the way in which
"traditional" knowledge (e.g., sailing techniques, fishing magic, martial
arts) and valued commodities (e.g., pearl-shell bonito lures, sorcery
"bottles") are transmitted. Thus owners of sermon exercise books generally
lend their *api* only to close kindred, preferably a member of their kin group
for whom they feel particular affection; thus an older man will typically lend

his *api* to his sister's son (*tuaatina*) or to his favorite grandson (*mokopuna*), because these relationships are normatively suffused with empathy and affection. These are also the kinship relationships along which traditional knowledge and commodities are typically transmitted. In short, written sermons are treated like these other manifestations of traditional culture, the transmission of which is carefully controlled by their owners. (Briggs 1988:331–6 describes fascinatingly similar patterns for rural Hispanic communities of Northern New Mexico, whose *cuadernos* "notebooks" of hymns and prayers are also transmitted within kin groups.)

Local explanations for the practice of writing out sermons also emphasize the particular role it plays in achieving orderliness in the church service. Earlier in this discussion I demonstrated that order, predictability, and consistency were particularly important in the church service. The written sermon contributes to this order in several ways. First, the written document can be thought of as an agenda: in fact, the order of the components of the service is often written out somewhere in the document, usually in the margin (even though this sequence is second nature to most members of the community, who have been going to church since they were children). The strong association of sermonic literacy with orderliness is particularly evident in one of my respondents' explication:

Ia, usu te pese, te mea e tafa atu, te lua mai tua o te pese, kee faitau ttusi tapu. Naa laa, koe e kilokilo ki tau pepa, koe e kilokilo. Naa laa, koo faitau ttusi tapu, toe kilo koe ki te polokalame teelaa, se aa te mea i te tolu? Te ttalo. [. . .] Teelaa te mea teelaa, se pepa teelaa e ttau kee kilokilo koe ki te fakosologa o te- o te lotu, kee tonu. I te mea maa oti aka te pese, koo puli iaa koe te pese koo oti ne usu, kae poi atu nei koo toe usu foki ssuaa pese.

[interviews:Ma 1990:3:B:254–274]

So, [they] are singing a hymn, what comes next, the second thing after the hymn, is Bible reading. So you look down at your piece of paper, you look down [at it]. So, there's Bible reading, [and] you look down at your program again, what comes in third place? The prayer. [. . .] So that's a piece of paper which you must look at to retrieve the sequencing of the- of the service, so that it's correct. Otherwise, the hymn could be over, and you forget that the hymn has already been sung, and to [everyone's] surprise [you ask for] another hymn.

Thus having a written program in front of oneself is a foolproof way to ensure that order and predictability will be achieved and that one will not embarrass oneself in front of the entire community.[14] The relevance of order to the written sermon is also evident in other ways. Lists, for example, are particularly prominent in written sermons, especially when rhetorical contrasts are involved:

I te Feagaiga Muamua, a te muna "alofa" se pati koo leva ne fakaaogaa ki vaega e uke i tona uiga:
(i) te alofa ki taugaasoa
(ii) te alofa ki maatua

(iii) te alofa ki tamataene ki tamaafine
(iv) te alofa e faipati e te poto ko Solomona.
[. . .]
I loto i te Feagaiga Foou, a te muna teenei, "alofa," e fakaasi i konei tona kaatoatoa
mai i te Feagaiga Muamua kee oko mai ki te Feagaiga Foou, koo kaatoatoa i ei te
muna "alofa."

[sermons:F 1985:405:1]

In the Old Testament, the word "love" is a word that had been used for a long time
for many types of meaning:
(i) love for one's friends
(ii) love for one's parents
(iii) love of a young man for a young woman
(iv) the kind of love that the wise Solomon talks about.
[. . .]
In the New Testament, this word, "love," is used with its full meaning, from that
used in the Old Testament to that used in the New Testament, its meaning is
complete.

Further symptoms of the pre-eminence of order in the written sermon
include the general neatness of the document, the salience of headings, and
the numbering of sections, all of which were described earlier.

There are other dimensions of the meaning of written sermons that do
not necessarily figure in the explicitly articulated picture that respondents
present to the ethnographer. In many respects, sermon notebooks resemble
another type of notebook, also called *api* (or *api logo* "notebook of
traditional knowledge" when they need to be distinguished from *api laauga*
"sermon notebooks"), in which certain members of the community write
down recipes, formulae, and instructions associated with various valued
technologies (see Chapter 3). There is an important difference between *api
laauga* and *api logo*, which explains in part why the parallel between the two
is not part of the "cover story" that Nukulaelae Islanders present to
outsiders: the technological knowledge recorded in *api logo* often includes
magical incantations and techniques to harness the power of spirits through
sorcery. Because Nukulaelae Islanders view anything having to do with the
world of spirits with a great deal of ambivalence and trepidation (Besnier
1992b), *api logo* are considered to be potentially dangerous possessions,
particularly if they fall into the hands of someone who is not entitled to
make use of the magical technology they spell out. No such feeling of
danger is associated with sermon notebooks.

However, the light in which Nukulaelae Islanders hold *api logo* is similar
to their attitudes towards sermon notebooks: both are jealously stored
among the owner's most prized possessions and are viewed as culturally
valued commodities, access to which the owner must carefully control.
Thus both sermon notebooks and *api logo* are typically passed on from
mother's brother to sister's son, or from a grandfather to his favorite
grandchild. Both types of notebooks are also motivated by the same belief

that "important" knowledge must be preserved as a written canon, even though the purpose of this canon is not dissemination.

Between literacy and orality

In this chapter, I have been concerned with the sociocultural "value" of written sermons, which straddle the boundary between the spoken and written modes. The sermon is the centerpiece of the church service, a social event that occupies an important place in the weekly routine of almost every member of the atoll community. Preachers take turns at preparing sermons in writing and delivering them in front of the community. In the transition from literacy to orality, sermons undergo various transformations, which bear witness to Nukulaelae Islanders' familiarity with the cognitive gambits associated with turning a written text into an oral performance.

I began this discussion by asking whether the Nukulaelae sermon should be considered an oral or a literate event. This question stems from a long tradition of viewing communicative contexts as ordered along a putative continuum between literacy and orality (see Chapter 1). This view generally assumes a common-sensical, pre-theoretical definition of the labels "literacy" and "orality," an assumption that is not devoid of problems. Ignoring these issues for a moment, let us evaluate the materials I presented in this chapter in light of the "continuum" hypothesis. Several characteristics of sermons suggest that they should be considered primarily as a literacy event. For example, the written form of sermons is in some ways more fundamental than the oral delivery, as the latter cannot take place without a written version. (However, a written sermon that is not delivered at once for one reason or another can be stored for later use.) Furthermore, the delivery of sermons resembles communicative activities that we are used to think of as "deeply literate": Nukulaelae Islanders can handle with great confidence the cognitively complex task of conducting an oral performance on the basis of a written document, extemporaneously transforming the latter as the performance unfolds. Nukulaelae sermons thus resemble academic lectures in the West. In Chapter 7, I will show that sermons centralize an individualistic sense of personhood and foreground concerns with logical reasoning and the search for the truth, characteristics also commonly associated with essayist literacy in "fully" literate traditions. Nukulaelae sermons thus bear many affinities to communicative practices, that have traditionally been considered "canonically literate."

At the same time, sermons are written out for the sole purpose of being delivered orally. No Nukulaelae Islander ever writes out sermons simply for the sake of doing so or for others to read them silently. In addition, the patterns of transmission associated with sermons are indistinguishable from patterns associated with tokens of "traditional" (i.e., orality-based) knowledge. Thus, according to a different set of criteria, the communicative practice is deeply embedded in an "oral" context and mentality.

Attempts to understand the nature of sermons in terms of an oral-literate continuum thus lead to a paradox, and capture little of the ways in which sermons are embedded in their sociocultural context. Instead, sermons should be understood in terms of the role they play in the church service, in terms of the cultural meaning of religious rituals, and in terms of their place in the community's symbolic market. Isolated from their context, written sermons appear to be superfluous objects, since most orators could dispense from them. Viewed in their context of performance, they suddenly acquire a richly polysemic texture: written sermons contribute directly to giving a sense of order to a ritual in which order is a major concern; they function as a commodity in intrafamilial structures of commodity transmission; they give preachers the sense of "readiness" upon which Nukulaelae ideology places so much emphasis; and, along with oral versions of sermons, they serve as the training ground for political oratory. In chapter 7, I will identify several other aspects of the meaning of sermons in both written and oral forms, showing that they play an important role in establishing authority and entitlement, and in defining a privileged relationship between the oral delivery and the truth. I will also demonstrate that these new dimensions shed light on the gendered nature of written sermons.

7
LITERACY, TRUTH, AND AUTHORITY

In Chapter 6, I analyzed the formal structure of written sermons and their relationship to oral performances, church services, and other forms of public discourse. In particular, I tackled the vexing problem of why written sermons exist at all, since there is ample evidence from other contexts in which public speaking figures prominently that many Nukulaelae preachers are accomplished orators with little use for written prompts. I demonstrated that written sermons are not just mnemonic tools, but that they carry a variety of more or less explicitly articulated cultural associations: they contribute to the sense of order in the church service; they are embedded in patterns of commodity exchange; and they have pedagogical functions. Yet their meaning is even more complex. In this chapter, I demonstrate that sermons (be they in oral or written form) have a particular relationship to the truth. Furthermore, the context of sermon performances is characterized by peculiar authority relations between participants and distinctive ways of defining personhood. Through an analysis of sermons as performances and texts, I will show that sermons contribute to the distinctiveness of the social context in which they are embedded.

In the following, I explore sermons as both literacy and orality events. When my discussion applies equally to both, I do not distinguish between them, and I illustrate my arguments with excerpts from both written and oral sermons without discussing the mode in which the data were produced.[1] This blurring of modal distinctions is justified: as argued in Chapter 6, the analysis of a genre like the Nukulaelae sermon can only be accomplished successfully by considering the entire life-history of the discursive genre. Thus the discussion that follows may appear at times to digress from a narrow focus on literacy practices. However, I return to the question of literacy in the conclusion of this chapter, where I show that the analysis developed presently provides further insights into the meaning of sermons as a literacy practice.

140

Sermons and the truth

Nukulaelae Islanders spend much time and effort talking about "the truth" (*te tonu*). Like members of many societies, they tacitly recognize, through their social actions and norms of interpretation (but not necessarily in their explanations to ethnographers), that what counts as "true" may differ from one social context to the other. For example, the concern for the truth is considerably more opaque in certain interactional contexts, such as gossip, where other factors like the creation and maintenance of conviviality are more important (Besnier 1994b). In addition, the truth "value" of linguistic actions depends crucially on authority and legitimacy, the latter being determined by complex norms that vary with the nature of discourse and context: what counts as true in a particular context is intimately bound to authority, hierarchy, and interpersonal and interfactional politics.

Within this symbolic market, the church service occupies an extreme position: here, the truth is a foremost concern, standards for evaluating the truth of utterances are most stringent, and the primary focus of words and actions is to uncover the truth. The religious context in which sermons are delivered is serious business. When delivering a sermon, the preacher's words must be carefully weighed, and he or she cannot slip. In contrast, whether what is said in the maneapa and other secular arenas is true or not matters less:

A ko te maneapa e ppau fua me se- me se fale fua e- e fai ei a pati, ka ne ssee tau pati, e llei fua me ssee fua peelaa.

[interviews:Ma 1990:3:A:231–233]

But in the maneapa it doesn't matter [what one says] because it's just a- a house in which words are spoken, if what you say is wrong, it's all right because it's just wrong [in the maneapa].

In this testimony, my respondent of course exaggerates a little for rhetorical effect, because in fact orators are expected to stick to certain standards of truthfulness in the maneapa. If they repeatedly violate these standards, even in jest, they are made fun of for being *gutu ppelo*, literally, "[endowed with a] lying mouth." Nevertheless, standards of truthfulness do seem less rigid and problematic in the maneapa than in church. The centrality of the truth in church services is bound to Nukulaelae's religious ideology, according to which the Scriptures are the ultimate arbiter of the truth. If they abide by the authority of God and the Bible, humans can gain access to the unambiguous truth that is otherwise beyond their reach (compare Christianized Ilongots' epistemological ideology as described in Rosaldo 1973). Ideally, social action should always refer to the Bible for evaluation and legitimation. However, the explanatory linkage between the Bible and the here-and-now is not always clear; crucially, it is the role of the sermon to clarify this connection.

Thus sermons are first and foremost exercises in the search for the truth, and this characterization leaves a strong imprint on sermons as both texts and performances. First, the term *tonu* "true, truth" appears very frequently in sermonic discourse:

*Ko tala i loto i te viu ko tala o te vavau, kolaa e filifili ei se mea **tonu** moo te talitonuga **tonu** ki te fakatuanakiga.*

[sermons:T 1991:1:A:390–392]

The stories in this foundational text are stories of ancient times, which is where [I] have chosen the **truth** about the **true** belief in faith.

*[...] ona koo **tonu** te koga e moe ei a Iaakopo, ona koo **tonu** te fatu teelaa e aluga ei a Iaakopo, koo matea ei nee ia te fakaasiga tafasili a te Atua. Moi moe faatea, moi aluga faatea, e see matea nee Iaakopo a fakaasiga tafasili a te Atua. Ala ake Iaakopo, ana muna, "E **tonu** eiloa a te Atua e nofo i konei!"*

[sermons:Se 1991:1:B:264–270]

[. . .] because where Jacob rested is the **truth**, because the stone upon which Jacob lay his head is the **truth**, through which he saw God's sublime revelation. Had he slept elsewhere, had he rested his head elsewhere, he would not have seen God's sublime revelation. Jacob woke up and said, "Surely the Lord is in this place!" [lit.: "It is indeed **true** that the Lord dwells here!"]

Second, much "space" in sermonic discourse is devoted to defining, qualifying, characterizing, and analogizing, rhetorical activities associated with truth-seeking in Nukulaelae ideology. Abstract concepts like "love" and "fear," as well as more concrete semiotic tokens like "the cross" and "resurrection," are invoked, defined, contrasted, morally evaluated, and associated with other notions and symbols:[2]

Manatu silisili: Te taimi o te fakaolataga.
Fesili: Se aa te taimi o te fakaolataga?

[sermons:F 1985:406:1]

Main theme: The time of resurrection.
Question: What is the time of resurrection?

The importance of conceptual manipulation is also evident in the high frequency of rhetorical questions, which often occur in series; questions posed during the delivery of a sermon are always rhetorical since the audience is silent:

A ko koe, ne aa mea e manavasee ei koe e fia maua nee koe? Ko meakkai, ko tupe, mo niisi koloa aka e uke?

[sermons:Ke 1991:9]

As for you, what do you worry about not getting? Food, money, other kinds of goods in great quantities?

Contrasts, not uncommonly in the form of lists, also play a major role (see Chapter 6). In the following excerpt, the preacher contrasts different types of worries (echoing Matthew 6:31–33), such as worrying for one's own welfare, worrying for the welfare of one's loved ones, and worrying about not finding God:

Ne aa mea koo fai moo mea e manavassee ei taatou io ttou olaga- ko mea e tausi ei? Muna a Ieesuu, "Saa manavassee!" Ko mea e iinu ei? E pei ei? Muna a Ieesuu, "Saa manavassee!" Ko ttou masaki ia taatou maa mmate? "Saa manavassee!" Ko te tino e ita mai? "Saa manavassee ki ei!" Ko tuupulaga o faanau i te fui fai? Kae maise ko te nofo maavaevae o maatua mo faanau? Muna a Ieesuu, "Saa manavassee!" Ko lau manafa mo koloa e uke o te olaga nei? "Saa manavassee!" [. . .] Kae kee muamua taatou o manavassee o ssala te Atua, ki tena maaloo mo tena aamio tonu.

[sermons:Ke 1991:18]

What are we focusing our worries on in our lives? The things that support [our lives]? Jesus says, "Do not worry!" What we drink? [What we] wear? Jesus says, "Do not worry!" The illnesses we might die from? "Do not worry!" [The fact that] someone is angry at us? "Do not worry!" Children who do not obey us? "Do not worry!" The abundance of land and goods? "Do not worry!" [. . .] Rather, let us first worry about seeking God, his kingdom and his righteousness.

The form of these contrasts is invariably iconic of a moral contrast: contrastive sets are arranged from least to most truthful, holy, and legitimate:

E seeai se alofa fakataugaasoa, seeai se alofa fakatautaaina, kae se alofa teelaa e isi se fakamoemoega ola i ei, ma kaa toe fakaolagina taaua i te ola e see gata mai.

[sermons:Ka 1991:1:B:152–155]

It is not love between friends, it is not love between siblings, but a [type of] love in which [one] can trust that there is living hope that we will again be reborn for ever and ever.

Finally, sermons contain many references to "completeness," a notion intimately associated to the truth. Several pieces of evidence bear witness to the conceptual kinship between these two notions. For example, the word *tonu* "true" commonly co-occurs with the word *kaatoatoa* "complete, whole," with which it frequently forms a doublet, *tonu kae kaatoatoa* "true and complete." This pattern is not just a rhetorical device, but is symptomatic of a conceptual linkage. A brief concrete example of the importance of this linkage, which I discuss in further detail elsewhere, will suffice here (Besnier 1994b). In 1985, the island pastor, knowing that I had been systematically collecting historical narratives from elderly people, asked me repeatedly to come and have a look at the church archives to "complete" them, because what they contained was *ssee* "wrong." In his words, the reason why they were wrong is that they were *see kaatoatoa* "not complete." For a narrative or body of narratives to be true, no detail must

be left out, and they must meet specific standards of "completeness" (the nature of these standards, of course, entails complex issues of authority and entitlement that I will not go into here). Not surprisingly, mentions of completeness and wholeness are frequent in the texts of sermons:

Te alofa fakatautaaina. [. . .] Se alofa teelaa e **tonu kaatoatoa**, *se alofa foki teelaa e* **kaatoatoa i ona feituu katoa**. *Se alofa teelaa e fakamaaonia i ei me e isi se fakamoemoega ola i ei.*

[sermons:Ka 1991:1:B:090–097]

Brotherly love. [. . .] [It is] a [type of] love which is **completely true**, a [type of] love which is **complete in all its aspects**. [It is] a [type of] love in which [one] can trust that there is living hope.

In short, many textual characteristics of sermons are indexical of the primary function of sermons, namely to seek out the truth as locally defined.

Sermons and authority

Whenever questions of truth arise, issue of authority, legitimacy, and ideology always lurk in the background, as many authors have shown (e.g., Bailey 1991, Bok 1979, Foucault 1981, Lindstrom 1992, Petersen 1993, Simmel 1950). I now turn to these questions in the context of Nukulaelae sermons. I first show that sermons centralize aspects of Nukulaelae identity that are underelaborated in other social contexts. I then show that, on the surface at least, sermon performances are imbued with extraordinary authority. I support the discussion of these questions with a microanalytic analysis of the linguistic and rhetorical structures of sermons, describing in turn pronoun use, patterns of reported speech, and prosodic structure.

Pronouns and personhood

A remarkable feature of sermonic texts is the highly individualized depiction of the social person that they invoke. In sermons, the basic unit of analysis is presented as the individual: the sermon is authored by an individual (even though in reality multiple authorship may have been involved in the production of the written text upon which the oral sermon is based), and it is addressed to each individual member of the congregation. When contrasted with other contexts of social life, where talk typically emphasizes communalism over individualism, sermons appear to involve a shift in identity. Symptomatic of this shift are patterns of pronoun use, which are very distinctive in sermonic discourse. That pronouns should be particularly revealing of shifts in identity is not surprising: in all societies, pronouns are complex shifters *par excellence*, whose meaning is highly context-bound, multifarious, and prone to subtle manipulations by language users (cf. Jakobson 1957; also Errington 1988, Friedrich 1972, Goffman 1979, Hanks 1990, Kuipers 1990, Silverstein 1976, Urban 1989).

To begin, first- and second-person singular pronouns (*au* "I," *koe* "you," and the sixteen corresponding possessive forms) are considerably more frequent in sermonic texts than in other genres of public discourse. Observe the salience of these pronouns in the following representative excerpts:

*Kaafai koo ttogi nee **koe** te mea tonu, tona uiga, ko **tou** see aava mo tou see alofa kiaa **koe** eeloa. Kaafai e ttogi atu nee **koe** te mea tonu, tona uiga, koo fakatau atu **tou** maalosi mo **tou** loto fuatua ifo, koo fakatau **tou** llei mo **tou** mmalu.*

[sermons:F 1985 (08/73)]

If **you** sell away what is true, that means that **you** have no respect and no love for **yourself**. If **you** sell away what is true, that means that **you** are selling **your** strength and **your** faith, **you** are selling **your** goodness and **your** dignity.

These pronouns often appear in contrasts between first-person referents and second-person referents:

*A **koe** se tino o te Eekaaleesia, **au** se fai laauga. A **koe** se tiaakono. Masaua **tau** feagaiga koo oti ne saina **tou** lima kee tusi ei **ttaa** igoa.*

[sermons:Ka 1991:1:B:168–170]

You are a member of the Congregation, I am a lay preacher. **You** are a deacon. Bear in mind the contract that **you** have signed with **your** hand in which [you] wrote down **both of our** names.

Such contrasts (of which I will provide more illustrations in this chapter) indicate that the pronouns indeed refer to first-and second-person entities, and are not non-specific indefinite pronouns with "generalized" referents comparable to *one* and certain uses of *you* in English. Also frequent is the first-person inclusive dual pronoun *taaua* "you and I" and its possessive forms:

*E aa **taaua**, taugaasoa fakalogollogo i te afiafi teenei? E aa te alofa fakataugaasoa peenei o **taaua**?*

[sermons:Ka 1991:1:B:071–073]

How about **the two of us**, my friends who are listening [to me] this afternoon? How about the friendship between **the two of us**?

*Seki lava te ola o **taaua** i te Atua? Aa! Taina Kelisiano i ttaeao nei, kaafai e manako **taaua** ki niisi talitonuga, taalofa!, i te tala llei a Ieesuu Keliso kaa fano o mate, ka see ola.*

[sermons:Se 1991:1:B:335–338]

Isn't life in God enough for **us both**? Ah! Christian brother this morning, if **we both** look for other religions, Heaven forbid!, Jesus Christ's good news will die away, and will not live.

In all other communicative contexts, plural pronouns are used whenever possible.[3] For example, in everyday conversation, care is always taken to choose pronouns that refer to the most inclusive and encompassing range of referents. If an individual performs a task in the presence of others, the activity is always described as having been performed by everyone present, even when the witnessing parties play no "active" role in the strict sense of the term. Thus if three people go angling in a canoe with fishing gear for only one person, an appropriate description of the activity is *maatou ne maattau i tua*, "We [three] angled outside [the reef]." A fuller description of the expedition might detail the division of labor, but the overall activity will be presented, through pronoun choice and otherwise, as having been performed by every adult present, including "inactive" parties. Similar linguistic patterns are found in the expression of possession and part–whole relationships: speakers refer to the kin group of which they are a member as *temotou kaaiga* "our [plural] kin group," rather than *toku kaaiga* "my kin group."[4] In light of these patterns, pronoun use in sermons emerges as highly unusual in comparison to other social contexts.

The discourse patterns observable in unmarked social contexts reflect the view that, in ideal circumstances, tasks are cooperatively tackled and accomplishments collectively achieved (see Duranti and Ochs 1986:221–2 for comparative materials on Samoa). In turn, this view is indexical of Nukulaelae Islanders' concern for consensus and inclusiveness. In Nukulaelae ideology, the act of *taapuaki* "ratified witnessing [a social situation]" is as important as the actual performance of the activity around which the social situation is centered. This is particularly true when the focal activity is a performance of some kind or another (e.g., a dance, a speech, a gossip narrative). In performance contexts, the audience that *taapuaki* the performance completes the dual organization that all ritualized activities ideally have: performers perform for an audience, one group competes with another group, and one person is another person's *nafa* "competing partner" in a ritualized exchange game. Nukulaelae orators occasionally allude approvingly to my recording activities in settings where speeches are made (particularly if I video-tape the performance), because recording is construed as a superb way of *taapuaki* oratory: it implies that the performance is being paid attention to by a party that "faces" the orator, both literally and figuratively.

Patterns of pronoun use in sermons have two additional characteristics that set them apart and further highlight the personal and individualistic orientation of the occasion. In all other communicative settings, coordinate constructions that involve pronouns (e.g., "you and I," "John and me") are most naturally structured so that a pronoun with widest referential scope appears in first position. For example, "John and me" is most naturally expressed as *maaua mo Ioane*, literally, "we [dual, exclusive] and John" (rather than *Ioane mo au*, literally "John and me," or *au mo Ioane*, literally "me and John"). What is important here is not the order of elements, but the referential scope of pronominal forms. The pattern used in sermons differs from all other contexts, and resembles the English pattern, in which the referents of coordinated nouns and pronouns are disjoint:

Ko te alofa o koe ki te Atua kee tuumau, ona ko tena fakatusa ne fai nee ia koe mo au kee oola taatou i ei.

[sermons:Te 1991:1:A:528–529]

Let your love for God be constant, for he created **your and me** in his image to enable us to live.

Closely related to this peculiarity is the preponderance of parallelisms where a verb with a pronominal subject appears twice, once with a second-person singular subject, and once with a first-person singular subject:

Masaua nee koe, masaua nee au ttaa pati fakataugaasoa ne fai?

[sermons:Ka 1991:1:B:087–088]

Don't you remember, don't I remember the promise of friendship that we made?

E iloa peefea nee koe, e iloa peefea nee au koo tonu te koga teenei ne moe ei a Iaakopo?

[sermons:Se 1991:1:B:242–244]

How do you know, how do I know that where Jacob slept was the right place?

In any other context, the referents of the two singular pronouns would be combined and expressed with the first-person inclusive dual pronoun *taaua* "we [two]," and the need to repeat the verb would be avoided. This type of parallelism is so intimately associated with sermonic discourse that it has the status of a stylistic shibboleth. In contrast to all other genres, sermonic discourse highlights the individuation of the person as an autonomous social unit. Whereas great emphasis is placed on the sociocentric nature of personhood in other social contexts, sermons centralize the separate individuality of the preacher and of each audience member.

A congruent emphasis on individuation permeates other aspects of religious life. For example, when they engage in prescriptive discourse on religion, Nukulaelae Islanders typically foreground individualized activities and intrapersonal affective experiences which, in other social contexts, are negatively valued and rarely talked about. Introspection is one such process. In most contexts, introspective contemplation is viewed as evidence of such negative emotions or character traits as shame (*maa*), sadness (*faanoanoa*), or anger (*kaitaua*), or of a person's refusal or inability to orient and accommodate to the social context (*kaugataa* "disobedient of societal directives," *solopuu* "to cling to the 'skirts' of one's parent or spouse"). In contrast, introspective contemplation is given a positive moral evaluation in religious contexts, as the following extract from an interview on religious ideology illustrates:

E peenaa eiloo te lalolagi teenei, e seeai se tino ne- ne tupu mai, faanau mai, te mea eiloo koo iloa. Kai, peenaa mo koe. Koe ne tupu mai, seei ei se mea e tasi e iloa, a koo taumafai katoa, fakaako i se koga, fakaakoako i se koga, koo ne fakaakoako, a koo maua ei te poto. A kaafai laa e fiifiileemuu koe, sagasaga, seeai laa se mea e maua nee koe. Seeai eiloo. Sagasaga fua peelaa mo te vaaivai mo te fakapalapala io mo te logo tonu o te- te moe. [. . .] E fai mai te Tusi Tapu, a te poto e ppau peelaa mo te aulo. Te mea e maua, a te aulo, te foitino o te aulo e maua i te koga tafasili i te ppoko, ppoko i loto i te laukele. Ia, te poto e ppau peelaa mo te peenina. A te peenina e maua i te moana i te koga ppoko ppoko. Tena uiga e keli, e keli te aulo i loto i te- i te laukele, kae uku a te peenina i loto i ttai.

[interviews:Ma 1990:3:B:112–133]

This is how the world is, no one came- came about, was born knowing. See, like you. [When] you were born, you knew nothing, but you kept trying, [you] learned here, [you] learned there, and once you'd learned, you became smart. But if you just sit there peacefully, you'll get nowhere. Nowhere. [You]'ll just sit there with all your weakness and just rot there, sleeping will feel so good [to you]. [. . .] The Bible tells us, knowledge is like gold. What one gets- gold, gold itself is obtained in the deepest of locations, deep inside the earth. Knowledge is also like a pearl. A pearl is obtained in the ocean in the deepest of places. Which means that [one has to] dig, dig for gold in the- in the ground, and dive for pearls in the sea.

In secular contexts, *fiileemuu* "peacefulness," the very trait that my respondent depicts in a negative light here, is talked about as a desirable personal quality, and the kind of inquisitive searching that he describes in glowing terms is at best viewed with suspicion. Sermons echo these valuations, as the following excerpt demonstrates:

Te fenua o te Atua i te taeao teenei! Teenei foki te fekau moo taatou i te taeao teenei, **kee taki sukesuke ifo te tagata kiaa ia eiloo,** *me peefea mai te fakattusa o te Atua ne faaite ei taaua.*

[sermons:Te 1991:1:A:543–546]

God's island this morning! Here is what we've come to say this morning, **that each man should investigate himself,** [to see] how God's image from which we [two] were made [looks].

Sermons frequently describe the person as having a personal answer to existentialist questions:

Se aa te mea kaa maua moo taaua i te ola see gata mai? Ko tau tali e iaa koe loa mo koe. [. . .] Nukulaelae i te taeao teenei- i te afiafi teenei! Se aa te filifiliga a te Atua moo koe? **E tofu taatou mo te tali.**

[sermons:P 1991:1:B:460–465]

What are the two of us going to get from eternal life? Your answer is to be found within you alone. [. . .] Nukulaelae in this morning- this afternoon! What has God chosen for you? **Each one of us has a different answer [to this question].**

Thus the individuated definition of the person in sermonic discourse contrasts sharply with the positive valuation of sociocentrism, at the expense of individualism, extant in other contexts.

Reported speech and scriptural authority

Reported speech, an area of inquiry frequently associated with issues of pronominal deixis (Goffman 1974, Goodwin 1990, Hanks 1990, Lucy, ed., 1993), is particularly interesting in sermons because virtually all quotes are from the Scriptures, the ultimate reference for all moral questions and social actions, and are thus charged with moral authority. In most other communicative contexts, directly reported speech (i.e., quotations purported to reproduce the exact wording of another utterance) is typically preceded by a speech-act verb or expression (e.g., *aku muna* "my words [were]," *koo fai mai* "[he] says to me"), or sometimes even two (Besnier 1992a). Reported-speech introducers are also found in sermonic discourse, where they take a variety of forms: *e fai peenei* "[it] is said thus," *muna a Ieesuu* "Jesus' words [are]," *muna mai te apositolo ko Paulo* "Paul the apostle tells us." However, in many instances, quotes from the Scriptures are left unmarked, particularly in the interpretive stages of the sermon, when the preacher has warmed up and is in the full swing of displaying the relevance of Scriptural authority to the audience's everyday concerns. Thus, for example, the highlighted quote in the following excerpt follows a comment by the preacher clarifying the first quote, and is not introduced by a speech-act introducer:

Muna a Ieesuu, "Iuutaia, ne aa mea konaa e manavassee ei koutou? Au ko te falaoa mai te lagi, a te tino e fakaaogaa nee ia, kae inu ki te toto, kaa toka a ia i te ola e see gata mai. Me i toku tino ko te meakkai tonu, toku toto ko te mea inu tonu." A Ieesuu koo faipati ki feituu e lua, te foitino mo te agaaga. "Ko au e toka ei koutou i mea e manavassee ei koutou i outou olaga faka-te-foitino. Ko au foki e toka ei koutou i ootou ola faka-te-agaaga."

[sermons:Ke 1991:10]

Jesus says, "Jews, what are you worrying about? I am the bread from heaven. Whoever eats my flesh and drinks my blood has eternal life, and I will raise him up at the last day. For my flesh is real food and my blood is real drink." Jesus speaks about both aspects, that of the body and that of the soul. **"I am where you find solace from your worldly fears. I am also where you find solace from your spiritual fears."**

Because Nukulaelae writers do not generally use punctuation, it is often difficult for an outside observer to distinguish between quoted and non-quoted discourse in the written forms of sermons. In oral performance, intonation does not necessarily distinguish biblical quotes from the preacher's comments and elaborations. In principle, most congregation members can pick out scriptural quotes from the rest of the discourse on account of their vast knowledge of the Bible, a defining characteristic of social maturity. However, despite the ultimate retrievability of the various voices, the optional use of otherwise obligatory speech-act introducers creates a particular effect comparable to that of the free indirect style of modern Euro-American literary genres, in which the quoted and quoting voices merge. This strategy enables the quoting voice to appropriate at least some of the authority associated with the quoted voice, without appearing to do so (Voloshinov 1978 [1929]). As a result, the voice of the preacher and the voice of divine authority are essentially blurred in Nukulaelae sermons.

Also prevalent in sermons are parallelisms between biblical quotes and non-quoted discourse. Preachers frequently pattern moral commentaries and explanations of the Scriptures so that their structure and wording echo that of biblical quotes. In the following excerpt, the preacher first provides the scriptural reading on which her sermon is based, and extracts from it a core idea:

Muna a te matua, "Saa mataku, faipati eiloa, saa fakavaaivai, i au e fakatasi mo koe." Te manatu maaluga, ko te fakaasiga faka-nui-manava.

[sermons:Si 1991:2:A:176–179]

The reading says, "**Do not be afraid**; keep on speaking, **do not be silent**, for I am with you." The main idea [of my sermons] is **the forbearing revelation**.

Further on in her sermon, she parallels both the theme and the structure of the reading and core idea in a question and exhortation addressed to the congregation:

E aa taatou mo te fakaasiga faka-nui-manava teenei? saa mataku, saa loto vaaivai ki mea fai a te vasega, i tau gaaluega ko te fakalauefaaga o te gaaluega a te Atua i luga o Tuuvalu teenei.

[sermons:Si 1991:2:A:210–215]

So what we do with this **forbearing revelation**? **Do not be afraid, do not be silent** in the organization's work, for what you are working on is the expansion of God's work in Tuvalu.

Such parallelisms between biblical discourse and the preacher's moral message are particularly effective, because they provide an iconic link between the biblical text and the statement of its relevance to contemporary life. Other comparable strategies are expansions from biblical quotes which do not involve parallelism. In the following, the preacher ingeniously intersperses scriptural quotes with questions:

*Fai mai te muna, "Koo filifili nee au koe." **Nukulaelae, moo aa?** "Moo tuku ei toku finagalo, ko te mea kee fanatu ei toku maainaaga, taalai atu ki feituu e faa o te lalolagi." **Moo aa?** "Ko te mea kee aumai a faanau a te Atua ki te Atua, kae see aumai a faanau a te Atua ki auala o te poouliga."*

[sermons:P 1991:1:B:473–477]

The Word says, "I chose you." **Nukulaelae, what for?** "So that my will be done, so that my light go forth, [and] be preached to the four corners of the world." **What for?** "So that God's children be led to God, and so that God's children not be led along the path of darkness."

In this dialogic simulation, the question *moo aa?* "what for?" is a prepositional phrase (rather than a full sentence) that can only be understood as a syntactic expansion of the previous utterance, i.e., of the biblical quote. This strategy creates a contrapuntal effect that dissolves the boundaries between the Scriptural voice and the preacher's voice and creates meaning through the joint "animation" (Goffman 1979) of both voices. In the above excerpt, in addition, some of the quoted passages appear to be paraphrases, even though pronominal deixis clearly frames them as quoted discourse; presenting paraphrases as direct quotes has the effect of further obscuring the separation of voices.

The blurring of voices is in fact part and parcel of Nukulaelae Islanders' religious ideology, and finds clear echoes in their prescriptive statements. In one of the interview excerpts I cited earlier, my respondent characterizes the preacher as *te tagata teelaa ne aumai te leo o te Atua* "the person who brought God's voice." Comparable metaphors are frequent: the preacher is often characterized as *te sui o te Atua* "God's representative," and sermons as *pati a te Atua* "God's words." As with fundamentalist Baptist Americans, for whom "preachers speak the word of God[, who] speaks through them" (Harding 1987:174), the preacher's voice and biblical voice merge (cf. also Zinsser 1986 on fundamentalist white middle-class American Bible schools, Rosenberg 1970a and G. Davis 1985 on African–American evangelical sermons, Stout 1986:34–5 on sermons in Colonial New England, and Hostetler and Huntington 1980:33–36 on Hutterite sermons).[5]

Antiphonal alternations

The powerful claim to authority embedded in quoting practices is echoed in another striking characteristic of oral sermonic performances, namely their prosodic structure. Preachers' voices frequently become extremely loud during sermons, so much so that the effort sometimes leaves the speaker hoarse after the service. Individuals who comport themselves meekly and unassumingly in other social arenas can take on a vociferous and overwhelming demeanor at the pulpit. What I call antiphonal alternation is a very peculiar delivery style, in which strings of words uttered in very loud voice alternate with strings spoken at regular volume. In the following illustrative extract, loudness is indicated with capitalization:

TAAVINI KI TE ALIKI, KEE OKO KI TE FAKAOTIGA, kee maua ei nee koe (mo au) a te ola e see gata mai. IEESUU KELISO, TE ATUA MO TENA FILIFILIGA, ne aumai nee ia a tena fua tasi KEE MATE KEE OLA KOE I TE TAEAO TEENEI,

*kee ola te lalolagi KEE OKO ATU EI TAATOU ki te ola e see gata mai, maafai
taatou e taavini ttonu ki te Atua. TE ALIKI TEELAA E MAUA EI NEE KOE A TE
OLA i te ola e see gata mai.*

[sermons:Me 1991:2:A:073–079]

SERVE GOD UNTIL THE END, so that you (and I) can live for ever and ever.
JESUS CHRIST, GOD AND HIS CHOICE, who brought [us] his only child TO
DIE IN ORDER FOR YOU TO LIVE THIS MORNING, in order for the world
to live SO THAT WE ALL LIVE for ever and ever, as long as we serve God as we
should. [This is] THE LORD THROUGH WHICH WE CAN LIVE for ever and
ever.

Alternations in voice quality occur at junctures between major syntactic
and semantic constituents, e.g., between superordinate and subordinate
clauses, or between topics and comments. However, there is no clear
relationship between voice quality and syntactic or informational structures. In the above extract, one finds subjunctive subordinate clauses
uttered in either normal voice (*kee maua ei nee koe (mo au) a te ola e see gata
mai* "so that you (and I) can live for ever and ever") or loud voice (e.g., *kee
mate kee ola koe i te taeao teenei* "to die in order for you to live this
morning"), and clauses in loud voice are neither more nor less information-
ally prominent than other clauses. So the meaning of antiphonal
alternations is not to be sought in the linguistic structures upon which it is
superposed, but rather in its overall effect.

Antiphonal alternations occur neither randomly nor consistently during
the performance. Rather, they tend to take place once the preacher has
"warmed up," generally half-way through the sermon or later (compare the
crescendo of intensity in Southern revivalist sermons discussed by
Rosenberg 1970b:5). Nukulaelae Islanders describe antiphonal patterns as
symptomatic of a trance-like state of excitement known as *matagi* (literally,
"wind, windy"), which can vary in intensity across contexts and individuals. Outside of church ceremonies, people typically experience *matagi*
during performances of *faatele*, a song-and-dance style which probably
originated in the late nineteenth century (Christensen and Koch 1964), and
in which the tension and tempo of the choreography and the volume and
tempo of the singing and percussion accompaniment gradually increase, to
finally come to an anti-climactic and abrupt end (the word *faatele* is a
borrowing from Samoan meaning "to increase, to multiply"). During a
faatele, dancers, spectators, and singers can be "hit" (*poko*) by a *matagi*
episode, which may vary in length and form: for example, a dancer may
"break frame" (Goffman 1974) from the normal tersely controlled
choreography by executing a brief twirl with arms extended while
whooping and smiling rapturously; a member of the chorus may get up and
lead the chorus with emphatic arm sweeps and loud and abrupt breath
exhalations; or an audience or chorus member may excitedly join in the

dancing. All these scenarios are taken to be manifestations of *matagi*. An entire *faatele* performance can also be judged to be *matagi* if the singing is particularly loud and well coordinated, and if the dancers apply themselves to enliven their performance with brief frame-breaking twirls and other embellishments. *Matagi* is the sign of a successful performance.

To understand the role that antiphonal voice alternations play in sermons, one must consider the range of expressive displays appropriate to church contexts on the one hand, and, on the other hand, the affective norms governing sermon performances. First, the kinetic repertoire that a preacher can draw upon is rather limited. One finds here none of the expressiveness and drama associated with religious performances in other ethnographic contexts, none of the walking about and dramatic gesturing comparable to that which take place during certain African–American revivalist sermons (e.g., Holt 1972). The preacher stands behind the elevated pulpit and does not leave that station (in fact, the structural configuration of the church does not afford much space for movement). Neither do preachers generally cry during their sermons, in contrast to the pastors of certain denominations in Tonga, for example. This is not to imply that preachers remain immobile: they often point fingers at their audiences and engage in dramatic hand gesturing, which typically cooccur with antiphonal voice alternations. At the same time, preachers are expected to offer some evidence that they are moved and inspired by the sermon, because, according to my respondents, it is only when this happens that their audience will pay attention to their message. Thus the voice becomes a prime index of affect in the relative absence of non-verbal channels.

Antiphonal alternations make for an impressive and powerful performance, particularly in conjunction with finger-pointing and the exhortative message of the sermon. By commanding the audience's attention, antiphonal performances are acts of raw communicative coercion. It is difficult to think of a blunter appropriation of a speaker's authority over his or her audience than the thunder of a preacher's voice in the midst of a *matagi* episode.

The preacher's authority

To recapitulate, sermons position the preacher and the audience in a highly specific configuration. Through a fine-grained analysis of the linguistic and discursive characteristics of sermons, I have shown that sermons foreground aspects of the participants' identity which are otherwise not emphasized, highlighting the individualistic, autonomous, and introspective qualities of the person. Furthermore, many communicative aspects of sermonic performances place the preacher in a position of great personal authority. I utilize here the notion of authority as it is commonly defined in classical social theory: authority characterizes a relationship between social entities in which one suspends private judgment, and in which the exercise of authority by the other entity is legitimized by some external criterion such as social role or status (cf. Lukes 1978:639–44). Thus authority involves some form of power (i.e., the ability to impose on others a particular definition of reality) and some form of institutionalization or other type of legitimacy (Barnes 1988:71–5). However, authority structures are always more complex than this distilled definition makes them out to be. In Nukulaelae sermon performances, the basic criteria of an authority structure are satisfied at some level: as the conduit of God's word, the preacher is entitled to speak directly to each and every member of the audience, who suspends the expression of his or her private judgment, at least in the immediate context of the service.

For a brief half hour, preachers claim God's voice for themselves and assume a position of immense assertiveness at the pulpit, in which asymmetries in power, knowledge, and morality between them and the congregation are emphasized. Because God's word is non-negotiable, sermonic discourse leaves no room for audience participation in the construction of meaning, and the congregation can only sit in stony silence. If any dialogism takes place, it can only involve God's and the preacher's voices. The preacher's assumption of unconditional authority, underscored by the thunder of antiphonal alternations, allows him or her to violate many of the rules of circumspection at play in other public encounters, which dictate that participants strive to maintain a non-directive, non-confrontational stance with each other. In other words, the preacher takes on a different identity in this context, and defines the identity of the audience in an equally marked fashion. This transformation has clear historical antecedents: the identity of the preacher is strongly reminiscent of the extreme personal, marginally divine authority of the Samoan pastor in the early days of missionization (Brady 1975, Munro 1978, 1982), which still colors the relationship between the contemporary pastor and the congregation, at least on the surface (Goldsmith 1989a). As they occupy the seat left vacant by the Samoan pastor, sermon performers are in a position from which they can harangue, impose their points of view, and accuse others of committing terrible sins in ways that would be perceived as extremely disruptive and inappropriate in other contexts.

The limits of sermonic authority

At the same time, the preacher's authority is fleeting, temporary, and allegorical, and in these respects resembles other forms of authority in this society. It is precisely because of its metaphorical nature that it can be displayed so dramatically in a society whose members are generally so

distrustful of overt manifestations of authority (Besnier 1991, 1993). I turn
here to the bounded nature of the preacher's authority, and analyze its
relationship to secular political authority.

First of all, the social context in which the preacher's authority is so
spectacularly exhibited is meticulously bracketed as a "special" context.
This bracketing has historical roots: church services in general and sermons
in particular were introduced from the outside by outsiders. While they are
now an integral part of what Nukulaelae Islanders view as tradition, the
social practices that accompany church services still retain an alien flavor.
For example, the church building is a tall and massive coral-stone building
in the dead center of the village, towering over the thatched or corrugated-
iron homes huddling around it, even dwarfing the contiguous maneapa (see
Figure 6). The church service is virtually the only social context in which
men have to wear a shirt, and sometimes also don a tie and Western-style
trousers, and women a long white muumuu; where the two gender groups
sit in segregated fashion; where respect is displayed by standing up rather
than sitting down; and where one sits on benches rather than mats. Literacy
contributes to the bracketing of church rituals as "different" from the rest
of life, a point to which I will return presently: for example, the service is the
one context where everyone carries books, namely, a Bible and a hymnal.
Until recently, the use of a foreign language, Samoan, was yet another
powerful indicator of the alien aura of religious ceremonies. The church
service is thus circumscribed by clear symbolic boundaries that isolate it
from ordinary life.

However, the preacher's authority is bracketed in an even more specific
manner. Despite its dramatic appearance, it is wedded to the immediate
context of the church service, and does not give rise to the cross-contextual
exertion of power and the imposition of dominance. Indeed, preachers
rotate at the pulpit, and every adult man (and, increasingly, many adult
women) is eventually entitled to get up and claim for him- or herself God's
voice, harangue the rest of the community, and point an accusatory finger
at each member of the congregation. Furthermore, who is at the pulpit on
any given Sunday is not something that preachers themselves control, in the
same way that turns at giving speeches are self-selected, for example.
Rather, it is the pastor's prerogative to choose preachers for any given
week. These patterns have a powerful levelling effect: after the performance, the preacher reverts to being an ordinary member of society, and
submits to the exhortations of the next preacher in line; and his entitlement
to pontificate at the pulpit is in the hands of a higher authority. Because
written sermons can be passed on from one person to the other (cf. Chapter
6), their authorship often becomes blurred, and thus their content ceases to
be associated with a particular individual. Thus ruled out is the possibility
that any one member of the community will claim privileged access to the

Figure 6   *The church building, built from coral rock and lime in the 1920s, towers at the center of the village. The water cistern in the foreground was for many years the only source of fresh water, until smaller cisterns were built next to each home in the early 1980s.*

truth and exert moral authority over others in a systematic and sustained manner.

The only person entitled to assume divinely inspired authority with any regularity is the pastor. The pastor not only chooses which lay preachers or deacons conduct two out of three services a week, but he also always conducts the Sunday morning service. However, as discussed in Chapter 2, the pastor is a stranger to the community and therefore a liminal figure, despite the enormous amount of prestige associated with his social status. Because of this liminality, his authority can ultimately be contained, and is in large part a social metaphor. When confined to religious contexts, the pastor's authority is heeded and even revered; but when a pastor attempts to exert any kind of political influence in secular contexts, his authority is viewed with very different eyes. On occasion, his opinion may be solicited on particular matters such as interpersonal or interfactional conflicts, but a wise pastor knows that any statement he makes must be confined to the moral implications of these issues. Ultimately, he is not entitled to a voice in the internal politics of the community, and not being native to the atoll offers a convenient justification for his exclusion from politics.

Many incidents of the atoll's history bear witness to the threatening nature of leakages between secular and religious authority. Even the authority of the Samoan pastors, whom Nukulaelae Islanders and Tuvaluans in general held in extreme reverence, was carefully controlled. The Samoan pastors were thought to perform their duty as long as they confined their authority to such matters as the imposition of prohibition and the surveillance of intimate details of people's lives (even though this authority is highly intrusive by modern Western standards). However, when they attempted to engage in economic transactions or control political processes, Tuvaluan congregations would ask the church authorities who supervised the pastors from Samoa to remove them (cf. Chambers, Chambers, and Munro 1978, Goldsmith 1989a:252–64, Goldsmith and Munro 1992b).

One may also recall from Chapter 6 that visiting or newly returned deacons and lay preachers are prime candidates for conducting the church service and giving the sermon on one of the first Sundays following their arrival. The ostensible reason for this practice is to introduce variety, to hear fresh ideas and styles, and to acknowledge the guest's or new returnee's presence in a respectful way. Yet there is also a clear covert agenda to the practice. New arrivals are also liminal figures who need to be ritually reintegrated into the community (in the case of returnees who are native to the atoll) or given some working connection to the community for the duration of their sojourn (in the case of visitors from another island). The sermon is a good ritual marker for this process. In addition, placing the liminal person in a position of extreme overt authority is a perfect way of bracketing the authority displays and controlling their ultimate relevance to more important areas of social life.[6]

Furthermore, the preacher's authority is topically bracketed, in that the themes addressed in sermons are normally confined to doctrinal matters over which everyone, as a good Protestant, is in agreement: that we are all sinners who need to be reminded of our wayward ways and castigated for them. This is not to say that sermons are entirely apolitical, quite the contrary. Skillful preachers know how to direct their sermons to "timely" issues, i.e., doctrinal topics of relevance to current circumstances, such as disputes, political rifts, and other socially disruptive happenings. They base their sermons on Scriptural passages that are relevant to ongoing events, and show in their exhortations how social problems can be solved through a close reading of the Bible. At the same time, sermons must be made to sound removed from the immediate secular context. Their messages must be opaque, metaphorical, and hidden:

Peelaa mo taku pati, ma kaafai hoki te faifeau e fai tena laauga, peelaa a ia e ttau fua o fakamatea maalie mai ua nee ia, nee?, nee ia ki tino, nee? Kae moo aa maa matea atu kaatoatoa te ata o tena faipatiiga, nee? [. . .] Me i tino laa fai maafaufau, e olo, koo leva loo ne olotou iloaga te kkano tonu o te faipatiiga teelaa, nee? A te mea paa koo too- koo too faipati, kae paa koo logo sala ki loto o tino, nee?

[interviews:Si 1991:1:A:103–109]

Like I said, when a pastor delivers a sermon, he sort of should just make people see [what he's getting at], right? He shouldn't reveal the entire picture of what he is [trying to] say, right? [. . .] Because people who have a good mind, as they go along, they'll certainly get the substance of what's being said, see? But when there's too much said, it doesn't feel right in people's hearts, see?

At first glance, the ideological makeup of sermons appears to present a fundamental contradiction. On the one hand, boundless authority is normatively displayed during sermon performances, while on the other hand this authority cannot be too transparently related to secular events. One possible account for this state of affairs would posit that a fundamental division between the religious and the secular is operative in social life, and that religious authority and secular authority are two distinct categories. However, this account is unsatisfactory in a number of respects: it is contradicted by the evidence of many leakages between the secular and the religious, and it fails to capture the intricate manner in which Christianity permeates tradition in contemporary Nukulaelae society.

Nevertheless, the seemingly paradoxical nature of sermonic authority does bear some relationship to the boundary between religious and political authority, the site of potential conflict between members of the religious cadres and the island community (compare Lambek 1990:33–5 on Islamic Mayotte in the Comoro Islands). When viewed against the background of attitudes towards political authority, a striking similarity emerges between the normative ambivalence underlying sermon performances and patterns found in political ideology. As I discussed briefly in Chapter 2 and in greater detail in a previous work (Besnier 1991), two broad strands can be discerned in the prescriptive schema for political action. On the one hand, one finds a yearning for an iron-fisted leadership which, when it operates legitimately, brings prosperity and peace to the community. At the same time, Nukulaelae Islanders also articulate a fierce spirit of egalitarianism, according to which everyone in the community is on the same footing and no one is entitled to exert authority over others. As a result, all positions of political authority on the atoll are fragile, temporary, and limited in scope. The same tension between two different ideologies is clearly evident in sermons. Despite their marked characteristics, sermons and their contexts are subjected to the same polarized pressures as social action in secular contexts.

Needless to say, finding a balance between these opposing forces, in sermon performances and elsewhere, presupposes sharply honed social skills, which not everyone is endowed with. On occasion, preachers misjudge their moves, triggering a strong negative reaction from the rest of the community. Elsewhere (Besnier 1993), I have analyzed the case of the leader of the Nukulaelae community on Nauru whose immoderate ostentation and abuses of power led him to be accused of being a sorcerer. Shortly after his demotion and forced return to the atoll, he was asked by the pastor to lead the Sunday afternoon service, in keeping with the tradition of asking new returnees to do so. During the service, he delivered an impassioned sermon on the topic of sorcery. Abandoning his written sermon half-way through his performance, dropping his Bible to the floor in the process (which a member of the congregation had to get up and retrieve), he became more and more pointed and precise in his allusions. Sobbing, he forcefully urged the congregation to abandon the ways of the *poouliga* "times of darkness," among which sorcery figures prominently (see Chapter 3):

NUKULAELAE I TTAEAO TEENEI! NUKULAELAE E PELE I MANATU, NUKULAELAE E TAGI KI EI TE LOTO, I TE AFIAFI TEENEI! [. . .] I TE AFIAFI TEENEI, E FAKAPILIPILI ATU, NUKULAELAE, NE AA LEO KONEI E TTAGI I LUGA I TE FENUA? [. . .] {voice breaking} *TE FILIFILIGA A TE ATUA, KOO TONU MOO KOE, Nukulaelae! E fakapilipili atu i te afiafi teenei, kee SEE TOE AUMAI NE MANATU SSEE, E FAKASSEEGINA EI TAATOU MO TTOU FAANAU! Koa oti tausaga o te poouliga. Koa oti tausaga o* {voice breaking} *te ifo ki tupua! Koo toi tausaga o te talittonu ki luga i- i fatu mo aa!*
[Sermons:P 1991:1:B:477–490]

NUKULAELAE THIS AFTERNOON! NUKULAELAE BELOVED IN ONE'S THOUGHTS, NUKULAELAE FOR WHICH THE HEART CRIES, THIS AFTERNOON! [. . .] THIS AFTERNOON, [GOD] IS REACHING OUT, WHAT ARE THOSE VOICES CRYING ON THE ATOLL? [. . .] {voice breaking} GOD'S CHOOSING IS RIGHT FOR YOU, Nukulaelae! [God] is reaching out to you this afternoon, DO NOT BRING UP ERRONEOUS THOUGHTS AGAIN, WHICH MAKE US AND OUR CHILDREN ERR! The years of darkness are over. The years of {voice breaking} the adoration of heathen gods are over! The years of beliefs in stone icons and whatever else are over!

However, the congregation saw in this overflow of emotionality nothing more than reproachable self-pity. Shuffling their feet and staring at the floor, congregation members murmured their disapproval audibly. Later, one respondent described her reaction to the sermon as follows:

Peelaa, hee fiafia au ki tena tagi i tena laauga! Paa me- ko tuulaga-, paa i tena faipatiiga, paa, fakamuli taa koo logo sala ei a tino, a ko ia koo vau foki mo tena tagi, nee? Peelaa aati koo fakauiga eeloo ana pati moo mea kolaa ne ttupu kiaa ia, koo tagi ifo oki eeloo, mo koo tagi o te ita, mo ko ttagi o te aa?, taa e fai nee ia i te afiafi, nee?
[interviews:Si 1991:1:A:129–134]

Like, I was not happy with the way he cried during his sermon! It was as if- it rested-, like, as he was speaking, like, later [in his sermon, he was saying things that] were offensive to people, and he was [aggravating it by] crying on top of it, see? It was like he was talking about what happened to him, and crying at the same time, were these tears tears of anger, or what [kind of] tears were they that he shed this afternoon, see?

The scorn and disapproval he brought upon himself through this sermon is a dramatic illustration of what can happen when the sermon performer transgresses the limits of sermonic authority.

Religious ritual and social context

The relationship between sermons, the religious rituals of which they are a part, and the broader context of Nukulaelae social life is complex. In certain conspicuous ways, sermons emerge as marked social events, in which many behavioral norms seem to be violated. In an attempt to understand the apparent exceptionality of sermons, I have shown in this chapter that sermons and the religious performances of which they are the central feature are indeed bracketed events. Some of this bracketing can be explained historically: as elsewhere in the Pacific, Christianity on the atoll still retains the imprint of its alien origins, despite the fact that tradition and religion are inextricably intertwined today. Nukulaelae Christianity probably maintained its foreign associations longer than it did in other Polynesian societies, where the church personnel was localized much sooner. Indeed, religious authority remained in the hands of Samoan "guest" pastors for almost a century, the last Samoan pastor having left the atoll only in 1958 (Nukulaelae was the last island of Tuvalu to have a Samoan pastor). Sermons today are suffused with these associations, which are clearly identifiable in their structural characteristics.

However, religious life and secular life are certainly not compartmentalized in this society. There are indeed many continuities between religious and secular events, several of which were described in Chapter 6: sermons are structured like secular speeches, the participant structure of church services resembles that of contexts in which secular speeches are made, preaching is "practice" for political oratory, and themes brought up in sermons can emerge in subsequent secular speeches. Furthermore, the very characteristics that appear unusual in a context-free analysis of the sermon can be shown to echo patterns of interaction in other contexts. For example, Nukulaelae Islanders subject each other's sermon performances to similar critical scrutiny as, say, political speeches and gossip. The authority of the preacher, which appears so boundless and overwhelming when observed *in vitro*, is in fact topically circumscribed, bounded to the immediate context of the church service, diluted by the sequential nature of authorship, and subjected to the same ideological constraints as secular authority.

What role does the emphasis on individualism play in the broader cultural context on sermons? The definition of personhood articulated in Nukulaelae sermons could be explained as an instantiation of Protestant doctrine, which Nukulaelae's brand of Christianity would share with comparable Protestant denominations: according to Evangelical precepts familiar from Western (particularly American) contexts, the individual is ultimately responsible for the fate of the soul and for establishing a personal relationship with God and Jesus (cf. Hunter 1983). However, religious events, religious discourse, and belief systems do not simply derive from the context-free implementation of religious doctrines. Rather, events, language, and beliefs articulate with sociocultural processes, and these processes determine the shape of religious ideology. It is noteworthy, for example, that Nukulaelae people do not foreground the notion of personal salvation in their explicit statements about religious ideology anywhere near as forcefully as Evangelical Christians do in Western societies, for whom "accepting Christ as one's personal savior" is an ever-recurring refrain. The concept of establishing a personal relationship with God out of one's own free will presupposes a certain conceptualization of the person that is not transparently echoed in Nukulaelae culture.[7] Yet, at some level, the person does emerge as an autonomous unit in Nukulaelae religious ideology. While commonalities are probably apparent between Nukulaelae religious events and church services in Western middle-class suburbs, these events do not occupy the same position in their respective sociocultural contexts, either from a sociological standpoint or from the point of view of individual experience.

Instead, I propose that Nukulaelae Islanders undergo an identity transformation in religious rituals, or at least a reorientation, and that the sermon is pivotal in bringing about this charge. I liken this metamorphosis to processes of identity transformation that have been described for many other religious institutions and rituals. An obvious example is the conversion experience familiar from Western (Harding 1987, Hartse 1993, Stromberg 1990) and non-Western settings (cf. Rosaldo 1973 and Watson-Gegeo and Gegeo 1991 on Pacific settings). As Stromberg (1990) demonstrates, the conversion experience is enacted whenever the experiencer tells the narrative of his or her conversion. The identity transformations triggered by a religious experience are thus not an isolated, once in a lifetime event, but rather emerge as a recursive and context-bound occurrence. While Nukulaelae differs considerably from the middle-class American setting that Stromberg describes, the identity transformations that members of both groups experience bear interesting similarities.

Even though the sermons' seemingly unusual characteristics are bound to a specific context, sermons should not be shrugged off as inconsequential "make-believe" behavior that members of this society engage in three times a week. Dismissing them as performed fiction trivializes the importance attached to sermons in this community and the seriousness with which Nukulaelae Islanders approach religious ceremonies. What takes place during the sermon is highly consequential for those involved, as is the particular way in which preachers and members of the congregation align themselves *vis-à-vis* such processes as authority, personhood, and access to the truth.

It is possible to account for these marked characteristics of sermons as images of the way that social life should *not* be organized outside the church building. According to this analysis, the person is depicted as an individualistic entity in sermons in order to display to the congregation how personhood should not be defined in secular contexts. Similarly, the dramatic authoritarianism displayed during sermon performances would demonstrate to those present how authority should not be performed elsewhere. Such dramatic instantiations of "what not to be" for negatively prescriptive purposes are common cross-culturally, as demonstrated by studies of symbolic reversals in performative events (e.g., Bakhtin 1984 on carnivals), social roles (e.g., Babcock-Abrahams 1974, E. Basso 1988, Pelton 1980, and Spinks 1991 on tricksters), and rituals (e.g., Babcock, ed., 1978, Scott 1990:156–82, and V. Turner 1969:166–203). However, this analysis is ill fitted to the context at hand, for several reasons. First, sermons are indeed bracketed social events, but not in the same fashion as, say, carnivals are. There is too much leakage between sermons and the rest of social life, as evidenced, for example, by similarities between the limits placed on the preacher's authority and the limits placed on political authority. Second, tricksters, rituals of reversals, and carnival-like festivals normally involve a suspension of social order: tricksters go out of their ways to violate behavioral norms, and carnivals are disorderly events during which, on the surface at least, "anything goes." In contrast, the sermon is a highly codified and rigidly structured event, hardly comparable to these other instances of anti-order. Finally, trickster roles, carnivals, and reversal rituals are always initiated by subordinated elements of society against dominant elements. While domination is of relevance to sermon-performance contexts at some level, the sermon is also a choice of display of high culture and hegemonic order. Clearly, the sermon cannot be analyzed as a ritual of reversal.

The individualistic identity that Nukulaelae Islanders foreground in religious contexts should not be seen as an anomaly or a deviation from the sociocentric identity foregrounded in other contexts. Rather, it is simply an illustration of the essentially context-dependent nature of personhood. Societies like Nukulaelae are often characterized in anthropology (and, increasingly, in some subfields of psychology) as having an understanding of the person as sociocentric and interactionally constructed (e.g., Geertz 1984, Heelas 1986, Markus and Kitayama 1991, Shweder and Bourne

1984). This understanding is commonly contrasted with views attributed to Western societies, where the person is conceptualized as situated in the individual.[8] The problem with this orthodox view is that members of societies which at first glance have "sociocentric" orientations are perfectly capable of articulating individualistic versions of their ethnopsychological understanding of personhood (Hollan 1992, A. Howard, 1985, Poole 1991, Spiro 1993). The holistic contrast between "individualistic" (read "Western") and "sociocentric" (read "non-Western") societies is thus a consequence of anthropologists' failure to attend to the importance of context-based variation in societies they study, and hence to capture the subtleties and complexities intrinsically associated with the sense of person in all cultures. The individualism that Nukulaelae Islanders elaborate in religious discourse, although undoubtedly distinct from Western middle-class individualism, is part and parcel of "the Nukulaelae sense of person."

Literacy again

The social and ideological characteristics of sermonic discourse have important implications for an understanding of church-related literacy practices, particularly written sermons. Written sermons both derive meaning from these associations and provide them with meaning in a variety of ways.

Written sermons play an important role in the truth-searching and truth-finding function of sermons. The fact that the sermonic performance is based on a written document heightens the privileged relationship between sermons and the truth. Specifically, preparing a written document ahead of time and referring to it during the sermon performance are thought of as ways of guaranteeing that what the preacher says during the performance is true, and not *ffuli ssee* "twisted around, inside out." This reasoning is particularly explicit in the following interview excerpt:

Me e maattaku a tino i au pati maa ssee. Teelaa laa, au mea koo oti katoa laa ne aa?, ne kkopi nee koe mai tua ki loto i te pepa. [. . .] Me i te mea teelaa e fanatu mai iaa koe, ko pati a te Atua. A ko tino laa kolaa e fakalogollogo mai, te sui o te Atua teelaa koo faipati mai, ko au pati kee ttonu eiloo, ma kaafai e ffuli ssee nee koe te pati, a ko tino kaa tausi nee laatou te mea ssee, see fakasala tino kae fakasala te- te tagata teelaa ne aumai te leo o te Atua.

[interviews:Ma 1990:3:A:548–565]

Because people [i.e., preachers] are afraid that they might say wrong things. So what you're going to say has been all- whatchamacallit?, all written out beforehand on a piece of paper. [. . .] Because what come through you are God's words. And there are people who listen to you, as God's representative in the process of speaking, so what you say had better be true, because if you twist words around, people [i.e., the congregation] are going to come away with wrong things, [and] people are not to blame, the- the person who's to blame is the one who brought God's voice.

The sermon being intimately associated with God's word, it is essential that every measure be taken to ensure that everything in it is true, and the presence of literacy during the performance gives it authority and truthfulness.

Written sermons are not the only literacy practice that have a special connection to the truth. Nukulaelae Islanders articulate the view that many manifestations of the written word, particularly as epitomized in the Bible and Church-sanctioned religious writings, has the potential of being maximally truthful, much more so than the spoken word. Not only is the Bible authored by God, an entity with undisputable universal legitimacy, but it is also the yardstick against which all actions should be evaluated. Children are socialized early to accept the written word as the bearer of truth, to be memorized and recited in the appropriate context: once a year in particular, on Children's Sunday (*te Aso o Tamaliki*), all children in the community take part in the church service, reciting memorized Bible passages and short sermons, or taking part in Scripture-inspired tableaux and plays, all of which are scripted.

Literacy is thought to give its users privileged access to the truth even when religious texts are not involved. For example, in discussions of oral history (a topic of great interest on the atoll), the potential truthfulness of literacy is frequently invoked. Islanders recognize that there are many coexisting but conflicting oral accounts of the past, each more or less subtly associated with particular interests and points of view. In practice, there is a general tolerance of these variations: competing historical accounts can be told in public without overt censorship. (Indeed, organized multivocality permeates many aspects of social life, as it both reflects and fuels valued egalitarianism.) Yet, at the same time, Nukulaelae thinkers often lament the resulting cacophony. These laments are often expressed in public speeches, and of course they are frequently voiced for the benefit of the ethnographer, who is the most literacy-oriented specimen that Nukulaelae people have ever encountered:

Naa laa, [. . .] vau a ttinoo, fakamatala, "E fai peelaa." Oti, kae vau ssuaa tino, fakamatala e tai kkese tena faipatiiga, peelaa mo koo tai kkese mo te- mo te fakamatalaaga a ssuaa tino. Ia, teelaa ko te tukumaiiga laa teenaa, koo mmai ei ki- ki taimi nei, nee? Koo maua ei a pepa konaa, teenaa laa koo tuku ki loto i pepa, kae faitau laa taatou, ai!, koo tai kkese maalie te tala a ttino teelaa! Ao, ko te mea ne- ne mmai taatou i taimi kolaa see iloa o tusi. [. . .] Teelaa laa, hee mafai o tonu. A moi ne mea, moi ne taimi ne paatusi eiloo ki loto!

[interviews:Ma 1990:3:B:356–387]

So [. . .] one person comes along, gives an account, "It happened this way." Once that's over, another person comes along, gives an account and what he says is slightly different, like it's slightly different from the first person's account. So that's how it would happen until today, see? [Now] we have paper, and we put [these stories] down on paper, and we read it, and, oh no!, that other person's account is slightly different! Yes, because it was handed down at a time when literacy was unknown. [. . .] That's why it can never be true. If only it had-, if only it had been written down right there and then!

As this excerpt illustrates, Nukulaelae Islanders blame the cacophony of historical accounts on their forebears' lack of literacy skills or, alternatively, on the fact that paper and writing implements were difficult to obtain in days bygone. Had history, while it was "going on," been "committed" (*fakamau*, literally, "made steadfast") to writing by someone entitled to do so, the resulting written text would have been maximally true and authoritative.

However, it is important to stress that not *all* forms of literacy are *inherently* truthful. To have a privileged relationship with the truth, the authorship of a written text must meet certain criteria of legitimacy that have little or nothing to do with literacy per se (e.g., it must be sanctioned by Church officialdom, and hence by God). What the written word carries is a strong *claim* of truthfulness. When this claim is substantiated by evidence of authorial legitimacy, literacy fulfills its social functions and is intrinsically more truthful than oral communication. In contrast, when Congregationalist Nukulaelae Islanders come across religious writings issued by the Baha'is or the Jehovah's Witnesses, for example, they see these writings as *ppelo* "lies" that usurp literacy's claim to truth and legitimacy, and their reaction can be ferociously critical and disparaging. No *oral* claim to legitimacy and truth is ever met with the disapproval that such writings encounter, even patently slanderous gossip. The extreme nature of these reactions bears witness to the privileged relationship between the truth and the written word.

So the link between literacy and the truth in Nukulaelae ideology is more complex than proponents of the ideological model of literacy have described it (see Chapter 1). These scholars have commonly viewed the search for objectivity, clarity, and truth as being intrinsically and universally related to literacy. The material I have just presented strongly suggests that Nukulaelae Islanders have a considerably more sophisticated understanding of the power of literacy than these writers do. Furthermore, it is now well established that, in many ethnographic and historical contexts, the written word is false and untrustworthy, is associated with secrecy, and is a tool for concealment, i.e., anything but a vehicle for the truth and its broad dissemination (e.g., Axtell 1987, Bledsoe and Robey 1986, Clanchy 1993, Ewald 1988, Kulick and Stroud 1990, Probst 1989). The social and epistemological associations of literacy are thus culture-specific and historically situated constructs that are constitutive of the sociocultural meaning of literacy. Literacy's privileged position in Nukulaelae's truth market should not be taken as a symptom of some transcendent characteristic of literacy itself, but must be understood in the context of particular literacy practices.

Literacy plays several other roles in church services. First, written sermons and other church-related literacy practices contribute to the bracketing of church services as distinctive social events. As mentioned earlier, for most inhabitants of the atoll, the church service is the only context in which books are regularly read from. The use of written sermons has similar connotations: the act of basing an oral performance on a piece of writing, as well as the act of listening to such a literacy-based performance, are peculiar to the church service, and stand out as unusual in the broader context of most people's lives.

Second, the privileged linkage between written sermons and the truth acquires an interesting twist when viewed in light of the complex dynamics that characterize sermonic authority. I described earlier how sermon performances are conspicuous displays of overt authority, a very marked practice in this community. I also showed how members of the community subject these displays to cynical scrutiny reminiscent of the scrutiny to which they subject all attempts to exert authority in secular contexts. In other words, the preacher's authority is fragile and potentially suspect, and it can afford all the legitimizing support it can get. The written sermon, with its special link to the truth, is one way of establishing the preacher as an authoritative figure in these potentially adverse circumstances. One characteristic of sermon writing as a literacy practice makes the written sermon a particularly attractive authority-endorsing object: written sermons often have multiple authors. Many hands and minds might have contributed to the message conveyed in the sermon in the course of its life history. On the one hand, this pattern of multiple authoring grounds the preacher's authority in the authority of his predecessors, thus giving it more authenticity. At the same time, it provides an indirect and equivocal quality to the association between the performer and the overt displays of authority that he or she engages in. In most cases, this indirection absolves the preacher of any potential allegation that he or she is trying to exert personal authority. Of course, if the preacher makes overt efforts to contextualize the sermon's message in contemporary secular events, the indirect quality that literacy lends to the performance is forgotten, and allegations of abuses of authority surface, as in the case I related earlier. As in Mayotte, "texts and their interpreters each lend authority to the other" (Lambek 1990:26); so if the preacher's authority is undermined by text-external factors, the text also loses its claim to authority.

This analysis adds a new perspective on the role that gender plays in the production and transmission of sermons notebooks. As noted in Chapter 6, women do not generally write their own sermons, but rather ask male relatives or friends to do so for them. So while men are both givers and receivers in the sermon-notebook market, women can only be receivers. They can pass on the sermons they have inherited from male relatives to women and younger men, but they themselves don't contribute to that market sermons they have authored.

Women are certainly not excluded from positions in which they can exert some form of authority in Nukulaelae society. Indeed, the Women's Council is a powerful body in the community's political scene, within which women have the potential of making their voices heard at least among themselves and of presenting their collective interests to the Council of Elders. In the 1950s, a Nukulaelae woman, Loine (phonemically, *Looine*), was the chief of the atoll community for a number of years, a position then known as *alii sili* (a borrowing from a Samoan expression for "paramount chief"). However, in typical fashion, women's authority is always bounded in one way or the other in this society: decisions reached in meetings of the Women's Council usually concern *mea a faafine* "women's things," in contrast with the resolutions of the Council of Elders, which by default apply to *te fenua* "the community," since the Council of Elders is a synecdoche for the community. Similarly, Loine was *alii sili* at a time when the position was considerably more ceremonial and devoid of power than it has become in recent years.

Women can thus *perform* sermons, because everyone knows that authority displays from the pulpit are ritually bracketed. This is particularly true of special "women-related" occasions, when this bracketing becomes even more salient, and when the message of the sermon is viewed as being primarily addressed to women. However, women do not *author* sermons, a more consequential act in which the writer stakes a claim to the truth. Were women to write sermons, men's privileged access to the truth would be threatened. It is important to add that no one on the atoll ever presented this analysis to me in explicit terms. Yet the patterns I observed in reference to sermon writing and gender are congruent with the gendering of political power and authority, and this congruence is not a coincidence. It is also important to point out that women are not *prevented* from writing sermons. Rather, they themselves contribute to the gendering of the practice, having bought into the "false consciousness" that they are not *maasani* "adept at, familiar with" sermon writing, and that their oratorical skills, Biblical knowledge, and understanding of the truth is inferior to that of men.[9] And one is indeed dealing with false consciousness: I have never seen or heard women actively challenge or decry their ideological exclusion from the production of sermonic texts, even though I have witnessed them perform many acts of resistance against other forms of male domination. Their exclusion is all the more immune to resistance in that it belongs to the realm of religion, a domain from which Nukulaelae people (particularly men, but not exclusively so) often draw powerful naturalizing arguments to justify or excuse gender hierarchies.

   To conclude, I have described several ways in which sermon writing as a literacy practice brings to the context in which sermons are performed significant characteristics, e.g., a special link to the Bible and truth, a gendered character, and the authority of multiple authorship. These attributes "bleed" onto the performance context and the church service, i.e., give them a specific meaning by association. In turn, sermon writing acquires meaning from the social attributes of the performance context to which it is ultimately aimed. For example, the bracketed flavor of religious services and the inherent fragility of the preacher's authority place sermon writing in a particular light for those that engage in it. In short, the relationship between written sermons and the context in which these texts are produced and consumed is bi-directional or *constitutive*: written texts not only give meaning to their context of use, but also acquire meaning from them.

[handwritten margin note:] acquiring meaning from context as well as give meanings to context.

8

CONCLUSION

In the foregoing chapters, I investigated the social, ideological, and textual characteristics of literacy on Nukulaelae, and explored the implications that the two principal types of literacy have for a theoretical understanding of literacy in its social and ideological context. In this conclusion, I turn to the questions that an examination of the full panoply of Nukulaelae literacy practices and events raises. In other words, having presented an event-centered examination of literacy on the atoll, I now analyze the same material from what I called in the introduction a comparative-ethnographic stance.

The ethnographic study of literacy is part and parcel of the broader concerns that have driven anthropological thought since its early formulation (cf. Tambiah 1990): do modes of thought (or "mentalities") share a common core in all societies? If so, what is this common core, and where is it located? If not, what is the quality of differences across modes of thought? What types of groups do the differences define? And are the differences mere elaborations of a universal grounding? To apply these questions to the investigation of literacy, one must first recognize that literacy, rather than *transcending* the social and the cultural, is *embroiled* in social and cultural processes. That literacy is entangled in social processes is demonstrated by the important role that it commonly plays in the formation and maintenance of inequality between social classes, women and men, and the center and the periphery. In the realm of culture, literacy is semiotically connected to many of the categories that social actors invoke to make sense of the world around them (e.g., personhood, emotionality, religious symbolism). No account of literacy, or for that matter of any other aspect of human nature, can ignore either social or cultural aspects of the phenomenon.

The problem that one faces is how to integrate the social and the cultural. The answer resides in an approach that foregrounds literacy as social practice. A practice-centered approach seeks to explain the relationship between human action and systemic categories located at the intersection of culture and society. As Ortner (1984) emphasizes, it starts from the recognition that human action and broader systemic categories determine

169

one another. How this dialectic determination works, and what its effects are, are complex empirical questions and the subjects of much theoretical debate. In the case of literacy, recognizing the dialectic nature of the relationship implies that literacy does not simply impose itself onto human action, and does not simply shape it without giving human actors a chance to shape it in turn. "Theory" in the study of literacy consists in making sense of the complex interweaving of literacy with society, culture, and individuals' cognitive and social makeup. In the course of this chapter, I identify certain categories at the intersection of the social and the cultural that are apt to play an important role in the process of giving meaning to literacy.

Restricted literacy

The first issue I must address is what type of literacy the Nukulaelae case is an example of. As noted in the introduction, it has become commonplace to characterize societies like Nukulaelae as situations of "restricted literacy." This phrase, which originated in the work of Goody,[1] refers to situations in which literacy is "restricted by factors other than the techniques of writing itself" (Goody 1977:198). However, the phrase has been applied to several types of situations, often without much attention being paid to the problems that this referential diversity gives rise to.

The first and best documented type of restricted literacy is societies in which only a small percentage of the population has access to literacy skills. For example, in many cultures where literacy and religious life are closely connected, only the clergy can read and write. These "demographically" restricted situations are frequently gendered: if literacy is controlled by an intellectual, political, or religious élite, this élite usually consists only of men, or sometimes of a mixture of women and men, but it is rarely if ever an exclusively female élite. The second way in which literacy can be restricted is illustrated by societies where everyone or nearly everyone knows how to read and write, but where literacy is used for a narrow and rigidly pre-set range of purposes or in limited (and usually well-defined) social contexts. Reading a set canon of religious texts, for example, can be the primary goal of learning literacy skills. Literacy production can be confined to composing lists or establishing legal or commercial contracts. Finally, the notion of "restricted literacy" is often invoked to describe literate societies which have not undergone the social and intellectual transformations that literacy is presumed to engender in "fully" literate individuals and groups. For example, Malagasy society is highly literate, but Malagasy attitudes towards knowledge do not correspond to what the autonomous model associates with literacy: thus written texts are not subjected to critical scrutiny, because written texts are akin to traditional forms of authoritative oratory, or *kabary* (Block 1989:18–26). Malagasy literacy would thus be described as "restricted."[2]

Restricted literacy has a number of general characteristics (Goody 1968:11–20). Members of restrictedly literate societies tend to have a protective attitude towards knowledge, including written knowledge. They frequently emphasize the memorization of texts. Literacy in such societies is often closely associated with religion, and written texts are often used for magico-religious purposes, e.g., in prayer wheels and as written charms. Restricted literacy contrasts with essayist literacy traditions, where literacy is "deeply interiorized" (Ong 1982:29) and where "true literacy" (Havelock 1982:203) prevails. The prime, and perhaps only, example of these traditions is Western middle-class literacy practices. With essayist literacy comes a much broader range of uses for writing: newspapers, magazines, and journals are used to disseminate articles and essays, to offer a forum for gentlemanly debate and poised reflection; memos and other forms of written communication take over the role fulfilled by verbal messages in restrictedly literate settings; and a general preference for written communication emerges for many purposes.

Invoking restricted literacy as an analytic or descriptive category raises a number of theoretical problems, as several authors have pointed out (e.g., Gough 1968a, 1968b, Messick 1983, Street and Besnier 1994). I will not go into the general arguments against it here, but instead will examine the contradictions that arise if one were to characterize Nukulaelae as a restrictedly literacy society. Indeed, Nukulaelae society can only be described as "steeped" in literacy. First, nearly all its members can produce and consume written texts with dexterity, a near universality that contrasts sharply with the situation found in most Western societies, one should add. Secondly, the ability to read and write is constitutive of personhood on the atoll. Third, from an intellectual perspective, Nukulaelae sermon performers can handle with great confidence the cognitively complex task of conducting an oral performance on the basis of a written document, extemporaneously transforming the latter as the performance unfolds. The reverse is also true: Nukulaelae Islanders take minutes of meetings associated with a multitude of groups and clubs, thereby demonstrating their ability to transform oral communication into writing. Fourth, from a social perspective, one form of literacy, namely letters, is deeply integrated in many aspects of everyday life, such as the workings of economic life and the maintenance of gossip networks. In all these respects, Nukulaelae literacy is "deeply interiorized" in social, ideological, and individual terms.

Furthermore, there is ample evidence that Nukulaelae Islanders orient themselves differently towards various literacy practices, and hence that the role literacy plays in their lives is varied and complex. For instance, they are deeply interested and invested in certain types of literacies, such as Bible reading and the exchange of letters, each of which is associated with very important aspects of life on the atoll. At the same time, they betray a complete lack of interest in other tokens of literate communication. For example, I discussed in Chapter 3 that few on the atoll try to decipher the meaning of slogans on imported tee-shirts, and that postings on notice boards are often ignored (such was the fate of the notice advertising my interest in collecting letters, as mentioned in Chapter 4). Later in this chapter, I will describe Nukulaelae Islanders' cool response to attempts to inscribe history, a coolness which is often tinged with indifference. Along the same lines, certain forms of literacy are viewed with skepticism and mistrust, while others are presented as the acme of trustworthiness and dependability. In the former category fall pamphlets that missionaries of "new religions" distribute, and, in a certain sense, letters, which can never be trusted completely to find their addressee. In the latter fall the Bible of course, but also written invitations to feasts (Chapter 3) and "signatures" (*saina*), which have become necessary and sufficient conditions for social commitments of various types. In other words, there is no such thing as *the* Nukulaelae attitude toward literacy, any more than there is an easily identifiable "Western" attitude toward reading and writing. Nukulaelae Islanders' orientation to literacy is as complex as white middle-class Americans'. Nevertheless, Nukulaelae literacy practices bear only a remote resemblance to the type of practices associated with essayist traditions. One does not find here a great deal of interest in writing or reading essays, in comparing different written accounts of the same events, or in disseminating knowledge and interpretations in the form of positions papers and other scholarly documents. Such practices are for the most part irrelevant to atoll life, and furthermore they presume access to resources far beyond the reach of the community. In short, characterizing this society as restrictedly literate fails to capture the complexities of Nukulaelae literacy.

Incipient literacy

While the notion of restricted literacy is of little descriptive or theoretical use in accounting for literacy traditions comparable to Nukulaelae's, Nukulaelae society is an example of a situation of *incipient literacy*, in that reading and writing on the atoll are recent innovations, having been brought in just a little over a century ago.[3] The category "incipient literacy" is of a different nature than "restricted literacy." It should not be seen as a homogeneous category, nor should it be viewed as a "stage" on an evolutionary scale. Rather, it is simply a way to recognize that Nukulaelae Islanders' exposure to the technology of literacy (and that of members of other similar societies) is a relatively recent phenomenon. There are different ways of defining the cut-off point between "incipient" and "established" literacy traditions, but the identification of this cut-off point is not problematic if the category "incipient literacy" is taken to be a convenient descriptive label, to which no theoretical claim is attached.

Can any general statement be made about situations of incipient literacy? Unfortunately, relatively little ethnographic information is available on how literacy takes root in newly literate societies. As a result, our understanding of relevant questions is still limited. Which communicative activities is literacy adapted to or excluded from in such situations? How do the circumstances under which it is introduced shape its path? To what extent do recipients "take over" the technology or keep it at a distance from their everyday lives? Attempts to generalize about the introduction of literacy to the pre-literate world have insisted on couching the question in terms of the "acceptance" or "rejection" of a monolithic model of literacy (e.g., Huebner 1987, Spolsky, Engelbrecht, and Ortiz 1983, Spolsky and Irvine 1982), and have thus failed to recognize that literacy may exist as a multifarious phenomenon right from its inception, upon which members of the "receiving" group can exert agentive control by shaping it and defining its meaning in novel and locally relevant ways. (Of course this definition can consist in a ruling that no form of literacy is relevant to their lives.) As Philips (1975) argues:

It might be possible to argue that in societies where literacy was not traditional, and has been introduced only through contact with the Western European tradition of literacy uses, one would encounter merely an unrevealing imitation and duplication of that tradition. However . . . it is more likely that in each of the various cultural situations into which literacy is introduced, there will be culturally varying responses to different uses of literacy and innovation in usage.

(Philips 1975:370)

In the case of Nukulaelae, many of the contexts in which literacy-producing practices take place today did not exist before the advent of literacy: the physical isolation of the atoll rendered long-distance communication with the rest of the world extremely infrequent prior to missionization, and aboriginal religious practices, about which very little is known (cf. Chapter 2), probably did not involve genres of religious discourse comparable to contemporary Christian sermons. (It is important to note that these contexts were not created by literacy, but rather that literacy was shaped to answer the needs created by these new contexts.) Yet today both practices are well integrated into the communicative repertoire of Nukulaelae society. This suggests that, in the course of one century, Nukulaelae Islanders have actively integrated literacy into their communicative repertoires. They have also redefined literacy from the narrow range of consumption-oriented activity which Samoan pastors introduced (i.e., reading the Christian scriptures) to a much broader range of activities involving both production and consumption. Furthermore, they have given to different literacy activities characteristics patterned on interpersonal dynamics in oral contexts, thus developing local definitions of literacy. These patterns shed serious doubt on the hypothesis that, "like many other aspects of modernization, literacy has become a source of confusion and doubt in the oral societies of the Pacific, and ... is contributing significantly to cultural erosion" (Topping 1992:30, a view also presented by Mühlhäusler 1990). There is anything but confusion and doubt in the way that Nukulaelae Islanders have empowered literacy to meet the social needs emerging from increased contact with the outside world, giving it a quintessential local meaning, and thoroughly absorbing it into the very fabric of social life and culture.

Interesting parallels emerge when one compares the Nukulaelae community's response to literacy and its reaction to other forms of social change triggered by its increasingly frequent relations with the outside world in the nineteenth century. At first blush, the atoll community appears to have been completely at the mercy of the authority of outsiders, be they Samoan pastors, German planters, colonial rulers, or, in more modern times, government and church officials from Funafuti. In some cases, the circumstances under which contact with the outside took place left Nukulaelae Islanders no control whatsoever over the course of events; such is the case of their brief and tragic encounter with Peruvian blackbirders. However, in other cases, there are always clear, if subtle, indications that Nukulaelae people took the lead in many of these encounters, and manipulated them to their own advantage. The same is true of literacy: rather than following what they were told literacy was for, they took control of the technology to monitor their economic links with the outside world, among other things.

Nukulaelae is not an isolated example of a society in which the social functions that introducing agents intend literacy to have diverge manifestly from the activities in which the recipients of the technology put it to use: similar patterns have been described in the small but growing body of literature from various areas of the world, including Papua New Guinea (Gewertz and Errington 1991, Kulick and Stroud 1990, Siegel 1981, 1984), Native North America (McLaughlin 1992, Philips 1983), and Aboriginal Australia (Ferguson 1987, Goddard 1990). For instance, literacy was brought to the Pitjantjatjara of Central Australia first by missionaries and later by governmental authorities in charge of education. To repeat a common pattern, these agents tried to encourage a passive and individualized orientation towards literacy, and, predictably, their efforts had little success. However, in the 1980s, several Pitjantjatjara communities began circulating newsletters in both Pitjantjatjara and English (Goddard 1990). These newsletters, which contain news of local interest, admonitory essays, narratives of various types, and announcements, have found an eager audience, in sharp contrast to Pitjantjatjara indifference toward Anglo-inspired school-related forms of literacy. Goddard suggests that the newsletters fill a gap left by the attrition of traditional consensus-seeking forms of public oratory on the one hand, and, on the other, the inability of new forms of face-to-face communication (e.g., church meetings) to fill the shoes of these older forms. While there are surface similarities between the form of Pitjantjatjara newsletters and comparable vehicles found in Western societies, the roles that these various forms play in people's lives are very different. Thus, to understand the shape that incipient literacy takes, one must examine how oral forms and social niches may have become realigned before or while literacy emerged onto the scene.

The ethnographic literature on Melanesia presents particularly fascinating illustrations of literacy empowerment. For example, the Chambri of the Middle Sepik Region of Papua New Guinea inherited literacy in the general context of governmental efforts to bring development to rural areas of the country (Gewertz and Errington 1991:147–68). (The Chambri, who are enthusiastic Catholics, have not been exposed to the onslaught of evangelical Christian missionizing efforts that one finds elsewhere in Papua New Guinea, in the context of which literacy is being introduced to many parts of the country.) The national ideology, which is brought to the Chambri primarily through schooling, places literacy in Tok Pisin (Neo-Melanesian Creole) or English in the foreground of the drive for development and concomitant national unity (echoing, as it were, the theoretical statements of Anderson 1991 and Gellner 1983). While the Chambri buy into this ideology, they also see in literacy a means to achieve certain aims, such as creating documents to enhance their individual prestige and their personal position on the village political map. The most straightforward examples are letters of recommendation, diplomas certifying that one is a "good sorcerer," and letters to the Queen of England requesting medals of recognition. During their sojourn among the Chambri, Gewertz and Errington were frequently approached by Chambri men with requests to type up such documents, as the Chambri place as much importance on the physical presentation of written documents as the audiences for which they are intended, even though which presentational details matter to them does not always match Western-style bureaucratic views (which details *do* matter from a Chambri perspective raises interesting questions). Chambri women also asked the anthropologists to write letters for them, although much less frequently, and their letters were of a more personal nature; for example, they frequently intended to send them to dead relatives (Gewertz, personal communication). Clearly, Chambri women and men are not the passive recipients of literacy; rather, they actively define what literacy means and can do for them.

The most important generalization that can be drawn from these cases is of a methodological nature. Rather than seeking to characterize the conditions under which literacy is "accepted" and "rejected" in incipiently literate settings, one should rather seek to understand which aspects of social life and which symbolic structures literacy becomes embedded in, and why. The Chambri have defined one form of literacy as an instrument for the manipulation of personal prestige. In contrast, for Nukulaelae Islanders, literacy itself has become a symbol of equality (see below for further discussion). These divergent paths are not haphazardly determined, but rather are tied to different priorities that manifest themselves elsewhere in the organization of society and its ideological scaffolding. The task of understanding the trajectory of reading and writing in incipiently literate societies must address why and how literacy acquires certain meanings and not others in each situation.

Literacy and hegemony

The creation, maintenance, and contestation of hegemonic structures are arguably the social processes with which literacy is most commonly embroiled, in both incipiently literate communities and societies where literacy has a long history. Early on, proponents of the autonomous model (e.g., Goody and Watt 1963) equated "widespread" literacy with the emergence of democratic institutions and the erasure of the inequality inherent to situations where certain segments of society have access to literacy, while others do not. Other authors concurrently maintained that literacy was by nature a hegemonic technology. The following oft-quoted passage from Lévi-Strauss' *Tristes Tropiques* is a powerful summary of this view:

> [A]t the moment when writing makes its débuts[,] it seems to favour rather the exploitation than the enlightenment of mankind. . . . If my hypothesis is correct, the primary function of writing, as a means of communication, is to facilitate the enslavement of other human beings. The use of writing for disinterested ends, and with a view to satisfactions of the mind in the fields either of science or the arts, is a secondary result of its invention – and may even be no more than a way of reinforcing, justifying, or dissimulating its primary function.
>
> (Lévi-Strauss 1964:292)

While it does manage to ground literacy in a social context, Levi-Strauss' characterization of literacy is as oversimplified as the images depicted by the autonomous model, in that it presents literacy as having inherent and universal instrumental powers, over which the dominated have no control. In short, both Goody and Watt's and Lévi-Strauss' representations rob human beings of agency. These mutually contradicting positions suggest that the relationship between literacy and hegemony cannot be summarized in any simple manner, and that it deserves close ethnographic scrutiny.

Although the very acts of reading and writing do not automatically create inequality, there is ample evidence that literacy easily lends itself to becoming a tool in the creation and maintenance of hegemonic structures. The clearest illustrations are provided by Western societies (the very contexts in which Goody and Watt see literacy as having socially levelling effects). In many complex societies of Europe, the Americas, and the Pacific Rim, the state exercises control over the little people with written documents, which by the same token are used to ground the legitimacy of the state. From parking tickets to acts of Congress, from school textbooks to university diplomas, written documents figure prominently among the tools with which the state machinery implements hegemony in such fields as education (Bourdieu 1988, 1990, 1991, Bourdieu and Passeron 1977), the legal world (Foucault 1977, 1980), and other bureaucratic and social institutions. Associated with these social arenas are scribal élites (e.g., attorneys, academics, art critics), whose *raison d'être* is to mediate between the masses and the state apparatus, by drafting and interpreting written documents. The fact that certain segments of society do not have access to sanctioned forms of literacy is further utilized to restrict their access to power and other resources. For example, the communicative styles of certain ethnic minorities are declared to be inappropriate for school literacy, and thus schooling becomes a gauntlet through which some segments of society are let through while others are rejected (Ogbu 1990). Similarly, both state discourse and popular thinking attributes poor job performance and joblessness among blue-collar workers to their lack of literacy skills, a notion which depends crucially on a very specific definition of what counts as literacy and what does not (Hull 1993).

Literacy is also directly involved in the reproduction of inequality in many non-Western contexts. Lambek's (1990, also 1993) analysis of religious written texts in Mayotte, on the Islamic periphery, is an exemplary case. As in many other parts of the Islamic world (e.g., Eickelman 1985, Gilsenan 1982, Messick 1993), the knowledge embedded in written texts is technically available to every Muslim Mayotte Islander, as Islamic ideology demands that knowledge be disseminated widely. However, in practice, only a handful of specialists (e.g., the *kutuba* "sermon reciters" and the *fundi* "religious teachers") understand Kuranic texts and sacred sermons. For instance, the *kutuba* are in charge of reciting religious texts to silent audiences, a brokering activity from which they derive a great deal of authority.[4] In the same manner, Islamic scholars derive a great deal of authority over other men from the knowledge and the recitation of texts, and from brokering activities crucial to the creation and maintenance of these texts.

In colonial situations, the picture is often further complicated by the fact that literacy commonly becomes a means through which the colonial power (and, at the post-colonial stage, the local élite that replaces it) controls and manipulates the colonized. This state of affairs is nicely illustrated by the case of Nukulaelae in the early days of contact. Visiting LMS missionaries tested the islanders' reading and writing skills as a condition for admission to the Church, using delaying strategies to heighten the prestige of both Church membership and literacy, and basing their evaluations of the Samoan pastors' performance on the results of these tests. Literacy was thus an instrument of domination in more than one way: not only did the individual's access to desirable symbolic resources depend on it, but so did the community's overall prestige and the Samoan pastors' livelihood. Later, colonial authorities chimed in by appointing scribes to keep detailed records of all political and legal events, and by requiring that island magistrates be literate, and literate in Samoan, demonstrating that language choice functioned as yet another instrument of domination.

However, when one explores the intricacies of these hegemonic structures and the role that literacy played in them, the situation becomes very complex. First, independently of literacy, the relationship between the various protagonists (Samoan pastors, LMS missionaries, colonial authorities, and the Nukulaelae community) were anything but clear-cut. In Chapters 2 and 7, I discussed how the Samoan pastors' authority was both curtailed by the community's subtle control and controlled by the LMS missionaries' not-so-subtle, but elusive, supervision. The power that colonial authorities yielded was so distant and mediated by so many factors that it is not clear that it had much impact on the community. Second, reading between the lines of the fragmentary historical evidence, literacy appears to have served as an instrument of resistance as much as domination. The very early emergence of letter reading and writing demonstrates that literacy was put to use for purposes that were quite different from what the religious authorities who introduced it had intended. Letters can thus be considered to be a mild form of resistance; at least, they represent a use of literacy that falls outside of the introducing agents' control. More speculatively, Nukulaelae people might have engaged in deceptive Scripture recitations from memory to fool LMS missionaries into thinking that they were proficient readers (see McKenzie 1985 on the Maori). Whether these practices took place with or without the collusion of the Samoan pastors, who were anxious to present a favorable veneer to the visitors, they ensured that it was the islanders who had the last laugh.

Whatever relationship literacy and hegemony may have had in historical times, there are few, if any, clearly discernible hegemonic connotations to contemporary uses of literacy on the atoll. Literacy does not even emerge as a simple marker of inequality in this community: everyone knows how to read and write, and everyone engages in roughly the same literacy activities, with the exception of sermon composition, to which I will return presently. In the course of its history, literacy quickly acquired equality-fostering qualities on Nukulaelae, as everyone became literate at roughly the same time. There are no classes of people who, because of their professional skills or other reasons, are defined as having privileged access to literacy practices. The inability to afford writing tools is the only obvious way in which an individual's access to literacy can be constrained. However, this situation is easily remedied by relying on one's reciprocity networks: asking one's relatives or neighbors for a sheet of paper and a pencil makes for a very reasonable request. The basic superficial equality between all members of the community that characterizes access to literacy, even if it is a cosmetic veneer that conceals more fundamental structures of inequality, is congruent with the egalitarian ethos that Nukulaelae Islanders emphasize in many institutions and in the social actions they perform. In the practice of everyday life, there are of course differences in power and authority between men and women, older people and younger people, and particularly individuals, as in all other societies including the most egalitarian.

Beneath a surface of equal access to literacy as a technology, there are two ways in which literacy as social practice can create and maintain inequality among adults. First, written sermons are composed almost exclusively by men. I will discuss the implications of this asymmetry in the next section, where I will demonstrate that it must be understood in the broader context of the gendering of various communicative practices. Second, literacy practices associated with secondary schooling, which is accessible by only a tiny fraction of the population, are associated with emergent school-derived opportunities for upward mobility, which in turn have created a salaried élite that lives on Funafuti, the capital. As shown in Chapter 3, proficiency in English literacy is a prerequisite for admission into secondary school, and this proficiency is readily available only on Funafuti. Thus a pattern familiar from the rest of the developing world appears to emerge, whereby a center-based élite is ensuring its own reproduction at the expense of the rural periphery. This pattern is very new, in that it results from changes associated with Tuvalu's independence in 1978, and still little can be said about the shape that it will take and the role of literacy in its formation. What can be noted about the current evidence is that caution should be exercised in interpreting its significance. Indeed, several processes are in place that counteract the emergence of inequality. Recall from Chapter 5 that salaried Nukulaelae Islanders in residence on Funafuti are besieged by their relatives' insistence that they produce the fruit of their labor for redistribution, a process in which, ironically, one form of literacy, namely letter writing, plays a central role. In some ways, salaried islanders are the community's beasts of burden, and their ability to situate themselves in a hegemonic relationship to the rest of the community is very tenuous. In short, the evidence that school-based literacy gives rise to inequality is at best equivocal.[5]

The conclusion one can draw from the Nukulaelae material is that literacy has neither inherently hegemonic nor equality-fostering qualities. Rather, it lends itself well to becoming a contesting ground between hegemony and resistance, as it did in nineteenth-century Nukulaelae, but it can become with equal ease a powerful symbolic banner of egalitarianism and a leveling instrument. The nature of the symbolic and social dimensions of literacy can vary greatly across different practices (letters are levelling instruments, sermons have hegemonic qualities), and they are crucially tied to dynamics that are independent of literacy as a technology, and yet are no less consequential in providing literacy with a specific meaning.

Literacy and gender

Like other parameters of social inequality, gender in many societies determines the extent to which individuals are given access to literacy. The gendering of literacy is classically illustrated by the seemingly typical situation in which literacy is men's exclusive prerogative. For example, in traditional Moroccan society (and probably much of the Islamic world), boys attended Qur'anic school where they learned to read the sacred texts, while girls were taught domestic skills in which there was no place for literacy (Wagner, Messick, and Spratt 1986:252–3). In other cases, the differences between women's and men's literacies may be less clear-cut: both women and men may be given access to literacy instruction, reading materials, and writing tools, but the range of reading and writing activities that women are allowed or expected to engage in is narrower than the range of literacy activities of men. Such was the case in many parts of Europe until very recently (N. Davis 1975, Schofield 1968, Stock 1983). Frequently, the gendered nature of literacy is the subject of naturalization, which helps justify and perpetrate resulting asymmetries. Among the Tamang of Nepal, for instance, literacy, the domain of men, is structurally opposed to weaving, which is women's work. Women weave because woven products signify exchange and mobility, which also characterize women in this patrilineal society that practices cross-cousin marriage, while men are associated with a fixity and permanence that resembles that of the Buddhist texts they read (Marsh 1983).

As the case of the Tamang suggests, the relationship between literacy and gender can exhibit considerable complexity. Thus gender is not relevant to literacy just because women in many societies read and write less than men. First, literacy skills and activities can be distributed in many different ways across gender lines. A particularly striking case is that of insular Southeast

Asia in the sixteenth and seventeenth centuries. In Sumatra, Java, the Philippines, and surrounding areas, the use of dēvanāgari-derived scripts was widespread, and was either equally distributed between women and men or primarily women's specialty (Reid 1988:215–25). Ironically, the growing Western colonial presence in the area contributed to both the decline of overall literacy rates and the redefinition of reading and writing as men's tasks. Similarly, in the rural Appalachian community that Puckett (1992) describes, women read and write considerably more than men do. However, when women act as the literacy brokers for the community, ideological constructs are frequently in place that devalue women's literacy practices or otherwise constrain their prestige: for example, in rural Appalachia, a woman has to walk a tightrope between presenting herself as a "proper" literate woman and not coming across as someone who "thinks she's better than we are" (Puckett 1992:143).

Second, in many contexts where the distribution of literacy across genders appears skewed at first glance, certain forms of literacy frequently emerge as tools of more or less covert resistance to gender-based hegemonic structures. As is typical of subversive action, these literacy practices frequently fail to attract the attention of those in power (as well as the attention of peripheral observers), or else are dismissed as inconsequential. Romance reading in Middle America (Radway 1991), which I describe in Chapter 1, is an example of such "invisible" subversive practices. Further examples are women's friendship letters in nineteenth-century America (Smith-Rosenberg 1975), the exchange of letters and poems between seventeenth-century Chinese women (Ko 1989), and many others (e.g., Long 1992, Quilligan 1991). Third, received characterizations of the distribution of literacy skills in many societies frequently fail to distinguish between the practice of everyday life and ideological evaluations of what counts as "worthwhile"or "true" literacy and what does not. Rockhill's (1987) ethnographic inquiry into the literacy practices of Hispanic women and men in Southern California is a revealing illustration of the care that one should exert in drawing conclusions about the gender-based distribution of literacy. In the Hispanic immigrant community that Rockhill focuses on, men view women as illiterate, poorly educated, and of inferior intelligence. Upon closer observation, women turn out to control many literacy tasks in the household, and to engage in reading and writing on a regular basis. However, because the contexts in which women read and write are part of the domestic sphere, which men devalue, women's literacy practices lack legitimacy in the eyes of men. One is thus driven to examine closely the ideological foundations of gender hierarchy in order to arrive at an adequate description of how literacy is distributed across gender boundaries. Stating that women in that society are illiterate while men are literate grossly oversimplifies the picture.

In the case of Nukulaelae, how literacy and gender interact is a complex question. As I discussed in Chapter 3, both women and men today have equal access to literacy instruction and to schooling in general. Until the 1970s, boys had greater access to secondary schooling than girls, but the impact of this inequality was somewhat mitigated by the fact that very few children, male or female, received secondary schooling anyway. As in many Western contexts, contemporary Nukulaelae girls perform better academically than boys, and their greater academic success has obliterated any repercussions that women's historical disadvantage might have had. As a result, there are no differences between men's and women's basic literacy skills. This fundamental equality is best reflected in letter-writing practices: as shown in Chapter 4, women and men send and receive letters with the same frequency (although younger women have a slight tendency to be keener letter writers than other segments of the community).

Yet a gender imbalance emerges when one investigates the semiotic associations of various literacy practices in greater depth. First, as I noted in Chapter 6, women deliver religious sermons (although much more rarely than men), but they do not normally compose their sermons in writing; instead, they generally call upon a male relative or friend to prepare their written sermons. In Chapter 7, I demonstrated that these practices must be understood in the context of the semiotic and social significance of written sermons. These documents are viewed as being in a privileged position with respect to the truth, and they implicitly make a strong claim of authority to assert and display this privileged position. In secular contexts, women can assert their authority, but the scope of this authority is limited by both concrete and metaphorical boundaries. Thus women engage in the oral performance of sermons, because the claims to authority embedded in these performances are ritually bracketed, but they do not compose sermons, because the composing process implies a much more serious claim to authority.

However, when placed in the context of the society's general authority structure, the exclusion of women from sermon-composing activities is less significant than other forms of gendering. It is indeed useful to compare religious sermons with political speeches, which I described briefly in Chapter 6. There are several ways in which the latter constitute a much more effective form of gendered dominance. While the delivery style in secular oratory is much more subdued than the blatant displays of authority that characterize sermonic performances, a much broader range of themes can be brought up in secular oratory than in sermons, and speeches are overall more frequent and less bracketed events than sermons. Thus the authority that can be exerted through speeches is potentially more consequential than that which can be exerted in sermons, and every time a man makes a political speech, the rest of the community is subtly reminded of the fact that only a subset of the community is entitled to make speeches, and in particular that women are for the most part excluded from engaging in oratorical performances.

Literacy is gendered in yet another way. In Chapter 5, I discussed that certain emotions, such as *alofa* "empathy," are particularly centralized in the letters that Nukulaelae people read and write. These emotions, as well as their presentation in letters and the emotional context of letter reading, all share a common feature: they highlight the vulnerability of the person who undergoes these emotional experiences. What I translate here as "vulnerability" is what Nukulaelae Islanders call *vaaivai*, which in its strictest sense means "weak(ness)." The term *vaaivai* is commonly contrasted with *maalosi* "strong, healthy, able-bodied" (cf. Mageo 1988 for comparative data on Samoa), but, when emotions are involved, a more appropriate antonym is *makeke* "hard." People are *vaaivai* when they lose control over their emotions, or when emotional experiences and social circumstances make them lose their composure. A typical context would be parting with a loved one; in all the excerpts of letters discussed in Chapter 5 in which writers allude to farewells, vulnerability is a major theme. *Vaaivai* can also characterize categories of persons: one becomes *vaaivai* when one gets elderly because the body weakens, but also because one tends to lose self-control more often (in fact, the most idiomatic way of stating that someone is old is to describe the person as *vaaivai*). Crucially, women are "by nature" more *vaaivai* than men: they break down more easily than men, they are more prone to being overpowered by emotional experiences, and they experience emotions associated with vulnerability, particularly *alofa*, more often and more powerfully. It is important to note that the polarization of women and men with respect to vulnerability is not a pretext for the devaluation of women's experiences. Nukulaelae Islanders do not universally place greater value on composure than on vulnerability for either men or women. Rather, they have a somewhat romantic attitude towards vulnerability, particularly when the context is appropriate, as in letters or during farewells, for example.

It is through these associative linkages that letter writing is gendered: letters centralize emotions and ways of experiencing emotions that are symptoms of vulnerability, and vulnerability in turn is a trait to which women have privileged access. These associations are of an indexical nature, and they therefore leave a lot of room for alternative readings of the mapping between literacy and gender. In particular, men can experience emotional vulnerability (the letter excerpts that thematize vulnerability in farewells cited in Chapter 5 all refer to men). It is true that a man who consistently foregrounds emotional vulnerability (in letters and elsewhere) will be viewed as lacking "manliness," as blurring gender signs in a way that exposes him to being labelled as a *pinapinaaine* "gender-liminal person" (cf.

Besnier 1994a). However, in Nukulaelae society, as elsewhere in Polynesia (e.g., Shore 1981), gender is like any other aspect of personhood, i.e., one facet of a multi-faceted entity. According to such understandings of personhood, both women and men can foreground or background signs of femaleness or maleness in certain cases. A striking example emerges in Samoan society, where high-ranking chiefs assume in certain ceremonial situations the sitting position of a woman, with one leg astride his opposite thigh in contrast to the normatively male tailor-fashion cross-legged posture (Milner 1968). Gendered emotions are no different from other gendered signs: men and women can foreground either woman-like or man-like emotions in appropriate contexts. There are of course normative restrictions: men are expected to foreground masculine traits more often and more consistently than women, and vice versa. Certain contexts may also restrict the amount of variation; such is the case of formal political meetings, in which men are expected to behave like men, as it were, under most circumstances. Where these boundaries reside is subject to variation and contestation between individuals and across social contexts. Letter reading and writing (as well as farewells) happen to be contexts in which men can safely "venture" far into the emotional territory primarily associated with women.

My analysis of the complex relationship between gender and literacy on Nukulaelae has several implications of theoretical and methodological import. First, it demonstrates the potential complexity of the role that gender plays in defining literacy. This role is located in semiotic forms, rather than in the absolute distribution of such processes as access to literacy. In fact, written communication is not the only sociocultural phenomenon with which gender is intermeshed in a very complex manner. As feminist anthropologists have convincingly demonstrated (e.g., di Leonardo 1991b, Meigs 1990, Morgen 1989), simplicity in social-scientific accounts of the meaning of gender is invariably suspect. Second, gender does not play any identifiable role in the meaning of Nukulaelae literacy per se, but it contributes to the definition of *specific literacy practices*. Thus the relationship between gender and literacy can only be made sense of through a practice-oriented approach. Third, gender and literacy practices are not in a simple symbolic relationship. Rather, the link between them is indexical (and hence potentially polysemic and ambiguous), and it is mediated by gendered situations, institutions, ideologies, and roles. As such, the role that gender plays in giving meaning to literacy is no different from the role that it plays in all other forms of verbal communication (Eckert and McConnell-Ginet 1992, Gal 1991, Ochs 1987, 1992, Sherzer 1987). Finally, gender and literacy practices do not map onto one another in a rigid fashion. Rather, the indexical nature of the mapping opens the possibility for leakages, as when men are "allowed" to take on "woman-like" social traits, as they do in letters, and for some contestation, as when women appropriate some (but not all) of the authority embedded in written sermons in sermonic performances.

Literacy and personhood

Returning to Gewertz and Errington's (1991) examination of literacy among the Chambri, the most fascinating testimony of the Chambri appropriation of literacy is the story of Godfried Kolly, one of Gewertz' research assistants during her first sojourn in Chambri. When they returned to Chambri for additional field research, Gewertz and Errington employed Godfried again, but the social status he had now gained demanded that he be given greater responsibility and autonomy. Accordingly, Godfried set out to write his autobiography. However, the project soon turned into his compiling a "Chambri Bible," i.e., a compilation of knowledge of importance to the Chambri, which would be identical to and on par with the Christian Bible, and through which the Chambri could represent their culture to themselves and the outside world. In the project, Godfried sought to reconcile conflicting accounts of Chambri history, and in particular the epistemological discrepancies between Catholic truth and truth as defined by *kastom*. Because the power associated with traditional knowledge diminishes when it is transmitted from one generation to the other, the Chambri approved of Godfried's project, in which they saw a way of arresting gradual amnesia. However, Godfried's project soon ran aground, as Chambri big men refused to provide him the ancestral stories he needed for inclusion in his Bible. Had they allowed Godfried to compile his canon, he would have become the most powerful Chambri to have ever existed, and "such a person would be intolerable since he would transcend and thus subvert the system of commensurate differences" (Gewertz and Errington 1991:166).

What is particularly revealing in Godfried's story is that the role which literacy plays in it is subordinated to local power dynamics and local conceptions of knowledge and personhood. How this is so becomes clear when one attempts to reframe the story in a Nukulaelae context. There are both compelling parallels and notable differences between the underpinnings of Godfried's actions and Nukulaelae Islanders' view of literacy and its relationship to truth and authority. First, as discussed in Chapter 7, Nukulaelae people frequently express the view that, had their ancestors bothered or been able to write down history as it was "going on," their knowledge of this history would now be less fragmented and more *kaatoatoa* "whole, complete." While the content of what is remembered or forgotten is a little different in the Chambri case, the relationship between literacy and memory is the same. However, in both cases, the purported anti-amnesiac power of writing remains an ideological construct, because powerful social forces prevent agents from translating it into practice. On Nukulaelae, very few people ever attempt to inscribe history or other types of knowledge for a public audience. When islanders compile *api logo* "notebooks of traditional skills" (see Chapter 3), the resulting product is carefully hidden from others. The few brave souls who have had the audacity to attempt to inscribe history (e.g., contributors to Laracy, ed., 1983, and Western historians and ethnographers including myself) expose themselves to constant criticism. Their accounts, in particular, can never pass the test of "completeness" (partly because the inscribers fail entitlement criteria), and hence never be true (cf. Chapter 7). For both Nukulaelae Islanders and the Chambri, literacy is thus Janus-faced: it has knowledge-preserving powers, but it cannot be used to preserve knowledge, particularly important knowledge. What is important is that neither characteristic is more important than the other in the definition of literacy for these two societies.

There is at least one major difference between the way in which Nukulaelae Islanders and the Chambri position themselves *vis-à-vis* literacy: had Godfried been a Nukulaelae Islander, it is very difficult to imagine how he would ever have attempted to compile his Bible. Leaving aside the fact that Nukulaelae people would consider the project sacrilegious, to assume single-handedly the role of cultural scribe presumes that individuals can claim the authority and display this authority in ways that would be unthinkable on Nukulaelae. In other words, the attempted project presumes the possibility of an entrepreneurial spirit which is intimately tied to a socially and politically constructed view of the person that is quintessential Chambri, and which also finds echoes in other Papua New Guinea societies (e.g., Kulick 1992:92–117). This spirit would be out of place, to say the least, in a Polynesian atoll society like Nukulaelae. Convergent patterns emerge when one compares other ways in which literacy has acquired different meanings for the Chambri and for Nukulaelae Islanders. As mentioned earlier, Gewertz and Errington are often asked to type up documents for the Chambri. Like them, I am also asked often to type up documents in the field. In 1990 and 1991, I took a solar-powered lap-top computer to the field, which further increased the prestige of documents I was asked to copy or compose. (Rumor had it that my computer could *fakasao maafaufauga* "correct [one's] thought.") However, Nukulaelae Islanders are more modest in their ambitions than the Chambri: they confine their requests to job applications, letters to the People's Lawyer on Funafuti, and sermons. Requesting a medal from the Queen of England and pushing forth letters of recommendation praising one's achievements and qualities would be considered acts of extraordinary *mata mua* "assertiveness" (literally, "forward-faced"). The contrast between the scopes of Chambri and Nukulaelae ambitions is in part a reflection of the differences between the two groups' familiarity with Western ways; but it also results, and I would say fundamentally so, from very different ways of constructing personhood.

The importance that personhood takes on in the local construction of the meaning of literacy in Chambri and on Nukulaelae (see also Chapters 5 and 7 for further examples of the latter) is not a fortuitous coincidence. I propose that, in all social groups, personhood as a sociocultural category plays a particularly important role in the process of giving literacy a specific meaning. This meaning piggy-backs, as it were, on local definitions of personhood, which itself is closely tied to political and economic processes. However, personhood is never a simple construct: it is often subjected to conflicting forces, and may be defined differently for different social contexts. For example, I argued in Chapter 7 that religious ceremonies on Nukulaelae foreground a very specific definition of personhood, which differs from definitions relevant to other social contexts, and which dictate what Nukulaelae Islanders put down on paper in written sermons (see also Kulick and Stroud 1990 for another example of how the complexities of personhood give rise to similar complexities in the practice of literacy).

In this work, I have attempted to clear a path toward explanatory generalizations within an ideological model of literacy. I have identified ways in which literacy and its context can be intertwined, and have singled out aspects of social life and culture that may be particularly prone to "interface" with literacy practices, i.e., to give meaning to these practices and acquire meaning from them. I singled out processes of inequality and equality, and in particular gender hierarchies, as well as personhood and the closely related area of affectivity, among the sociocultural categories that are particularly relevant in characterizing the social value of literacy in the specific ethnographic context I focused on. In the foregoing discussion, I used comparative material from other contexts to demonstrate that the privileged relationship between literacy and these other categories is not particular to Nukulaelae.

The generalizations that the ideological approach to literacy seeks are different in nature from the types of generalizations that proponents of more traditional models of literacy have typically proposed. Ideological generalizations can be described as "systemic": the model explores how literacy interacts with social categories and communicative processes, and how changes from pre-literacy to literacy go hand-in-hand with changing social dynamics. At the same time, these generalizations open the door for a rich understanding of the relationship between norm and practice, between structure and agency, and between group and individual.

NOTES

Transcription conventions and orthography

1 The following abbreviations appear in the word-by-word interlinear glosses: *Anp* "anaphora," *Cmp* "complementizer," *Cnt* "contrastive," *Dxs* "deictic," *Erg* "ergative," *Foc* "focus," *Fut* "future," *Itj* "interjection," *Neg* "negative," *Nps* "non-past," *Sbj* "subjunctive," *i* "inclusive," *3* "plural," and + "morpheme boundary."

1 Introduction

1 The model is sometimes called the Cognitive Divide model (Frake 1983), the Strong-Text model (D. Brandt 1990:13–32), or the Great Divide model, although scholars like Goody protest vehemently against being associated with these designations. The term "autonomous" refers to the view that literacy itself has the power to bring about fundamental changes in societies, cultures, and persons. It also echoes the notion that written communication, unlike oral communication, has an existence independently of its context of production and consumption. Variants of the same model have been developed also, at various times and more or less independently of Goody's work, in the writings of many thinkers outside of anthropology (e.g., Illich 1991, Illich and Sanders 1988, Innis 1972, Ong 1967, 1971, 1977, 1982). Particularly conspicuous among these scholars are members of the Toronto School, which, following the lead of McLuhan (1962) and Havelock (1963, 1976, 1982, 1986), is best represented today in the writings of educational psychologist David Olson (1977, 1984, 1986, 1991, Olson and Torrance 1981; see Halverson 1991 for a critical overview of Olson's work).

2 Scholars have traditionally distinguished between three major kinds of writing systems: *logographic* systems, in which each symbol represents a word; *syllabic* systems, in which symbols refer to syllables; and *alphabetic* systems, in which symbols refer to contrastive sound units, or phonemes. Orthodox models maintain that these types represent three stages in a purported evolutionary scheme. Recent scholarship has demonstrated the artificiality of these proto-types and the problems associated with their evolutionary ordering (cf. Coulmas 1989, R. Harris 1986, and Sampson 1985 for detailed treatments, and Street and Besnier 1994:528–32 for a succinct overview).

3 There are striking parallels in the roles that anthropologists have traditionally

188

assigned to literacy and to money. "Regardless of cultural context and of the nature of existing relations of production and exchange," write Bloch and Parry (1989) about the latter, "it is often credited with an *intrinsic* power to revolutionise society and culture, and it is sometimes assumed that this power will be recognised in the way in which the actors themselves construct money symbolically" (1989:3, emphasis in original). The word "literacy" could easily substitute "money" in this statement.

4 The term "ideological" refers to the view that reading and writing as communicative activities are particularly tied to ideological processes that give them social meaning. Problems with this label arise when one considers the diversity of meanings that have been attached to the term "ideology" (Eagleton 1991, Thompson 1984, 1990:28–73, Wuthnow 1987:145–85). My use of this designation is an expedient compromise; in a sense, my purpose here can be taken to be attempt to clarify the meaning of "ideology" in the particular ethnographic context I focus on.

5 Reed-Danahay's (1995) careful critique of Bourdieu's (1977) celebrated North African research demonstrates that Bourdieu sets up Kabylia as the prototype of a pre-literate and unschooled society. Yet he never mentions the colonial schools and barely alludes to the Qur'anic schools that were well established in Kabylia at the time of his field work.

6 Some writers have argued that the presence or absence of *print* literacy determines whether a society is "truly" literate or not. This hypothesis is most clearly articulated in Eisenstein's writings (1969, 1979, 1981, 1983), and is also found in a slightly different form in Anderson (1991). However, it is vulnerable to the same criticisms as the traditional versions of the autonomous model (see, e.g., J. Parry 1989), and the problems I outline here in reference to the autonomous model can easily be shown to apply to this hypothesis as well.

7 This concept is inspired from the notion of "speech event" developed in the Ethnography of Communication tradition (Hymes 1974, also Duranti 1985, 1988). It should be noted that this tradition of inquiry has been criticized for its lack of attention to political dimensions of communication (e.g., Grillo, Pratt, and Street 1987). My endorsement of "literacy event" as a useful analytic unit does not preclude a critical analysis of communicative acts, which on the contrary I want to foreground in this work.

8 Some readers have reproached Heath for what they view as her lack of a critical perspective on the systems of educational reproduction that filter out Roadville and Trackton children (DeCastell and Walker 1991, Rosen 1985, see also Heath 1993). In *Ways With Words*, Heath's purpose is to show that children from traditionally disadvantaged groups are exposed to rich learning experiences at home (but see Heath 1990 for a follow-up with a different conclusion). However, her critics saw in the book yet another indictment of home learning among disenfranchised groups as "deficient," citing as evidence the unfortunate preponderance of negatively worded characterizations of Trackton and Roadville communicative practices (which my own summary reflects), in contrast to the preponderance of positive illustrations when dealing with Maintown. For a poised evaluation of the strengths and limitations of the theoretical stance represented in Heath's work, see Erickson (1987).

9 Sociolinguistic investigations of literacy to date have also suffered from the virtual lack of a cross-cultural and cross-social perspective, being largely based on the speaking and writing activities of Western middle-class academic élites. This has led researchers to confuse cognitive behavior and sociocultural norms that have become, in the process of a long sociohistorical evolution, "naturalized," i.e., made to appear as if they were the only valid way to communicate through the medium of literacy. For example, Biber's (1988) widely quoted study analyzes large computerized textual data-bases that are commonly referred to as "standardized corpora." These corpora are made up of such texts as transcripts of conversations and lectures in academic settings, excerpts from novels and magazine articles, and so on. However, Biber (and the many other users of these materials) never pauses to consider how these data "fit" in the context of the full range of the spoken and written output of the society which these data purport to represent, and does not attend to the social and political implications of analyzing these corpora as "standardized."(While the corpora were initially conceived as widely available data-bases with which theories could be confirmed or falsified, they have come to be taken as "standards" in a broader sense, i.e., as prescriptive references on language use; for example, they have been used as prototypes against which scholastic and non-native writing can be compared for stylistic and grammatical sophistication.) To declare that a body of text is standardized is an example of naturalization, even when it is based on empirical observations. As many social theorists have demonstrated (e.g., Bourdieu and Passeron 1977, Bowles and Gintis 1976, Giroux 1981, Willis 1977), naturalization is used to control access to such institutions as schooling, and is thus pivotal in the maintenance of sociocultural hegemony.

10 Throughout this study, while I strive to discuss the oral contexts in which literacy practices are embedded, space considerations preclude a *detailed* investigation of the larger communicative system extant in the community I focus on. I have chosen to focus primarily on literacy practices, and give priority to discussions and examples of reading and writing, sometimes at the expense of a more thorough treatment of language use in general, which must await another study.

2 The ethnographic context

1 Sixty Nukulaelae Islanders were enumerated on Funafuti in the 1979 census (Iosia and Macrae, eds., 1980:205). The 1991 census (Kaitu, Balkaran, and Telupe, eds., 1992) notes a 23 percent increase in the country's total population to 9043, but Nukulaelae's population remained stable at 353. This census enumerated 71 Nukulaelae Islanders on Funafuti, although this figure only includes individuals of at least 15 years of age. The importance of this off-island subcommunity for an understanding of Nukulaelae literacy practices will be demonstrated in Chapter 4.

2 Workers from Japan and China were also imported to Ocean Island (between 1908 and 1918 and after 1921 respectively), while Chinese laborers comprised the largest group of immigrants on Nauru until the late 1940s. On both islands,

East Asian recruits were eventually replaced by recruits from the Gilbert and Ellice Islands Colony, which became the mainstay of the phosphate work force after World War II. For a detailed history of the Ocean Island and Nauru phosphate industry and its labor practices, see Williams and Macdonald (1985) and Shlomowitz and Munro (1992).

3   What I translate here as "chief" is in fact any of several terms, some of which are used as synonyms while others characterize particular historical periods. The term *aliki*, a cognate of words in other Polynesian languages that are usually translated as "chief," appears to have been the original designator for the chiefly role; but a borrowing from Samoan, *tupu*, commonly rendered in English as "king" (although the felicity of the gloss is debatable), is also used retroactively to refer to the chief of pre-Christian days. Nineteenth-century Western visitors commonly used the English term "king" in their accounts of Nukulaelae social structure, which allowed them to deride the anachronism of a "king" ruling over a few dozen subjects (e.g., David 1899:280–91). Today, the terms *ulu fenua* "head of the atoll community" and, less frequently, *ulu aliki* "head chief" are in common usage. Of course, whether or not one is dealing with a chiefly institution in the strict sense of the term is an open question.

4   The conflict between authoritarian hierarchy and a communal, egalitarian, and anti-individualistic ethos is certainly not unique to Nukulaelae in the region, in that it characterizes probably all Polynesian political systems (Marcus 1989). Indeed, behind-the-scenes political action by the less powerful can have a great deal of influence on decision-making even in the most hierarchy-conscious Polynesian societies such as Tikopia (R. Firth 1964) and Samoa (e.g., Shore 1991). Where Nukulaelae differs from better documented cases in the region is the extent to which the discourse of egalitarianism can gnaw at the very base of the authoritarian edifice, because Nukulaelae lacks a built-in system of political inequality based on the inheritance of chiefly prerogatives and the complex system of entitlement one finds in a society like Samoa. On Nukulaelae, authoritarian action and the exercise of power lack a solid foundation, which, even if it existed prior to contact, has been thoroughly undermined by the tormented history of the atoll since the mid-nineteenth century.

5   At first blush, these patterns appear to be instances of what is frequently referred to as "symbolic domination" (Bourdieu 1984) or "cultural hegemony" (Gramsci 1971), whereby subordinated groups consent to the hegemonic structuring of society, which they view as ultimately beneficial to their interests despite all evidence to the contrary (see Scott 1990:85–96 and Thompson 1990:85–97 for critical summaries). It is true that coercive practices scapegoat women and younger men, since they are responsible for the harder and dirtier work. However, there is no clearly identifiable hegemonic entity in the community. For example, it is usually women themselves who place demands on women (as in the underwear example cited here). Furthermore, there is a high turn-over rate in positions of authority (e.g., the chieftainship), which makes it impossible to point to a particular person or group as the beneficiaries of hegemonic structures. Thus symbolic domination and its near synonyms are not very useful in explaining Nukulaelae authoritarianism.

6   As Sahlins (1957) notes, such radical restructuring of all aspects of social and

economic life are not uncommon on atolls of Polynesia, which are vulnerable to dramatic population changes because of their small size and exposure to the elements. In Nukulaelae's case, restructuring was of course not solely a consequence of climatic and ecological vulnerability.

7 Elekana's drift voyage was probably not as extraordinary an event as the religious literature of the time makes it out to be. Today, unexpected bad weather blows off course at least one canoe or dinghy every year from the Tuvalu Group; in many but not all cases, these craft are found before they get too far on the open sea. In some cases, however, they drift away, and only a few lucky drifters reach land many hundreds of miles away, in the Solomon Islands or Wallis and Futuna, for example. Setting off alone in a canoe is a favorite way to commit suicide, and it was one method that atoll communities employed to deal with adulterers, murderers, and other trouble-makers in former, but not too distant, times (cf. G. Turner 1876:4–5).

8 Eventually, Tuvaluans would join the ranks of Pacific Island missionaries for the LMS in Papua New Guinea and the Torres Straits Islands (Wetherell 1980, 1993).

9 The missionaries' complete lack of interest in and attention to inter-island differences is nicely summarized in the following comment that a missionary made in his report of a visit to Funafuti:

> I need not remark particularly on the appearance, manners, customs, &c., of the natives, seeing that they are Samoans, and that in all essential respects they are one with the people from whom they are descended. Long separation from their fatherland has led to some slight diversity in language, manners, dress, and some other things.
>
> (Murray 1865:340)

There were clear practical advantages in emphasizing cultural and linguistic similarities over differences. Among other things, it saved the cost and effort of translating the Scriptures into another language, a fact that some attributed to divine providence:

> Again, the *quarter whence God is causing the light of life to shine forth upon these islands* is worthy of notice. Samoa . . . is the fatherland. Hence there is a common language, not to mention minor advantages. The Gospel can be intelligibly preached at once, while our books and translations are ready to put into their hands. An immense advantage this, which it would not be easy to over-estimate.
>
> (Murray 1865:344, emphasis in original)

Indeed, money was very much in the foreground of LMS missionaries' thinking, as witnessed by the journals they wrote, some of which (e.g., G. Turner 1861) read like veritable account books, replete with detailed tallies of expenses, donations, and saved souls.

10 The condescending attitudes of British LMS missionaries towards their Samoan trainees is particularly strident in the journals that some published. Witness George Turner, the founder of the mission school at Mālua:

> People in England hearing of a *native teacher and preacher*, are apt to think of an *educated* man, fully qualified for the work which his name indicates; but such is by no means always the case. . . . Take, for example, the teachers in the district where I commenced my labours in Samoa: if I asked them to write down on a slate *fifteen*, three-fourths of them would write X5, or perhaps 105. That, too, is a fair specimen of what they were in Bible

knowledge. At that early stage, also, it is common to find out that the strangest errors have been made, and propagated as Scripture truth. I discovered one day that some of the teachers had been preaching up and down the district, giving poor Nebuchadnezzar a tail, snout, and hoof, and declaring that he had been actually changed into a *real* four-footed beast!

(1861:121, emphasis in original)

11 Only two resident European missionaries spent any time in Tuvalu before modern times. An English missionary, Henry Bond James, was the principal of Motufoua School on Vaitupu between 1912 and 1917. In 1912, another English missionary, Sarah Jolliffe, who had spent time in Samoa, established a girls' school, Papa Elise, on an islet of Funafuti, where she stayed until 1920 (Garrett 1992:217–19).

12 I borrow the term "liminality" from V. Turner's (1967, 1969, also 1992) elaboration on a concept originally theorized by van Gennep (1909). Liminal events and persons have three distinguishing characteristics: they are located "betwixt and between"; they have the status of outsiders; and they are socially inferior. In addition, liminality has a special affinity to performance and rituals of reversal. Of these characteristics, only one does not apply uncontroversially to the pastor on Nukulaelae, namely social inferiority. But the other characteristics capture the essence of his status rather nicely, as I will further elaborate in Chapters 6 and 7.

13 Rose's vilification by the missionaries should be taken with a grain of salt (Goldsmith 1989a:132, Goldsmith and Munro 1992a:33). Similar allegations were made against the trader Jack O'Brien on Funafuti, the next island to be visited by the slavers, and here again the evidence is open to controversy (Munro 1982:69–71).

14 The tragic discontinuities consequent to this event may explain why contemporary Nukulaelae Islanders' genealogical records stop abruptly with individuals who were alive in the mid-nineteenth century, in contrast to the minute details with which genealogies from that time on are remembered (these genealogies often are the topic of disagreement and contention, but they are nevertheless very detailed). However, the memory void prior to the mid-nineteenth century may have other explanations. For example, it is possible that Nukulaelae Islanders only became concerned about genealogical records under the influence of the Samoan pastors (genealogies have always been a favorite Samoan obsession). It is also possible that the written genealogies that Nukulaelae people began to keep after the introduction of literacy provided a useful mnemonic tool. Needless to say, literacy itself did not create a sudden interest in keeping genealogical records, nor did it eliminate the possibility of conflicting accounts.

15 Population exchanges between Nukulaelae and the rest of the world were not unidirectional. Very early after contact, islanders probably went to work on plantations in Queensland and Fiji and became sailors on Western ships, as mentioned earlier. No documentation exists on labor out-migrations from Nukulaelae specifically, but in the late nineteenth century twenty-five Tuvaluans were reported to be working in Queensland and "a few" in Fiji (Munro 1982:271). Labor recruitment never became a major force in Tuvalu as it did in

many other parts of the Pacific, because the LMS and later British colonial authorities strongly discouraged it. Nevertheless, recruitment must have made an impact on the very small atoll populations, even if the numbers recruited were tiny.

16 It is important not to equate secondary school literacy with a reified notion of "Tuvaluan" literacy, as Vetter (1991) appears to do unproblematically.

3 The domains of reading and writing

1 One important question is how the Nukulaelae dialect managed to survive after the Peruvian slave raid in 1863, which depleted the population so severely. Unfortunately, no information whatsoever is available that could shed a glimmer of understanding on this matter.

2 In contrast, the disappearance of Gilbertese will be slower on Funafuti, because many people formerly in the employ of the colonial administration in Tarawa now form a bureaucratic élite in Tuvalu's capital. They and their children are typically fluent in Gilbertese, particularly if a Gilbertese spouse is part of the picture (a not uncommon situation among post-Separation returnees from Tarawa), and still keep the language alive. One should also not forget that a dialect of Gilbertese is the first language of the inhabitants of Nui atoll, where it does not appear to be giving way to Tuvaluan. Its status as the mother tongue of part of Tuvalu's population keeps it in the foreground as a lively auxiliary language in the capital of the country.

3 A number of these borrowings form doublets with native words, some of which have been coined recently, and to which the borrowings have often lost ground. Thus one finds both *vii* "song of praise" and *viki* "to praise," *aaoga* and *aakoga* "schooling, school-related," *apa* and *kaapa* "tin can, corrugated iron," *faamasino* "judge" and *fakamasino* "to judge," and *fua* and *fuka* "flag."

4 Elekana reports that the first three letters he taught two Nukulaelae boys upon first arrival were "k," "u," and "a," "the three together 'kua'. They asked for another word. That, I said, is 'm', that 'a', that 'i', that 'r', and that 'a' – the five 'maira' " (Elekana 1872:148). These phonemes indicate that the language he was teaching them was a dialect of Cook Island Maori, most likely Rarotongan, the written language used throughout the Cook Islands at the time.

5 For example, as early as 1866, "The Sabbath-school was in keeping with other things. There were thirty children present – *all on the island who were of an age to attend*" (Murray 1876:401, emphasis added).

6 There is no clear historical evidence of gender-based differences in access to primary schooling and basic literacy. Missionary reports that specify the number of girls and boys receiving instruction in the Samoan pastors' school suggest a numerical balance between the two genders. Nor was literacy ever unequivocally associated with personal status. In fact, the scanty evidence suggests the opposite: recall from the last chapter that the chief who signed the deed of cession to Britain did so with a cross, in contrast to four of the five magistrates, who signed their full names.

7 A girls' school, Papa Elise, operated on Funafuti from 1912 until 1920. Before 1912 and after 1920, girls had to go to Samoa for secondary schooling, and the

expenses involved severely restricted their access to education. So for many decades there was gender-based discrimination in relative access to secondary schooling, in contrast to primary schooling, although one must also bear in mind, however, that very few boys attended secondary school. Since Motufoua became coeducational in 1970, the gendering of secondary education has disappeared, and today more girls than boys are generally admitted to the school. For a concise but informative discussion of this and other issues relating to the history of schooling in Tuvalu, see Sapoaga (1983).

8 These figures are probably distorted by the fact that many Nukulaelae Islanders who have attended secondary school have salary-earning jobs, and hence live on Funafuti or elsewhere. No separate figures for the educational standards of the Nukulaelae community on Funafuti are available.

9 Murray (1876:382) would later state that Nukulaelae people carried with them these pages when the blackbirders persuaded them to board their ships.

10 One detail casts serious doubt on LMS reports of the rapidity and thoroughness with which Nukulaelae Islanders learned literacy: two of six signatories of the Treaty of Cession to Britain, including the chief, were obviously unable to write in 1892, since they had to sign their names with a cross (compare McKenzie 1985:32–5 on Maori literacy and the Treaty of Waitangi).

11 The proverbial Samoan preoccupation with decorum and expertise in performances of all kinds (Shore 1982) must have come in very handy in such contexts. On Nukulaelae today, there are regular occasions when the community displays itself, as it were, through performances for visiting dignitaries. During preparations for such occasions, which can last more than a year in some cases, older men frequently exhort, cajole, and threaten *ad nauseam* the rest of the community to put on a good performance. These exhortations are very likely to be the direct descendants of what the Nukulaelae community must have been subjected to in the early days of Samoan pastors.

12 Nineteenth-century travelers frequently mistransliterated place names in the Pacific, and the maps they drew helped perpetrate these mistransliterations. Such is the case of the forms "Nukulailai" in the following quote (also "Nukuleilei" and "Nukurairai"), the result of English-speaking travelers' inability to identify a mid-high vowel [e] following a low vowel [a]. Unfortunately, the result means "dirty home-island" in Tuvaluan, and Nukulaelae Islanders are not fond of it. The fact that even colonial officials made these mistakes is revealing of their attitudes towards the communities whose interests they claimed to look after.

13 The origin of this convention can probably be traced back to the practice of sending written invitations to formal governmental receptions, which some Nukulaelae adults probably witnessed while in the employ of the colonial and later national administrations on Ocean Island, Tarawa, and Funafuti.

4 Letter writing and reading

1 The writer was the adolescent daughter of a Funafuti woman and of a European trader, which explains why her family had the means to send her to Samoa to get an education. The original of this letter has not survived, although the Funafuti

File of the Edgeworth David papers in the Mitchell Library, Sydney, contain several of Vitolia's letters in Samoan to Mrs. David, all of which are in the same tone.

2 Why my offer was taken up may have implications for how Nukulaelae people viewed the transaction, or it may suggest that the saving of letters is not as significant an act as it seems on the surface. I do not have any clear explanation for it.

3 I do not wish to assert that letters addressed to me are entirely indistinguishable from letters addressed to Nukulaelae Islanders, since my position in the economic structure of Nukulaelae society, among others, is radically different from that of members of the community. (As I will show presently, letter writing and exchange are intimately related.) However, it would be a mistake to assert that letters addressed to me represent a completely different genre from other letters. A study of the letters I have received over the years would constitute a very interesting piece of reflexive ethnography, but it is unfortunately beyond the scope of this book.

4 In 1981–2, a sea-plane service was in operation between Nukulaelae and Funafuti, but the experiment, which was funded by foreign aid, was too costly and was discontinued. Nukulaelae's small population and the fact that few people can afford the fare means that passenger volume for such a service is very restricted.

5 Through the analysis of a corpus of English-language letters and postcards exchanged sequentially by people involved in a correspondence network (in an unspecified speech community), DeRycker (1991) demonstrates that letter writing is subject to a turn-taking organization comparable to informal conversation (cf. Sacks, Jefferson, and Schegloff 1974), and that it should be studied as such. While the point is well taken, the difficulties associated with collecting a sequence of Nukulaelae letters and following up on the methodological suggestion are unsurmountable. Furthermore, the assertion that letter writing is sequentially organized assumes the availability of a reliable, regular, and easily accessible message-conveying infrastructure, which is not the case here. It is not clear that Nukulaelae people perceive sequential organization as a basic property of letter-writing activities. What seems to be more basic for them is the uncertainty and unreliability of the medium.

6 On the occasion of one of my departures from the atoll, a middle-aged Nukulaelae woman entrusted me a letter to be delivered on Funafuti on my way out of the country. When she proceeded to spell out the oral message to be delivered along with the letter, I committed the *faux-pas* of responding that the addressee would know from reading the letter the nature of the message, hoping to free myself of the responsibility of yet another message to remember. The writer was clearly puzzled and slightly annoyed at this response, and simply went on to repeat the message again, explaining that I had to make sure that it was clear (*manino*) to the recipient.

7 These patterns, particularly the dramatic skewing in the number of younger women recipients, is probably in part due to the way my sample was collected. Younger women were much less likely to feel *maa* "ashamed" to bring me their letters than younger men, and younger people than older people (although I did

obtain substantial numbers of letters from older people who know me well). However, the patterns that my corpus reflects do correspond to my own informal observations of who writes and receives letters in the community.

8 I do not wish to imply that physical distance *determines* whether people communicate orally or by letter, since there is much evidence that demonstrates that the choice of communicative medium is dictated by factors other than the copresence of one's interlocutor or some abstract notion of communicative "convenience" (*contra* Thompson 1990:168–71 and many others). Shuman (1986:91–6) and Bennett and Berry (1991:102, also Berry and Bennett 1991:19) discuss instances of letter writing between persons who are within earshot of one another amongst American school children and in a Cree community in Northern Ontario respectively. In both Shuman's and Bennett and Berry's ethnographic settings, letters are written to perform communicative acts which would be judged socially inappropriate (e.g., too hostile, direct, or face-threatening). However, when asked about why letters are not "internally" written on the atoll, Nukulaelae Islanders invariably invoke the small size of their home island: why take the trouble to write a letter when a child can be sent over to convey a message? Yet one must mention here written invitations to feasts, which Nukulaelae residents send to one another. These invitations, which are clearly distinct from letters in form and social function, are discussed in Chapter 3.

9 This young woman had the poor judgment of striking a number of very sensitive chords in the letter she wrote, the full details of which were not revealed to me because I am theoretically her taboo classificatory brother. First, ringworm affliction is one of Nukulaelae's *pona* "stigmata" in the eyes of the rest of Tuvalu. Ringworm is indeed endemic on the atoll, and the phonological similarity between the word for ringworm, *lafaa*, and Nukulaelae's nickname, Laeva, does not help. To add insult to injury, ringworm frequently affects the genital area in both women and men. Second, the young woman was gossiping about her own kin to someone from another island, thereby reinforcing yet another of Nukulaelae's stigmata, according to which Nukulaelae people are inveterate gossips who will dirty the name of one of their own to total strangers. Third, the situation is aggravated by the fact that the young woman is only "half" Nukulaelae because her mother comes from another island of Tuvalu. She was told during the meeting that, as a *fakaalofa* "stranger" (literally, "object of empathy"), she should be even more on her best behavior than "true" (*tonu*) Nukulaelae people.

10 The telephone is enormously popular as a means of communication among urbanized immigrant groups from Pacific countries in New Zealand, Australia, and the United States. Many immigrant households have their phone cut off periodically because members of their extended families run up huge phone bills for international calls that cannot be paid.

11 Men and unmarried women usually take their father's first name as their own last name, while married women commonly use their husband's father's first name for this purpose. In face-to-face interactions, last names are only mentioned in official contexts, or when the need arises to distinguish between people with the same first name. In such cases, a descriptive expression like *te*

tama a X "X's child" or *te aavaga a Y* "Y's spouse" is commonly used, rather than a first-name-last-name combination, although for men at least the result is roughly identical.

5 Letters, economics, and emotionality

1 The importance of lists in the history of literacy has been noted by many scholars, most notably Goody (1977:74–111), who maintains that drawing up lists was one of the functions for which writing was invented. On Nukulaelae, lists are found in many written contexts. For example, they emerge in the written versions of sermons, as noted in Chapter 6. Nukulaelae Islanders also often put pen to paper to establish rosters, record debts, and keep genealogical records (see Chapter 3), activities in which listing figures prominently.

2 See Brady (1970, 1974, 1976) for an analysis of economic life in Tuvalu in general, in which the role of emotionality is described succinctly, and Chambers (1975, 1983) for comparative material from Nanumea. The patterns I describe here also apply to many other Polynesian societies in one form or the other.

3 The gossiping patterns illustrated here are strikingly similar to the patterns that Goodwin (1990) describes among urban working-class African-American children in the United States. Unfortunately, space and confidentiality concerns do not permit a full analysis of these materials. But see various analyses of different aspects of Nukulaelae gossip I have presented elsewhere (Besnier 1989b, 1990b, 1991, 1992a, 1992b, 1993).

4 The emergence in letters of affect-denoting expressions like "my liver is eaten up by pity" and, elsewhere, "the heart is satisfied" (e.g., letter 1985:522, this chapter) and "the desire to chat is not about to end" (letter 1985:591, Chapter 4) could be seen as an attempt to create a more "detached" text, because they describe emotions in somatic fashion, as experiences that are somewhat depersonalized and physically removed from the experiencer's seat of emotions. This explanation would support the hypothesis that many researchers have advanced (e.g., Chafe 1982) to the effect that written language is intrinsically more detached than spoken language. However, these constructions are common ways of expressing emotions in both spoken and written Nukulaelae Tuvaluan, as well as many other experiences and cognitive processes (see Cook 1993 and Talmy 1985 for discussions of the linguistic aspects of this cross-linguistically familiar pattern).

5 Bennett and Berry (1991) and Berry and Bennett (1991:19) describe similar uses of letter writing among the Cree of Northern Ontario, who are extremely disapproving of face-threatening acts like direct requests. The Cree use letters to communicate what would be deemed embarrassingly pushy and socially inappropriate. For example, letter writing has become an ideal way to initiate marriage negotiations. (See also Kulick and Stroud 1990 for some fascinating material on the uses of letters among the Gapun of the Lower Sepik area of Papua New Guinea.)

6 The same remark applies to many other Polynesian societies (see Love 1985 on Samoan farewells). However, the possibility that departing relatives will never return is probably even more real for Nukulaelae people than for other Pacific Islanders, given the paucity of links of communication and the restricted size of

the kinship networks that link the community to the outside world (compared, for example, to the vast Samoan and Tongan kinship networks in the industrialized Pacific Rim).

6 Between literacy and orality: the sermon

1 Copies of the Bible can usually be obtained from the pastor for A$5 each, which is rather steep for many.
2 I will argue in this chapter and the next that sermons constitute a gendered genre in this society, in that they are strongly associated with men despite women's occasional "encroachments." As a result, I will use male pronouns generically to refer to preachers except in specific cases when the preacher I am writing about is a woman.
3 Some of these activities are sometimes outrageously mirthful and, at least superficially, chaotic. For example, in May 1990, during the centennial celebrations of the return of Niuoku Islet to the Nukulaelae community (see Chapter 2), the master of ceremonies asked that all people over the age of fifty play *uga puulou*, a children's game, in the maneapa. In this game, two players of opposite gender are designated by their respective teams; the woman hides under a mat, and the man tries to guess her identity by feeling the mat and groping at the hidden body, or vice versa. This game is extremely risqué because the two players may turn out to be "taboo" cousins who are expected to avoid each other's presence at all times, a norm that older people are particularly sensitive to. When this turns out to be the case, the audience disintegrates in roars of uncontrollable laughter and deafening whoops.
4 The Tuvaluan version of the Bible in use during my 1991 field work, when this recording was made, is the first complete translation of the text into Tuvaluan (Suva, Fiji: South Pacific Bible Society, 1987). English translations of biblical passages cited in this chapter and the next are taken from *The NIV Study Bible: New International Version* (Grand Rapids, MI: Zondervan, 1985).
5 On occasion, some members of the congregation will continue reading in automatic fashion beyond the passages that the preacher requested. When this occurs, other congregation members shoo the transgressors in well-orchestrated unison, with a scandalized, barely muffled, and heavily aspirated *tteeeee!* The same interjection is used when someone (usually a child) transgresses a social norm in a particularly blatant manner. Clearly, any violation of the preset order of events during the service is viewed with strong disapproval.
6 All conductors during my various sojourns in the field were men. A good friend who sometimes conducts the choir once castigated me light-heartedly for smiling at him while he was conducting during a church service, saying that I almost succeeded in making him break the impassive demeanor he had to maintain during the performance. However, during choir performances on festive occasions, someone (frequently an elderly woman) occasionally takes over the leadership of the choir and clowns about, imitating the style of particular conductors in an exaggerated and sometimes outrageous fashion (e.g., lifting her skirt at the end of the hymn). These frame-breaking episodes never take place during church services, and can be thought of as generally

reinforcing rather than undermining of the normative rigidity of choir performances in all other contexts, much as rituals of comic reversal do in many cultures (cf. Babcock, ed., 1978, Babcock-Abrahams 1974, Bakhtin 1984, V. Turner 1969). I also have witnessed occasions when the clowning "goes overboard" and arouses general disapproval, which indicates that these practices bear the seed of subversion.

7 A young Nukulaelae woman once listened to the copy of the wonderfully romantic recording of Bach's *Matthäuspassion* performed by the Berliner Philharmoniker conducted by Von Karajan (on DGG 419 789–2) that I usually take to the field. Her response to the lyricism of the recording was that the singers were *fakavalevale* "crazy, lacking in social skills," an evaluation she supported by describing the tremulousness of the solo voices, the ornamentations, and what she considered to be an ever-varying tempo.

8 It should be noted that what the oratorical genre referred to as *lāuga* in Samoa, as described by Duranti (1984) and others, appears to differ significantly from Nukulaelae sermons and speeches.

9 Michael Goldsmith (personal communication) points out that these patterns contribute to the fact that Nukulaelae Islanders who leave the Church of Tuvalu for other religious denominations also write themselves out of the political life of the atoll by the same token.

10 The distinction between religious and secular oratory is slightly more problematic than I have depicted here in one situation, namely when a pastor or former pastor delivers a secular *laauga*. At times, these speeches bear many stylistic similarities to sermons. The interesting questions that this caveat raises cannot be addressed here for lack of space. For a thought-provoking description of pastors in the maneapa, see Goldsmith (1989a:259–64).

11 Because Nukulaelae was the first atoll of Tuvalu to become acquainted with and accept Christianity, Nukulaelae Islanders frequently talk about their community as having been "chosen"by God. The reference in this example is a typical instance.

12 Harvey Whitehouse (personal communication) asks which features of a sermon performance are taken as particularly memorable, leading to the denunciation of the sermon as recycled. I do not know the answer to this interesting question and doubt that it can be investigated hypothetically, although I look forward to the opportunity of hearing such a denunciation in future field work, which will enable me to query my respondents about it. In my discussion of the differences between written and spoken sermons, I did not deal with transformations that written sermons undergo when they are recycled or passed on to another person. To what extent do various versions of the "same" sermon differ across preachers and events? Unfortunately, I have not had access to the longitudinal data to allow me to compare different oral renditions of the same written sermon across speakers and events, and am unable to say anything about the important issues that the practice raises.

13 The term "market" in its strictest economic sense is generally defined as "the social institution of exchanges where prices or exchange equivalencies exist" (Plattner 1989:171). My use of this term here, which follows Bourdieu (1985 and

elsewhere), takes the category "exchange equivalencies" to include symbolic commodities.

14 From the vast canon of historical anecdotes about their foreparents, Nukulaelae people tell the story of man called Uele, who remained unmarried all his life (a condition which is already the mark of social deficiency). Once upon a time, Uele was designated to conduct the service, but when the time came to deliver his sermon, he was only able to utter one semisensical sentence (*Ia! Pulapula koutou tuupulaga, koutou i aso nei koo mmafi eiloo ki te mea peelaa!*, "So! You just stare ahead, all of you younger people, you are all good at doing things like that!"); "faced with the dignified congregation, his mind went dark, and he suddenly knew nothing. People laughed at him, and he left," relates one of my respondents. The salience of this well-known parable in the community's collective historical memory suggests that "forgetting" how to conduct oneself when one is in the limelight is a particularly horrifying prospect.

7 Literacy, truth, and authority

1 The form of the excerpt reference that precedes the translation indicates whether an excerpt is from an oral or written sermon. See "Transcription Conventions and Orthography" (p. xiv) for a key to the form of these references.

2 One grammatical construction associated with definitions and qualifications is only found in sermonic and other religious discourse. It consists of an equational construction in which the order of topic and comment is reversed from the usual pattern. For example, in the sentence *Tasi o tuulaga faigataa teenei, [. . .] ko te manavasee*, literally, "One of [the most] difficult states this [is, that of] fear" (sermons:Ke 1991:9), the comment comes first, and the topic last. In this construction, the qualification or definition is in a position of greater informational prominence than the reference of that which is qualified or defined, which highlights its textual importance. The stylistic specialization of inversion makes it a clear index of the sermonic genre.

3 An apparent exception to this pattern is the cross-linguistically unusual use of dual pronouns as forms of respect in political and recreational oratory. In the course of a speech, dual pronouns can be used to refer to speakers or the group they represent, to addressees, and to third parties, whether the referent is a singular, dual, or plural entity. However, this pattern differs in several respects from the frequent occurrence of dual pronouns in sermons. Most saliently, only the first-person exclusive dual pronoun *taaua* occurs with any frequency in sermons, while in secular oratory all dual pronouns other than *taaua* appear as respect forms.

4 If a Nukulaelae Islander says *toku kaaiga* "my kin group," the reference is understood to be limited to the speaker's spouse and children, rather than to an extended kin group. Even then, the expression *temaa kaaiga* "our [dual] kin group," in which the pronoun refers to a couple, is preferred.

5 Echoes of this state of affairs are also found in spirit mediumship sessions, which were extremely important in Nukulaelae's pre-Christian religion and still continue today despite being frowned upon by Christian authorities. In spirit

mediumship, the voice of the spirit merges with that of the medium, as discussed further in Besnier (1992b). Whether a historical link should be established between sermons and spirit mediumship is an open question.

6 There are other reintegration rituals besides sermons, the most important being the feasts that village sides put on to greet their returning members. During these feasts, the returnee is expected to make a monetary gift to the village side and to give at least one speech to describe what he or she has done during her absence (narrations of encounters with other Nukulaelae Islanders overseas are particularly relished in these speeches). What is interesting is that even young people who ordinarily do not speak in public are expected to give these speeches. Thus, here too, the liminality of the returnee is marked by a suspension of ordinary norms of conduct.

7 The concept of being "born again" is not unknown to Nukulaelae Islanders, who think it is a very good idea in principle but are not about to incorporate it into their lives. Evangelical Christianity has appeared on the religious scene on Funafuti, and Nukulaelae people are exceedingly scornful of the views and practices that have been imported with it (e.g., glossolalia, religious healing, rejection of church hierarchies, etc.).

8 Scholars of different theoretical persuasions (feminism, critical theory, social constructionism) have argued convincingly that, while individualism plays a pivotal role in Western ethnopsychological models, it does so in the context of a specific middle-class idealization of self-reliant upward mobility (cf. di Leonardo 1991a, Ehrenreich 1989, Ortner 1991, Sennett and Cobb 1972, and many others). In other words, the individualism of Western personhood is an ideological construct, and its promotion to the status of key symbol of the West in anthropological thinking instantiates the tendency in anthropological writings to reify Western culture, a tendency that Carrier (1992, 1995) aptly labels "occidentalism."

9 The polysemy of the term *maasani* is particularly interesting in this context: indeed, women have no *maasani* "familiarity" with delivering sermons because they are not in the habit of doing so, although many certainly have *maasani* "aptitude," in that they have all the oratorical skills that the task demands.

8 Conclusion

1 A number of other terms, like "conditional literacy," "functional literacy," and "'bush' literacy," have been used more or less interchangeably with "restricted literacy" by various authors. In their original statement, Goody and Watt (1963) appear to equate restricted literacy with non-alphabetic literacy, although this equation becomes blurred in subsequent reformulations.

2 One additional way of restricting literacy is by burning books or engaging in comparable acts of censorship, as Barton (1994:76) reminds us.

3 I use the word "innovation" rather than "import" to reflect the fact that literacy underwent a redefinition after being introduced to the atoll, as it probably does in all similar cases.

4 Recitation is one of the central features that Goody (1968:13–14) and Ong (1982:115–16) ascribe to "oral residues" in not quite fully literate societies (cf.

also Lord 1960 and M. Parry 1971). Messick (1993) has a nicely worded answer to this view:

This recitational emphasis is perhaps better understood as a complex motif of a fully realized type of civilizational literacy. Muslim societies elaborated diverse, historically specific textual worlds, central elements of which were their particular understandings, and relative valuings, of the recited and the written. It is only with the application of Western-modeled yardsticks for complex forms of literacy and for universal (evolutionary) routes of oral-to-written shifts that cases such as the Muslim one can be made to appear incomplete, marked by residuals, or stalled in development.

(1993:24–5)

5 Young men who work as seamen on foreign ships are probably better off than salaried islanders in the capital: not only do they make considerably more money, but they are also too isolated to form a sub-community that would immediately begin to engage in fund-raising activities comparable to the activities that the Nukulaelae community on Nauru engages in. However, seamen are generally not well educated, and their access to monetary resources has little to do with literacy.

REFERENCES

Akinnaso, F. Niyi. 1982. On the Differences Between Spoken and Written Language. *Language and Speech* 25:97–125.
1992. Schooling, Language, and Knowledge in Literate and Nonliterate Societies. *Comparative Studies in Society and History* 34:68–109.
Anderson, Benedict O'G. 1991. *Imagined Communities: Reflections on the Origin and Spread of Nationalism*, 2nd edition. London: Verso.
Arno, Andrew. 1993. *The World of Talk on a Fijian Island: An Ethnography of Law and Communicative Causation*. Norwood, NJ: Ablex.
Atkinson, J. Maxwell and John Heritage. 1984. Transcript Notation. In *Structures of Social Action: Studies in Conversation Analysis*, J. Maxwell Atkinson and John Heritage, eds., pp. ix–xvi. Studies in Emotion and Social Interaction Series. Cambridge: Cambridge University Press. Paris: Editions de la Maison des Sciences de l'Homme.
Axtell, James L. 1987. The Power of Print in the Eastern Woodlands. *William and Mary Quarterly* 44:301–9.
Babadzan, Alain. 1985. From Oral to Written: The *Puta Tupuna* of Rurutu. In *Transformations of Polynesian Culture*, Antony Hooper and Judith Huntsman, eds., pp. 177–93. Memoirs of the Polynesian Society, 45. Auckland: The Polynesian Society.
Babcock, Barbara A., ed. 1978. *The Reversible World: Symbolic Inversion in Art and Society*. Ithaca, NY: Cornell University Press.
Babcock-Abrahams, Barbara A. 1974. "A Tolerated Margin of Mess": The Trickster and His Tales Reconsidered. *Journal of the Folklore Institute* 11:147–86.
Bailey, F.G. 1983. *The Tactical Uses of Passion: An Essay on Power, Reason and Reality*. Ithaca, NY: Cornell University Press.
1991. *The Prevalence of Deceit*. Ithaca, NY: Cornell University Press.
Bakhtin, Mikhail. 1984. *Rabelais and His World*, Helen Iswolsky, trans. Bloomington, IN: Indiana University Press.
Barnes, Barry. 1988. *The Nature of Power*. Urbana, IL: University of Illinois Press.
Barton, David. 1991. The Social Nature of Writing. In *Writing in the Community*, David Barton and Roz Ivanič, eds., pp. 1–13. Written Communication Annual, 6. Newbury Park, CA: Sage.
1994. *Literacy: An Introduction to the Ecology of Written Language*. Oxford: Blackwell.
Basso, Ellen B. 1988. The Trickster's Scattered Self. *Anthropological Linguistics* 30:292–318.
Basso, Keith H. 1974. The Ethnography of Writing. In *Explorations in the Ethnography of Speaking*, Richard Bauman and Joel Sherzer, eds., pp. 425–32.

204

Cambridge: Cambridge University Press.
Bauman, Richard. 1975. Verbal Art as Performance. *American Anthropologist* 77:290–311.
1977. *Verbal Art as Performance*. Prospect Heights, IL: Waveland Press.
1986. *Story, Performance, and Event: Contextual Studies of Oral Narrative*. Cambridge Studies in Oral and Literate Culture, 10. Cambridge: Cambridge University Press.
Bauman, Richard and Charles L. Briggs. 1990. Poetics and Performance as Critical Perspectives on Language and Social Life. *Annual Review of Anthropology* 19:59–88.
Baynham, Mike. 1993. Code Switching and Mode Switching: Community Interpreters and Mediators of Literacy. In Street, ed., pp. 294–314.
Bedford, Richard, Barrie Macdonald, and Doug Munro. 1980. Population Estimates for Kiribati and Tuvalu, 1850–1900: Review and Speculation. *Journal of the Polynesian Society* 89:199–246.
Bennett, Jo Anne and John W. Berry. 1991. Cree Literacy in the Syllabic Script. In *Literacy and Orality*, David Olson and Nancy Torrance, eds., pp. 90–104. Cambridge: Cambridge University Press.
Berry, John W. and Jo Anne Bennett. 1991. *Cree Syllabic Literacy: Cultural Context and Psychological Consequences*. Cross-Cultural Psychology Monographs, 1. Tilburg: Tilburg University Press.
Bertram, I. Geoffrey and Ray F. Watters. 1985. The MIRAB Economy in South Pacific Microstates. *Pacific Viewpoint* 26:497–519.
Besnier, Niko. 1988. The Linguistic Relationships of Spoken and Written Nukulaelae Registers. *Language* 64:707–36.
1989a. Literacy and Feelings: The Encoding of Affect in Nukulaelae Letters. *Text* 9:69–92. (Reprinted in Street, ed., 1993, pp. 62–86.)
1989b. Information Withholding as a Manipulative and Collusive Strategy in Nukulaelae Gossip. *Language in Society* 18:315–41.
1990a. Language and Affect. *Annual Review of Anthropology* 19:419–51.
1990b. Conflict Management, Gossip, and Affective Meaning on Nukulaelae. In *Disentangling: Conflict Discourse in Pacific Societies*, Karen A. Watson-Gegeo and Geoff White, eds., pp. 290–334. Stanford, CA: Stanford University Press.
1991. Authority and Egalitarianism: Discourses of Leadership on Nukulaelae Atoll. Paper presented at the Conference on Leadership and Change in the Western Pacific: For Sir Raymond Firth on the Occasion of his Ninetieth Birthday, London School of Economics.
1992a. Reported Speech and Affect on Nukulaelae. In *Responsibility and Evidence in Oral Discourse*, Jane H. Hill and Judith T. Irvine, eds., pp. 161–81. Studies in the Social and Cultural Foundations of Language, 15. Cambridge: Cambridge University Press.
1992b. Heteroglossic Discourses on Nukulaelae Spirits. Paper presented at the Annual Meeting of the Society for Social Anthropology in Oceania.
1993. The Demise of the Man Who Would Be King: Sorcery and Ambition on Nukulaelae Atoll. *Journal of Anthropological Research* 49:185–215.
1994a. Polynesian Gender Liminality Across Time and Space. In *Third Sex, Third Gender: Beyond Sexual Dimorphism in Culture and History*, Gilbert Herdt, ed., pp. 285–328, 554–66. New York: Zone Books.
1994b. The Truth and Other Irrelevant Aspects of Nukulaelae Gossip. *Pacific Studies* 17(3):1–39.
Biber, Douglas E. 1988. *Variation Across Speech and Writing*. Cambridge:

Cambridge University Press.
Bilaniuk, Laada. 1989. Samplers: Embroidery as Literacy and Literacy Acquisition Through Embroidery. Senior Essay, Department of Anthropology, Yale University.
Bledsoe, Caroline and Kenneth M. Robey. 1986. Arabic Literacy and Secrecy Among the Mende of Sierra Leone. *Man* (n.s.) 21:202–26. (Reprinted in Street, ed., 1993, pp. 110–34.)
Bloch, Maurice. 1989. Literacy and Enlightenment. In *Literacy and Society*, Karen Schousboe and Mogens T. Larsen, eds., pp. 15–38. Copenhagen: Akademisk Forlag for the Center for Research in the Humanities, Copenhagen University.
  1993. The Uses of Schooling and Literacy in a Zafimaniry Village. In Street, ed., pp. 87–109.
Bloch, Maurice and Jonathan Parry. 1989. Introduction: Money and the Morality of Exchange. In *Money and the Morality of Exchange*, Jonathan Parry and Maurice Bloch, eds., pp. 1–32. Cambridge: Cambridge University Press.
Bloome, David and Judith L. Green. 1992. Educational Contexts of Literacy. *Annual Review of Applied Linguistics* 12:49–70.
Bok, Sissela. 1979. *Lying*. New York: Vintage.
Bourdieu, Pierre. 1977. *Outline of a Theory of Practice*, Richard Nice, trans. Cambridge: Cambridge University Press.
  1984. *Distinction*, Richard Nice, trans. Cambridge, MA: Harvard University Press.
  1985. The Market of Symbolic Goods. *Poetics* 14:13–44.
  1988. *Homo Academicus*, Peter Collier, trans. Stanford, CA: Stanford University Press.
  1990. *In Other Words: Essays Towards a Reflexive Sociology*, Matthew Adamson, trans. Cambridge: Polity Press.
  1991. *Language and Symbolic Power*, Raymond Gino and Matthew Adamson, trans., John B. Thompson, ed. Cambridge: Polity Press.
Bourdieu, Pierre and Jean-Claude Passeron. 1977. *Reproduction in Education, Society, and Culture*, Richard Nice, trans. Sage Studies in Social and Educational Change, 5. London: Sage.
Bowles, Samuel and Herbet Gintis. 1976. *Schooling in Capitalist America: Educational Reform and the Contradictions of Economic Life*. New York: Basic Books.
Brady, Ivan A. 1970. Land Tenure, Kinship and Community Structures: Strategies for Living in the Ellice Islands of Western Polynesia. Ph.D. dissertation, Department of Anthropology, University of Oregon.
  1972. Kinship Reciprocity in the Ellice Islands: An Evaluation of Sahlins' Model of the Sociology of Primitive Exchange. *Journal of the Polynesian Society* 81:290–316.
  1974. Land Tenure in the Ellice Islands: A Changing Profile. In *Land Tenure in Oceania*, Henry P. Lundsgaarde, ed., pp. 130–78. Association for Social Anthropology in Oceania Monographs, 2. Honolulu: University of Hawaii Press.
  1975. Christians, Pagans and Government Men: Culture Change in the Ellice Islands. In *A Reader in Culture Change*, Ivan A. Brady and Barry L. Isaacs, eds., vol. 2, pp. 111–45. New York: Schenkman.
  1976. Socio-Economic Mobility: Adoption and Land Tenure in the Ellice Islands. In *Transactions in Kinship: Adoption and Fosterage in Oceania*, Ivan A. Brady, ed., pp. 120–63. Association for Social Anthropology in Oceania

Monographs, 4. Honolulu: University of Hawaii Press.

1978. Stability and Change: Wherewithal for Survival on a Coral Island. In *Extinction and Survival in Human Populations*, Charles Laughlin, Jr. and Ivan A. Brady, eds., pp. 245–81. New York: Columbia University Press.

Brandt, Deborah. 1990. *Literacy as Involvement: The Acts of Writers, Readers, and Texts*. Carbondale, IL: Southern Illinois University Press.

Brandt, Elizabeth A. 1983. Native American Attitudes Toward Literacy in the Southwest. *Journal of the Linguistic Association of the Southwest* 4:185–95.

Bridge, Cyprian. 1886. Cruises in Melanesia, Micronesia, and Western Polynesia, in 1882, 1883, and 1884, and Visits to New Guinea and the Louisiades in 1884 and 1885. *Proceedings of the Royal Geographic Society and Monthly Record of Geography* 9:545–67.

Briggs, Charles L. 1988. *Competence in Performance: The Creativity of Tradition in Mexicano Verbal Art*. Conduct and Communication Series. Philadelphia: University of Pennsylvania Press.

Briggs, Charles L. and Richard Bauman. 1992. Genre, Textuality, and Social Power. *Journal of Linguistic Anthropology* 2:131–72.

Brodkey, Linda. 1987. *Academic Writing as Social Practice*. Philadelphia: Temple University Press.

Butinov, N.A. 1982. *Polineziytsy ostrovov Tuvalu* [The Polynesian Tuvalu Islands]. Moscow: Glavnaya Redaktsiya Vostochnoy Literatury, Izdatel'stvo Nauka.

Callender, Christine and Deborah Cameron. 1990. Responsive Listening as Part of Religious Rhetoric: The Case of Black Pentecostal Preaching. In *Reception and Response: Hearer Creativity and the Analysis of Spoken and Written Texts*, Graham McGregor and R.S. White, eds, pp. 160–78. London: Routledge.

Campbell, I.C. 1989. *A History of the Pacific Islands*. Christchurch: University of Canterbury Press.

Carrier, James G. 1992. Occidentalism: The World Turned Upside-Down. *American Ethnologist* 19:195–212.

1995. Introduction. In *Occidentalism: Images of the West*, James G. Carrier, ed. Oxford: Oxford University Press.

Cassirer, Ernst. 1946. *Language and Myth*, Suzanne K. Langer, trans. New York: Harper.

Chafe, Wallace L. 1982. Integration and Involvement in Speaking, Writing, and Oral Literature. In *Spoken and Written Language: Exploring Orality and Literacy*, Deborah Tannen, ed., pp. 35–54. Advances in Discourse Processes, 9. Norwood, NJ: Ablex.

1986. Evidentiality in English Conversation and Academic Writing. In *Evidentiality: The Linguistic Coding of Epistemology*, Wallace L. Chafe and Johanna Nichols, eds., pp. 261–73. Advances in Discourse Processes, 20. Norwood, NJ: Ablex.

1992. Written Language: Writing vs. Speech. In *International Encyclopedia of Linguistics*, William Bright, ed., vol. 4, pp. 257–9. New York: Oxford University Press.

Chafe, Wallace L. and Jane Danielewicz. 1987. Properties of Spoken and Written Language. In *Comprehending Oral and Written Language*, Rosalind Horowitz and S.J. Samuels, eds., pp. 83–113. New York: Academic Press.

Chafe, Wallace L. and Deborah Tannen. 1987. The Relation Between Written and Spoken Language. *Annual Review of Anthropology* 16:383–407.

Chambers, Anne F. 1975. *Nanumea Report: A Socio-Economic Study of Nanumea Atoll, Tuvalu*. Victoria University of Wellington Rural Socio-Economic

Survey of the Gilbert and Ellice Islands. Wellington: Department of Geography, Victoria University of Wellington.

1983. Exchange and Social Organization in Nanumea, a Polynesian Atoll Society. Ph.D. dissertation, Department of Anthropology, University of California at Berkeley.

Chambers, Keith S. and Anne F. Chambers. 1980. Distribution of Lands. In Iosia and Macrae, eds., pp. 86–91.

Chambers, Keith S., Anne F. Chambers, and Doug Munro. 1978. Sapolu, S. Percy Smith, and a Tale From Nanumea. *Journal of the Polynesian Society* 87:29–40.

Christensen, Dieter and Gerd Koch. 1964. *Die Musik der Ellice-Inseln*. Veröffentlichunger des Museum für Völkerkunde, Neue Folge 5, Abteilung Südsee 2. Berlin: Museum für Völkerkunde.

Clanchy, Michael T. 1987. Review of *Literacy in Theory and Practice*, by Brian Street. *History of Education* 16:309–10.

1993. *From Memory to Written Record: England 1066–1307*, 2nd edition. Oxford: Basil Blackwell.

Cleave, Peter. 1979. The Languages and Political Interests of Maori and Pakeha Communities in New Zealand During the Nineteenth Century. Ph.D. dissertation, Wolfson College, University of Oxford.

Cole, Michael and Ageliki Nicolopoulou. 1992. Literacy: Intellectual Consequences. In *International Encyclopedia of Linguistics*, William Bright, ed., vol. 2, pp. 343–6. New York: Oxford University Press.

Conklin, Harold C. 1949. Bamboo Literacy on Mindoro. *Pacific Discovery* 2(4):4–11.

1991. *Doctrina Christiana, en Lengua Española y Tagala*, Manila 1593. In *Vision of a Collector: The Lessing J. Rosenwald Collection in the Library of Congress*, Kathleen Mang and Peter Van Wingen, eds., pp. 36–40. Washington, DC: Library of Congress.

Connell, John. 1986. Population, Migration, and Problems of Atoll Development in the South Pacific. *Pacific Studies* 9(2):41–58.

Cook, Kenneth W. 1993. A Cognitive Analysis of the Samoan Absolutive Construction. Paper presented at the First International Conference on Oceanic Linguistics, Vila, Vanuatu.

Cook-Gumperz, Jenny. 1986. Introduction. In *The Social Construction of Literacy*, Jenny Cook-Gumperz, ed., pp. 1–15. Studies in Interactional Sociolinguistics, 3. Cambridge: Cambridge University Press.

Coulmas, Florian. 1989. *The Writing Systems of the World*. Oxford: Basil Blackwell.

Crawford, Ronald J. 1977. The Lotu and the Fa'aSamoa: Church and Society in Samoa, 1830–1880. Ph.D. dissertation, Department of History, University of Otago.

David, Mrs. Edgeworth [Lady Caroline M. David]. 1899. *Funafuti, or Three Months on a Coral Island: An Unscientific Account of a Scientific Expedition*. London: John Murray.

Davies, S.H. 1873. Letters. South Sea Letters 34/2/D, Records of the London Missionary Society, School of Oriental and African Studies Library.

Davis, Gerald L. 1985. *I Got the Word and I Can Sing It, You Know: A Study of the Performed African-American Sermon*. Philadelphia: University of Pennsylvania Press.

Davis, Nathalie A.Z. 1975. *Society and Culture in Early Modern France: Eight Essays*. Stanford, CA: Stanford University Press.

DeCastell, Suzanne and Tom Walker. 1991. Identity, Metamorphosis, and Ethnographic Research: What *Kind* of Story is *Ways With Words? Anthropology and Education Quarterly* 22:3–20.

De Certeau, Michel. 1984. *The Practice of Everyday Life*, Stephen Rendall, trans. Berkeley, CA: University of California Press.

De Rycker, Teun. 1991. Turns at Writing: The Organization of Correspondence. In *The Pragmatic Perspective: Selected Papers From the 1985 International Pragmatics Conference*, Jef Verschueren and Marcella Bertucceli-Papi, eds., pp. 613–47. Pragmatics & Beyond Companion Series, 5. Amsterdam: John Benjamins.

di Leonardo, Micaela. 1991a. Habits of the Cumbered Heart: Ethnic Community and Women's Culture as American Invented Traditions. In *Golden Ages, Dark Ages: Imagining the Past in Anthropology and History*, Jay O'Brien and William Roseberry, eds, pp. 234–52. Berkeley, CA: University of California Press.

1991b. Introduction: Gender, Culture, and Political Economy: Feminist Anthropology in Historical Perspective. In *Gender at the Crossroads of Knowledge: Feminist Anthropology in the Postmodern Era*, Micaela di Leonardo, ed., pp. 1–48. Berkeley, CA: University of California Press.

Duranti, Alessandro. 1984. *Lāuga* and *Talanoaga*: Two Speech Genres in a Samoan Political Event. In *Dangerous Words: Language and Politics in the Pacific*, Don Brenneis and Fred Myers, eds., pp. 217–42. New York: New York University Press.

1985. Sociocultural Dimensions of Discourse. In *Handbook of Discourse Analysis*, Teun A. Van Dijk, ed., vol. 1, pp. 193–230. New York: Academic Press.

1988. Ethnography of Speaking: Toward a Linguistics of the Praxis. In *Linguistics: The Cambridge Survey*, Frederick J. Newmeyer, vol. 4, pp. 210–28. Cambridge: Cambridge University Press.

Duranti, Alessandro and Elinor Ochs. 1986. Literacy Instruction in a Samoan Village. In *The Acquisition of Literacy: Ethnographic Perspectives*, Bambi Schieffelin and Perry Gilmore, eds., pp. 213–32. Advances in Discourse Processes, 21. Norwood, NJ: Ablex.

Durkheim, Emile and Marcel Mauss. 1903. De quelques formes primitives de classification. *L'Année Sociologique* 6:1–72.

Eagleton, Terry. 1991. *Ideology: An Introduction*. London: Verso.

Eckert, Penelope and Sally McConnell-Ginet. 1992. Think Practically and Look Locally: Language and Gender as Community-Based Practice. *Annual Review of Anthropology* 21:461–90.

Edwards, Jane A. 1993. Principles and Contrasting Systems of Discourse Transcription. In *Talking Data: Transcription and Coding in Discourse Research*, Jane A. Edwards and Martin D. Lampert, eds., pp. 3–31. Hillsdale, NJ: Lawrence Erlbaum.

Ehrenreich, Barbara. 1989. *Fear of Falling: The Inner Life of the Middle Class*. New York: Pantheon.

Eickelman, Dale F. 1985. *Knowledge and Power in Morocco*. Princeton, NJ: Princeton University Press.

Eisenstein, Elizabeth L. 1969. The Advent of Printing and the Problem of the Renaissance. *Past and Present* 45:19–89.

1979. *The Printing Press as an Agent of Change: Communications and Cultural Transformations in Early Modern Europe*. Cambridge: Cambridge University Press.

1981. Some Conjectures About the Impact of Printing on Western Society and Thought: A Preliminary Report. In *Literacy and Social Development in the West*, Harvey J. Graff, ed., pp. 53–68. Cambridge Studies in Oral and Literate Culture, 3. Cambridge: Cambridge University Press.

1983. *The Printing Revolution in Early Modern Europe*. Cambridge: Cambridge University Press.

Elekana. 1872. Elikana's [*sic*] Story. *The Juvenile Missionary Magazine* June–October: 101–5, 123–7, 147–50, 175–7, 196–8.

Ellice Islands Protectorate. 1894. *Tulafono o le Atu Elisa* [Laws of the Ellice Islands]. Suva: Edward John March, le Lomitusi a le Malo [in Samoan].

Erickson, Frederick. 1987. Transformation and School Success: The Politics and Culture of Educational Achievement. *Anthropology and Education Quarterly* 18:335–56.

Errington, J. Joseph. 1988. *Structure and Style in Javanese: A Semiotic View of Linguistic Etiquette*. Conduct and Communication Series. Philadelphia: University of Pennsylvania Press.

Ewald, Janet. 1988. Speaking, Writing, and Authority: Explorations in and from the Kingdom of Taqali. *Comparative Studies in Society and History* 30:199–224.

Fabian, Johannes. 1983. *Time and the Other: How Anthropology Makes Its Object*. New York: Columbia University Press.

Fardon, Richard. 1990. General Introduction. In *Localizing Strategies: Regional Traditions of Ethnographic Writing*, Richard Fardon, ed., pp. 1–35. Edinburgh: Scottish Academic Press. Washington, DC: Smithsonian Institution Press.

Ferguson, Charles A. 1987. Literacy in a Hunting-Gathering Society: The Case of the Diyari. *Journal of Anthropological Research* 43:223–37.

Finnegan, Ruth. 1988. *Literacy and Orality: Studies in the Technology of Communication*. Oxford: Basil Blackwell.

Firth, Raymond. 1964. Authority and Public Opinion in Tikopia. In *Essays on Social Organization and Values*, pp. 123–44. London School of Economics Monographs in Social Anthropology, 28. London: Athlone Press.

Firth, Stewart. 1973. German Firms in the Western Pacific Islands, 1857–1914. *Journal of Pacific History* 8:10–28.

Foucault, Michel. 1977. *Discipline and Punish: The Birth of the Prison*, Alan Sheridan, trans. New York: Pantheon.

1980. *Power/Knowledge: Selected Interviews and Other Writings, 1972–1977*, Colin Gordon, ed., Colin Gordon *et al.*, trans. New York: Pantheon.

1981. The Order of Discourse. In *Untying the Text: A Post-Structuralist Reader*, Richard Young, ed., pp. 48–78. Boston: Routledge & Kegan Paul.

Frake, Charles O. 1983. Did Literacy Cause the Great Cognitive Divide? *American Ethnologist* 10:368–71.

Frank, Stephen M. 1992. "Rendering Aid and Comfort": Images of Fatherhood in the Letters of Civil War Soldiers from Massachusetts and Michigan. *Journal of Social History* 26:5–32.

Friedrich, Paul. 1972. Social Context and Semantic Feature: The Russian Pronominal Usage. In *Directions in Sociolinguistics: The Ethnography of Communication*, John J. Gumperz and Dell Hymes, eds., pp. 270–300. New York: Holt, Rhinehart and Winston.

Gal, Susan. 1991. Between Speech and Silence: The Problematics of Research on Language and Gender. In *Gender at the Crossroads of Knowledge: Feminist*

Anthropology in the Postmodern Era, Micaela di Leonardo, ed., pp. 175–203. Berkeley, CA: University of California Press.

Garrett, John. 1992. *Footsteps in the Sea: Christianity in Oceania to World War II.* Geneva: World Council of Churches. Suva: Institute of Pacific Studies, University of the South Pacific.

Geertz, Clifford. 1984. From the Native's Point of View: On the Nature of Anthropological Understanding. In *Culture Theory: Essays on Mind, Self, and Emotion*, Richard A. Shweder and Robert A. LeVine, eds., pp. 123–36. Cambridge: Cambridge University Press.

Gellner, Ernest. 1983. *Nations and Nationalism*. Ithaca, NY: Cornell University Press.

Gewertz, Deborah and Frederick Errington. 1991. *Twisted Histories, Altered Contexts: Representing the Chambri in a World System*. Cambridge: Cambridge University Press.

Gibson, R.P. 1970. *Samoa 1830–1900: The Politics of a Multi-Cultural Community*. Melbourne: Oxford University Press.

Gilbert and Ellice Islands Colony. 1916. *Revised Native Laws of the Gilbert, Ellice, and Union Groups*. Suva: S. Bach, Printer to the Government of His Britannic Majesty's High Commission for the Western Pacific.

Gilbert and Ellice Islands Protectorate. 1913. *Report for 1911*. Annual Colonial Reports, 753. London: His Majesty's Stationery Office.

Gilbert, G.N. and Michael Mulkay. 1984. *Opening Pandora's Box: A Sociological Analysis of Scientists' Discourse*. Cambridge: Cambridge University Press.

Gilsenan, Michael. 1982. *Recognizing Islam*. London: Croom Helm.

Gilson, R.P. 1970. *Samoa 1830–1900: The Politics of a Multi-Cultural Community*. Melbourne: Oxford University Press.

Giroux, Henry. 1981. *Ideology, Culture, and the Process of Schooling*. Philadelphia: Temple University Press.

Goddard, Cliff. 1990. Emergent Genres of Reportage and Advocacy in the Pitjantjatjara Print Media. *Australian Aboriginal Studies* 1990(2):27–47.

Goffman, Erving. 1974. *Frame Analysis: An Essay on the Organization of Experience*. New York: Harper and Row.

1979. Footing. *Semiotica* 25:1–29.

1981. The Lecture. In *Forms of Talk*, pp. 160–96. Conduct and Communication Series. Philadelphia: University of Pennsylvania Press.

Goldsmith, Michael. 1985. Transformation of the Meeting-House in Tuvalu. In *Transformations of Polynesian Culture*, Antony Hooper and Judith Huntsman, eds., pp. 151–75. Memoirs of the Polynesian Society, 45. Auckland: The Polynesian Society.

1989a. Church and State in Tuvalu. Ph.D. dissertation, Department of Anthropology, University of Illinois at Urbana-Champaign.

1989b. Time, Space and Bodies: Missionary Discourse and Colonialism in Tuvalu. Unpublished manuscript, Department of Politics, University of Waikato.

1993. New Gods in Another Age: The Transformation of Religion in Tuvalu and the Pacific. Unpublished manuscript, Department of Politics, University of Waikato.

Goldsmith, Michael and Doug Munro. 1992a. Encountering Elekana Encountering Tuvalu. In *Pacific History: Papers From the 8th Pacific History Association Conference*, Donald H. Rubinstein, ed., pp. 25–41. Mangilao, GU: University of Guam Press and Micronesian Area Research Center.

1992b. Conversion and Church Formation in Tuvalu. *Journal of Pacific History* 27:44–54.

Goodwin, Marjorie H. 1990. *He-Said-She-Said: Talk as Social Organization Among Black Children*. Bloomington, IN: Indiana University Press.

Goody, Jack. 1968. Introduction. In Goody, ed., pp. 1–26.

1977. *The Domestication of the Savage Mind*. Themes in the Social Sciences Series. Cambridge: Cambridge University Press.

1986. *The Logic of Writing and the Organization of Society*. Studies in Literacy, the Family, Culture, and the State. Cambridge: Cambridge University Press.

1987. *The Interface Between the Written and the Oral*. Studies in Literacy, the Family, Culture, and the State. Cambridge: Cambridge University Press.

Goody, Jack, ed. 1968. *Literacy in Traditional Societies*. Cambridge: Cambridge University Press.

Goody, Jack and Ian Watt. 1963. The Consequences of Literacy. *Comparative Studies in Society and History* 3:304–45. (Reprinted in Goody, ed., 1968, pp. 27–68.)

Gough, Kathleen. 1968a. Implications of Literacy in Traditional China and India. In Goody, ed., pp. 70–84.

1968b. Literacy in Kērala. In Goody, ed., pp. 70–84.

Graeffe, Eduard. 1867. Reisen nach verschiedenen Inseln der Südsee. *Das Ausland* 48:1139–44, 49:1159–64, 50:1184–91.

Graff, Harvey J. 1979. *The Literacy Myth: Literacy and Social Structure in the Nineteenth Century*. New York: Academic Press.

Gramsci, Antonio. 1971. *Selections from the Prison Notebooks*, Quentin Hoare and Geoffrey N. Smith, trans. and eds. London: Lawrence & Wishart.

Grillo, Ralph, Jeff Pratt, and Brian V. Street. 1987. Anthropology, Linguistics and Language. In *New Horizons in Linguistics: An Introduction to Contemporary Linguistic Research*, John Lyons, Richard Coates, Margaret Deuchar, and Gerald Gazdar, eds., vol. 2, pp. 268–95. London: Penguin.

Gumperz, John J. 1968. The Speech Community. In *International Encyclopedia of Social Sciences*, David L. Sills, ed., vol. 9, pp. 381–6. New York: Macmillan and the Free Press.

Gumperz, John J. and Norine Berenz. 1993. Transcribing Conversational Exchanges. In *Talking Data: Transcription and Coding in Discourse Research*, Jane A. Edwards and Martin D. Lampert, eds., pp. 91–121. Hillsdale, NJ: Lawrence Erlbaum.

Guss, David M. 1986. Keeping It Oral: A Yekuana Ethnology. *American Ethnologist* 13:413–29.

Halverson, John. 1991. Olson on Literacy. *Language in Society* 20:619–40.

1992. Goody and the Implosion of the Literacy Thesis. *Man* (n.s.) 27:301–17.

Hanks, William F. 1987. Discourse Genres in a Theory of Practice. *American Ethnologist* 14:64–88.

1990. *Referential Practice: Language and Lived Space Among the Maya*. Chicago: University of Chicago Press.

Harbsmeier, Michael. 1988. Inventions of Writing. In *State and Society: The Emergence and Development of Social Hierarchy and Political Centralization*, John Glendhill, Barbara Bender, and Mogens T. Larsen, eds, pp. 253–76. London: Unwin Hyman.

Harding, Susan F. 1987. Convicted by the Holy Spirit: The Rhetoric of Fundamentalist Baptist Conversion. *American Ethnologist* 14:167–81.

Harris, Roy. 1986. *The Origin of Writing*. London: Duckworth.

Harris, William V. 1989. *Ancient Literacy*. Cambridge, MA: Harvard University Press.

Hartse, Caroline M. 1993. On the Colony: Social and Religious Change Among Contemporary Hutterites. Ph.D. dissertation, Department of Anthropology, University of New Mexico.

Havelock, Eric A. 1963. *Preface to Plato*. Cambridge, MA: Belknap Press of Harvard University Press.

1976. *Origins of Western Literacy*. OISE Monograph Series, 14. Toronto: Ontario Institute for Studies in Education.

1982. *The Literate Revolution in Greece and its Cultural Consequences*. Princeton, NJ: Princeton University Press.

1986. *The Muses Learn to Write*. New Haven, CT: Yale University Press.

Haviland, Jeannette M. 1984. Thinking and Feeling in Woolf's Writing: From Childhood to Adulthood. In *Emotions, Cognition, and Behavior*, Carroll E. Izard, Jerome Kagan, and Robert B. Zajonc, eds., pp. 515–46. Cambridge: Cambridge University Press.

Heath, Shirley B. 1983. *Ways With Words: Language, Life, and Work in Communities and Classrooms*. Cambridge: Cambridge University Press.

1990. The Children of Trackton's Children: Spoken and Written Language in Social Change. In *Cultural Psychology: Essays on Comparative Human Development*, James W. Stigler, Richard A. Shweder, and Gilbert Herdt, eds., pp. 496–519. Cambridge: Cambridge University Press.

1993. The Madness(es) of Reading and Writing Ethnography. *Anthropology and Education Quarterly* 24:256–68.

Heelas, Paul. 1986. Emotion Talk Across Cultures. In *The Social Construction of Emotions*, Rom Harré, ed., pp. 234–66. Oxford: Basil Blackwell.

Hollan, Doug. 1992. Cross-Cultural Differences in the Self. *Journal of Anthropological Research* 48:282–300.

Holt, Grace S. 1972. Stylin' Outta the Black Pulpit. In *Rappin' and Stylin' Out: Communication in Urban Black America*, Thomas Kochman, ed., pp. 189–204. Urbana, IL: University of Illinois Press.

Hooper, Antony. 1969. Socio-Economic Organization of the Tokelau Islands. In *Proceedings of the VIIIth International Congress of Anthropological and Ethnological Sciences*, vol. 2, pp. 238–40. Tokyo: Science Council of Japan.

Hostetler, John A. and Gertrude E. Huntington. 1980. *The Hutterites in North America*. Case Studies in Cultural Anthropology. New York: Holt, Rinehart and Winston.

Howard, Alan. 1985. Ethnopsychology and the Prospects for a Cultural Psychology. In *Person, Self, and Experience: Exploring Pacific Ethnopsychologies*, Geoffrey M. White and John Kirkpatrick, eds., pp. 401–20. Berkeley, CA: University of California Press.

Howard, Irwin J. 1981. Proto-Ellicean. In *Studies in Pacific Languages and Cultures in Honour of Bruce Biggs*, Jim Hollyman and Andrew Pawley, eds., pp. 101–18. Te Reo Monographs. Auckland: Linguistic Society of New Zealand.

Howe, Nicholas. 1992. The Cultural Construction of Reading in Anglo-Saxon England. In *The Ethnography of Reading*, Jonathan Boyarin, ed., pp. 58–79. Berkeley, CA: University of California Press.

Huebner, Thom. 1987. A Socio-Historical Approach to Literacy Development: A Comparative Case Study from the Pacific. In *Language, Literacy, and Culture: Issues in Society and Schooling*, Judith A. Langer, ed., pp. 178–96. Norwood, NJ: Ablex.

214   *References*

Hull, Glynda. 1993. Hearing Other Voices: A Critical Assessment of Popular Views on Literacy and Work. *Harvard Educational Review* 63:20–49.

Hunter, James D. 1983. *American Evangelicalism*. New Brunswick, NJ: Rutgers University Press.

Hymes, Dell. 1968. Linguistic Problems in Defining the Concept of "Tribe." In *Essays on the Problem of Tribe: Proceedings of the 1967 Annual Spring Meeting of the American Ethnological Society*, June Helms, ed., pp. 23–48. Seattle: University of Washington Press.

———. 1974. *Foundations in Sociolinguistics: An Ethnographic Approach*. Conduct and Communication Series. Philadelphia: University of Pennsylvania Press.

———. 1975. Breakthrough Into Performance. In *Folklore: Performance and Communication*, Dan Ben-Amos and Kenneth S. Goldstein, eds., pp. 11–74. The Hague: Mouton.

Illich, Ivan. 1991. A Plea for Research on Lay Literacy. In *Literacy and Orality*, David Olson and Nancy Torrance, eds., pp. 28–46. Cambridge: Cambridge University Press.

Illich, Ivan and Barry Sanders. 1988. *ABC: The Alphabetization of the Popular Mind*. San Francisco: North Point Press.

Innis, Harold A. 1972. *Empire and Communications*, 2nd edition. Toronto: University of Toronto Press.

Iosefa, Suamalie N.T., Doug Munro, and Niko Besnier. 1991. *Te Tala o Niuoku: The German Plantation on Nukulaelae Atoll, 1865–1890*, 2nd edition. Suva: Institute of Pacific Studies, University of the South Pacific.

Iosia, Simeona and Sheila Macrae, eds. 1980. *A Report of the Results of the Census of the Population of Tuvalu, 1979*. Funafuti: Government of Tuvalu.

Irvine, Judith T. 1979. Formality and Informality in Communicative Events. *American Anthropologist* 81:773–89.

Jackson, Michael. 1975. Literacy, Communications and Social Change: A Study of the Meaning and Effect of Literacy in Early Nineteenth Century Maori Society. In *Conflict and Compromise: Essays on the Maori Since Colonisation*, I.H. Kawharu, ed., pp. 27–52. Wellington: A.H. and A.W. Reed.

Jakobson, Roman. 1957. *Shifters, Verbal Categories, and the Russian Verb*. Cambridge, MA: Harvard University Russian Language Project.

Kaitu, Hellani M., Sundat Balkaran, and Tulaga Telupe, eds. 1992. *Report on the 1991 Population Census of Tuvalu*, vol. 1 (Basic Information). Funafuti: Government of Tuvalu.

Kennedy, Donald G. 1931. *Field Notes in the Culture of Vaitupu, Ellice Islands*. Memoirs of the Polynesian Society, 9. New Plymouth: Polynesian Society.

———. 1946. *Te Ngangana a Te Tuvalu: Handbook of the Language of the Ellice Islands*. Suva: Government Printer.

Khan, Farida A. 1993. Cognitive Organization and Work Activity: A Study of Carpet Weavers in Kashmir. *Quarterly Newsletter of the Laboratory of Comparative Human Cognition* 15:48–53.

Ko, Dorothy Yin-Yee. 1989. Towards a Social History of Women in Seventeenth-Century China. Ph.D. dissertation, Department of History, Stanford University.

Koch, Gerd. 1961. *Die Materielle Kultur der Ellice-Inseln*. Veröffentlichungen des Museums für Völkerkunde, Neue Folge, 3, Abteilung Südsee, 1. Berlin: Museum für Völkerkunde. (Translated [n.d.] by Guy Slatter as *The Material Culture of Tuvalu*. Suva: Institute of Pacific Studies, University of the South Pacific.)

1962. Kulturwandel bei den Polynesien des Ellice-Archipels. *Sociologus* 12:128–41.

1963. Notizen über Verwandtschaft, Adoption und Freudschaft in Ellice-Archipel (Westpolynesien). *Bässler-Archiv* (n.s.) 11:107–14.

Koskinen, Aarne A. 1957. On the South Sea Islanders' View of Christianity. *Studia Missiologica Fennica* 1:7–16.

1965. **Tuhi*: A Polynesian Word with Magic Connotations. *Temenos* 1:122–41.

Kuipers, Joel C. 1990. *Power in Performance: The Creation of Textual Authority in Weyéwa Ritual Speech*. Conduct and Communication Series. Philadelphia: University of Pennsylvania Press.

Kulick, Don. 1992. *Language Shift and Cultural Reproduction: Socialization, Self, and Syncretism in a Papua New Guinea Village*. Studies in the Social and Cultural Foundations of Language, 14. Cambridge: Cambridge University Press.

Kulick, Don and Christopher Stroud. 1990. Christianity, Cargo, and Ideas of Self: Patterns of Literacy in a Papua New Guinea Village. *Man* (n.s.) 25:286–303. (Reprinted in Street, ed., 1993, pp. 30–61.)

Kuper, Adam. 1988. *The Invention of Primitive Society: Transformations of an Illusion*. London: Routledge.

Lambek, Michael. 1990. Certain Knowledge, Contestable Authority: Power and Practice on the Islamic Periphery. *American Ethnologist* 17:23–40.

1993. *Knowledge and Practice in Mayotte: Local Discourses of Islam, Sorcery, and Spirit Possession*. Toronto: University of Toronto Press.

Laracy, Hugh, ed. 1983. *Tuvalu: A History*. Suva: Institute of Pacific Studies and Extension Services, University of the South Pacific. Funafuti: Ministry of Social Services, Government of Tuvalu.

Larsen, Mogens T. 1988. Introduction: Literacy and Social Complexity. In *State and Society: The Emergence and Development of Social Hierarchy and Political Centralization*, John Glendhill, Barbara Bender, and Mogens T. Larsen, eds., pp. 173–91. London: Unwin Hyman.

Latouche, Jean-Paul. 1984. *Mythistoire tungaru: Cosmologie et généalogies aux îles Gilbert*. Langues et Cultures du Pacifique, 5. Paris: Société d'Etudes Linguistiques et Anthropologiques de France.

Lave, Jean. 1988. *Cognition in Practice*. Cambridge: Cambridge University Press.

Lawless, Elaine J. 1988a. *Handmaidens of the Lord: Pentecostal Women Preachers and Traditional Religion*. Publications of the American Folklore Society (n.s.), 9. Philadelphia: University of Pennsylvania Press.

1988b. *God's Peculiar People: Women's Voices and Folk Tradition in a Pentecostal Church*. Lexington, KY: University of Kentucky Press.

Leach, Edmund R. 1956. *Political Systems of Highland Burma: A Study of Kachin Social Structure*. London: G. Bell & Son.

1983. Correspondence: Imaginary Kachins. *Man* (n.s.) 18:191–7.

Leap, William L. 1991. Pathways and Barriers to Indian Language Literacy-Building on the Northern Ute Reservation. *Anthropology and Education Quarterly* 22:21–41.

Lévi-Strauss, Claude. 1962. *La pensée sauvage*. Paris: Plon.

1964. *Tristes Tropiques: An Anthropological Study of Primitive Societies in Brazil*, John Russel, trans. New York: Atheneum.

Levy, Robert I. 1984. Emotion, Knowing, and Culture. *Culture Theory: Essays on Mind, Self, and Emotion*, Richard A. Shweder and Robert A. LeVine, eds., pp. 214–37. Cambridge: Cambridge University Press.

Lévy-Bruhl, Lucien. 1910. *Les fonctions mentales dans les sociétés inférieures*. Paris: Alcon.

Lindstrom, Lamont. 1990. *Knowledge and Power in a South Pacific Society*. Smithsonian Series in Ethnographic Inquiry. Washington, DC: Smithsonian Institution Press.

——— 1992. Context Contests: Debatable Truth Statements on Tanna (Vanuatu). In *Rethinking Context: Language as an Interactive Phenomenon*, Alessandro Duranti and Charles Goodwin, eds., pp. 101–24. Studies in the Social and Cultural Foundations of Language, 11. Cambridge: Cambridge University Press.

Linell, Per. 1985. Language and the Communication of Emotion. In *Papers on Language and Literature Presented to Alvar Ellegård and Erik Frykman*, Sven Bäckman and Göran Kjellmer, eds., pp. 264–73. Gothenburg Studies in English, 60. Göteborg: Acta Universitatis Gothoburgensis.

——— 1988. The Impact of Literacy on the Conception of Language: The Case of Linguistics. In *The Written World: Studies in Literate Thought and Action*, Roger Säljö, ed., pp. 41–58. Berlin: Springer-Verlag.

Long, Elizabeth. 1992. Textual Interpretation as Collective Action. In *The Ethnography of Reading*, Jonathan Boyarin, ed., pp. 180–211. Berkeley, CA: University of California Press.

Lord, Albert B. 1960. *The Singer of Tales*. Cambridge, MA: Harvard University Press.

Love, Jacob W. 1985. "Oh, I Never Will Forget You": A Samoan Farewell. In *Music and Context: Essays for John Milton Ward*, Anne D. Shapiro, ed., pp. 453–76. Cambridge, MA: Harvard University Press.

Lucy, John A., ed. 1993. *Reflexive Language: Reported Speech and Metapragmatics*. Cambridge: Cambridge University Press.

Lukes, Stephen. 1978. Power and Authority. In *A History of Sociological Analysis*, Tom Bottomore and Robert Nisbet, eds., pp. 633–76. New York: Basic Books.

Luria, Aleksandr R. 1976. *Cognitive Development: Its Cultural and Social Foundations*, Martin Lopez-Morillas and Lynn Solotaroff, trans., Michael Cole, ed., Cambridge, MA: Harvard University Press.

Lutz, Catherine. 1988. *Unnatural Emotions: Everyday Sentiments on a Micronesian Atoll and Their Challenge to Western Theory*. Chicago: University of Chicago Press.

Macdonald, Barrie. 1982. *Cinderellas of the Empire: Towards a History of Kiribati and Tuvalu*. Canberra: Australian National University Press.

McGinnis, Mary. 1986. Preachin': A Black Speech Event. *Southern California Occasional Papers in Linguistics* 11:99–123.

McKenzie, D.F. 1985. *Oral Culture, Literacy and Print in Early New Zealand: The Treaty of Waitangi*. Wellington: Victoria University Press and Alexander Turnbull Library Endowment Trust.

McLaughlin, Daniel. 1992. *When Literacy Empowers: Navajo Language in Print*. Albuquerque, NM: University of New Mexico Press.

McLean, R.F. and Doug Munro. 1991. Late 19th Century Tropical Storms and Hurricanes in Tuvalu. *South Pacific Journal of Natural Science* 11:203–19.

McLennan, John F. 1876. *Studies in Ancient History*. London: Macmillan.

McLuhan, Marshall. 1962. *The Gutenberg Galaxy: The Making of Typographic Man*. Toronto: University of Toronto Press.

Mageo, Jeannette. 1988. *Mālosi*: A Psychological Exploration of Mead and Freeman's Work and of Samoan Aggression. *Pacific Studies* 11(2):25–65.

Maine, Henry S. 1873[1963]. *Ancient Law: Its Connection With the Early History of Society and Its Relation to Modern Ideas.* Boston: Beacon Press.

Marcus, George. 1989. Chieftainship. In *Development in Polynesian Ethnology*, Alan Howard and Robert Borofsky, eds., pp. 175–211. Honolulu: University of Hawaii Press.

Markus, Hazel R. and Shinobu Kitayama. 1991. Culture and the Self: Implications for Cognition. *Psychological Review* 98:224–53.

Marsh, Kathryn S. 1983. Weaving, Writing and Gender. *Man* (n.s.) 18:729–44.

Martin, John. 1817[1981]. *An Account of the Natives of the Tonga Islands, in the South Pacific Ocean, with an Original Grammar and Vocabulary of Their Language, Compiled and Arranged from the Extensive Communications of Mr. William Mariner, Several Years Resident in Those Islands*, 4th edition. Neiafu, Vava'u: Vava'u Press.

Maude, Harry E. 1981. *Slavers in Paradise: The Peruvian Labour Trade in Polynesia, 1862–64.* Canberra: Australian National University Press.

Meigs, Anna. 1990. Multiple Gender Ideologies and Statuses. In *Beyond the Second Sex: New Directions in the Anthropology of Gender*, Peggy R. Sanday and Ruth G. Goodenough, eds., pp. 99–112. Philadelphia: University of Pennsylvania Press.

Messick, Brinkley. 1983. Legal Documents and the Concept of "Restricted Literacy" in a Traditional Society. *International Journal of the Sociology of Language* 42:41–52.

1993. *The Calligraphic State: Textual Domination and History in a Muslim Society.* Comparative Studies on Muslim Societies, 16. Berkeley, CA: University of California Press.

Milner, George B. 1958. Aspiration in Two Polynesian Languages. *Bulletin of the School of Oriental and African Studies* 21:368–75.

1968. Problems of the Structure of Concepts in Samoa: An Investigation of Vernacular Statement and Meaning. Ph.D. dissertation, University of London.

Miyoshi, Masao. 1988. The "Great Divide" Once Again: Problematics of the Novel and the Third World. *Culture & History* 3:7–22.

Modleski, Tania. 1984. *Loving With a Vengeance: Mass Produced Fantasies for Women.* Hamden, CT: Archon.

Møller, Peter U. 1990. From Russia With Love: Letters in a National Literary Heritage. *Culture & History* 8:69–86.

Moresby, John. 1876. *New Guinea and Polynesia: Discoveries and Surveys in New Guinea and the d'Entrecasteaux Islands; A Cruise in Polynesia and Visits to the Pearl-Shelling Stations in Torres Straits of H.M.S. Basilick.* London: J. Murray.

Morgen, Sandra. 1989. Gender and Anthropology: Introductory Essay. In *Gender and Anthropology: Critical Reviews for Research and Teaching*, Sandra Morgen, ed., pp. 1–20. Washington, DC: American Anthropological Association.

Mühlhäusler, Peter. 1990. "Reducing" Pacific Languages to Writing. In *Ideologies of Language*, T.J. Taylor, ed., pp. 189–205. London: Routledge.

Mulkay, Michael. 1985. Agreement and Disagreement in Conversations and Letters. *Text* 5:201–27.

1979. *Science and the Sociology of Knowledge.* London: Allen.

Munro, Doug. 1978. Kirisome and Tema: Samoan Pastors in the Ellice Islands. In *More Pacific Islands Portraits*, Deryck Scarr, ed., pp. 75–93. Canberra:

Australian National University Press.
1982. The Lagoon Islands: A History of Tuvalu, 1820–1908. Ph.D. dissertation, Department of History, Macquarie University.
1985. On the Lack of English-Speaking Tuvaluans in the Nineteenth Century. In *Papers in Pidgin and Creole Linguistics*, vol. 4, pp. 133–41. Canberra: Pacific Linguistics A–72.
1986. Lutelu: The Tongan of Nukulaelae. *Word of Mouth* 10:15–9.
1990a. Transnational Corporations of Kin and Their MIRAB System: The Case of Tuvalu. *Pacific Viewpoint* 31:63–6.
1990b. Migration and the Shift to Dependence in Tuvalu: A Historical Perspective. In *Migration and Development in the South Pacific*, John Connell, ed., pp. 29–41. Pacific Research Monographs, 24. Canberra: National Centre for Development Studies, Research School of Pacific Studies, Australian National University.
1990c. The Peruvian Slavers in Tuvalu, 1863: How Many Did They Kidnap? *Journal de la Société des Océanistes* 90:43–52.
Munro, Doug and Richard Bedford. 1980. Historical Background. In Iosia and Macrae, eds., pp. 1–13.
1990. Labour Migration From the Atolls: Kiribati and Tuvalu. In *Labour in the South Pacific*, Clive Moore, Jacqueline Leckie, and Doug Munro, eds., pp. 172–7. Studies in Melanesian History Series, 1. Townsville: James Cook University.
Munro, Doug and Niko Besnier. 1990. The German Plantation at Nukulaelae Atoll. In *Labour in the South Pacific*, Clive Moore, Jacqueline Leckie, and Doug Munro, eds., pp. 178–80. Studies in Melanesian History, 1. Townsville: James Cook University.
Munro, Doug and Stuart Firth. 1986. Towards Colonial Protectorates: The Case of the Gilbert and Ellice Islands. *The Australian Journal of Politics and History* 32:63–71.
1990. Company Strategies – Colonial Policies. In *Labour in the South Pacific*, Clive Moore, Jacqueline Leckie, and Doug Munro, eds., pp. 3–29. Studies in Melanesian History, 1. Townsville: James Cook University.
Murray, A.W. 1865. Missionary Voyage to the Lagoon Islands. *Missionary Magazine* December: 335–45.
Missionary Voyage Among the Islands of Ellice's & Other Groups in October, November & December 1866. South Sea Journals 157, Records of the London Missionary Society, School of Oriental and African Studies Library.
1876. *Forty Years' Mission Work in Polynesia and New Guinea, From 1835 to 1875*. London: James Nisbet.
Noricks, Jay S. 1981. Niutao Kinship and Social Organization. Ph.D. dissertation, Department of Anthropology, University of Pennsylvania.
Nugent, David. 1982. Closed Systems and Contradiction: The Kachin In and Out of History. *Man* (n.s.) 17:508–27.
1983. Correspondence: Imaginary Kachins. *Man* (n.s.) 18:197–206.
Ochs, Elinor. 1979a. Transcription as Theory. In *Developmental Pragmatics*, Elinor Ochs and Bambi B. Schieffelin, eds., pp. 43–72. New York: Academic Press.
1979b. Social Foundations of Language. In *New Directions in Discourse Processing*, Roy O. Freedle, ed., pp. 207–21. Advances in Discourse Processes, 2. Norwood, NJ: Ablex.
1987. The Interaction of Stratification and Socialization on Men's and Women's Speech in Western Samoa. In *Language, Gender, and Sex in Comparative*

Perspective, Susan U. Philips, Susan Steele, and Christina Tanz, eds., pp. 50–70. Studies in the Social and Cultural Foundations of Language, 4. Cambridge: Cambridge University Press.

1988. *Culture and Language Development: Language Socialization in a Samoan Village*. Studies in the Social and Cultural Foundations of Language, 6. Cambridge: Cambridge University Press.

1992. Indexing Gender. In *Rethinking Context: Language as an Interactive Phenomenon*, Alessandro Duranti and Charles Goodwin, eds., pp. 335–58. Studies in the Social and Cultural Foundations of Language, 11. Cambridge: Cambridge University Press.

Ochs, Elinor and Bambi B. Schieffelin. 1989. Language Has a Heart. *Text* 9:7–25.

Ogbu, John U. 1990. Cultural Mode, Identity, and Literacy. In *Cultural Psychology: Essays on Comparative Human Development*, James W. Stigler, Richard A. Shweder, and Gilbert Herdt, eds., pp. 520–41. Cambridge: Cambridge University Press.

O'Keeffe, Katherine O. 1990. *Visible Song: Transitional Literacy in Old English Verse*. London: Methuen.

Olson, David R. 1977. From Utterance to Text: The Bias of Language in Speech and Writing. *Harvard Educational Review* 47:257–81.

1984. "See! Jumping!" Some Oral Language Antecedents of Literacy. In *Awakening to Literacy*, Hillel Goelman, Antoinette Oberg, and Frank Smith, eds., pp. 185–92. Exeter, NH: Heinemann Educational Books.

1986. The Cognitive Consequences of Literacy. *Canadian Psychology* 27:109–21.

1991. Literacy and Objectivity: The Rise of Modern Science. In *Literacy and Orality*, David Olson and Nancy Torrance, eds., pp. 149–64. Cambridge: Cambridge University Press.

Olson, David R. and Nancy Torrance. 1981. Learning to Meet the Requirements of Written Texts: Language Development in the School Years. *Writing: The Nature, Development, and Teaching of Written Communication*, Carl H. Fredericksen and Joseph F. Dominic, eds., vol. 2, pp. 235–55. Hillsdale, NJ: Lawrence Erlbaum.

Ong, Walter J. 1967. *The Presence of the Word*. New Haven, CT: Yale University Press.

1971. *Rhetoric, Romance, and Technology*. Ithaca, NY: Cornell University Press.

1977. *Interfaces of the Word*. Ithaca, NY: Cornell University Press.

1982. *Orality and Literacy: The Technologizing of the Word*. New Accents Series. London: Methuen.

Ortner, Sherry. 1984. Theory in Anthropology Since the Sixties. *Comparative Studies in Society and History* 26:126–66.

1991. Reading America: Preliminary Notes on Class and Culture. In *Recapturing Anthropology: Writing in the Present*, Richard G. Fox, ed., pp. 163–89. Santa Fe, NM: School of American Research Press.

Parry, Jonathan. 1989. The Brahmanical Tradition and the Technology of the Intellect. In *Literacy and Society*, Karen Schousboe and Mogens T. Larsen, eds., pp. 39–71. Copenhagen: Akademisk Forlag for the Center for Research in the Humanities, Copenhagen University.

Parry, Milman. 1971. *The Making of Homeric Verse*. London: Clarendon Press.

Parsonson, George S. 1967. The Literate Revolution in Polynesia. *Journal of Pacific History* 2:39–57.

Pattison, Robert. 1982. *On Literacy: The Politics of the Word from Homer to the Age of Rock*. London: Oxford University Press.

Pawley, Andrew K. 1966. Polynesian Languages: A Subgrouping Based on Shared Innovations in Morphology. *Journal of the Polynesian Society* 75:39–64.

1967. The Relationships of the Polynesian Outlier Languages. *Journal of Polynesian Society* 76:259–96.

Pawley, Andrew K. and Frances H. Syder. 1983. Natural Selection in Syntax: Notes on Adaptive Variation and Change in Vernacular and Literary Grammar. *Journal of Pragmatics* 7:551–79.

Pedersen, Poul. 1990. Anxious Lives and Letters: Family Separation, Communication Networks and Structures of Everyday Life. *Culture & History* 8:7–19.

Petersen, Glenn. 1993. *Kanengamah* and Pohnpei's Politics of Concealment. *American Anthropologist* 95:334–52.

Pelton, Robert D. 1980. *The Trickster in West Africa: A Study of Mythic Irony and Sacred Delight.* Hermeneutics: Studies in the History of Religions, 8. Berkeley, CA: University of California Press.

Philips, Susan U. 1975. Literacy as a Mode of Communication on the Warm Spring Indian Reservation. *Foundations of Language Development*, Eric H. Lenneberg and Elizabeth Lenneberg, eds., vol. 2, pp. 367–82. New York: Academic Press. Paris: UNESCO.

1983. *The Invisible Culture: Communication in Classroom and Community on the Warm Springs Indian Reservation.* New York: Longman.

Plattner, Stuart. 1989. Markets and Marketplaces. In *Economic Anthropology*, Stuart Plattner, ed., pp. 171–208. Stanford, CA: Stanford University Press.

Poole, Fitz John Porter. 1991. Cultural Schemas and Experiences of the Self Among the Bimin-Kuskusmin of Papua New Guinea. In *The Psychoanalytic Study of Society*, L. Bryce Boyer and Ruth M. Boyer, eds., vol. 16, pp. 55–85. Hillsdale, NJ: The Analytic Press.

Popper, Karl R. 1959. *The Logic of Scientific Discovery.* New York: Basic Books.

Prelli, Lawrence J. 1989. The Rhetorical Construction of Scientific Ethos. In *Rhetoric in the Human Sciences*, Herbert W. Simons, ed., pp. 48–68. Inquiries in Social Construction Series. London: Sage.

Probst, Peter. 1989. The Letter and the Spirit: Literacy and Religious Authority in the History of the Aladura Movement in Western Nigeria. *Africa* 59:153–67. (Reprinted in Street, ed., 1993, pp. 198–219.)

Puckett, Anita. 1992. "Let the Girls do the Spelling and Dan will do the Shooting": Literacy, the Division of Labor, and Identity in a Rural Appalachian Community. *Anthropological Quarterly* 65:137–47.

Quilligan, Maureen. 1991. *The Allegory of Female Authority: Christine de Pizan's Cité des dames.* Ithaca, NY: Cornell University Press.

Radford, Jean. 1986. *The Progress of the Romance: The Politics of Popular Fiction.* London: Routledge & Kegan Paul.

Radway, Janice A. 1991. *Reading the Romance: Women, Patriarchy, and Popular Literature*, 2nd edition. Chapel Hill, NC: The University of North Carolina Press.

Rafael, Vicente L. 1988. *Contracting Colonialism: Translation and Christian Conversion in Tagalog Society Under Early Spanish Rule.* Ithaca, NY: Cornell University Press.

Reder, Stephen and Karen R. Green. 1983. Contrasting Patterns of Literacy in an Alaskan Fishing Village. *International Journal of the Sociology of Language* 42:9–39. (Reprinted as Literacy Development and Ethnicity: An Alaskan Example, in Street, ed., 1993, pp. 176–97.)

Reed-Danahy, Deborah. 1995. The Kabyle and the French: Occidentalism in

Bourdieu's Theory of Practice. In *Occidentalism: Images of the West*, James G. Carrier, ed. Oxford: Oxford University Press.

Reid, Anthony. 1988. *Southeast Asia in the Age of Commerce, 1450–1680*, vol. 1. New Haven, CT: Yale University Press.

Ring, Betty. 1983. *Let Virtue Be a Guide to Thee: Needlework in the Education of Rhode Island Women, 1730–1830*. Providence, RI: The Rhode Island Historical Society.

———. 1993. *Girlhood Embroidery: American Samplers and Pictorial Needlework, 1650–1850*, 2 vols. New York: Alfred A. Knopf.

Roberts, R.G. 1958. Te Atu Tuvalu: A Short History of the Ellice Islands. *Journal of the Polynesian Society* 67:394–423.

Rockhill, Kathleen. 1987. Gender, Language, and the Politics of Literacy. *British Journal of the Sociology of Education* 8:153–67. (Reprinted in Street, ed., 1993, pp. 156–75.)

Rosaldo, Michelle Z. 1973. I Have Nothing to Hide: The Language of Ilongot Oratory. *Language in Society* 2:193–223.

———. 1980. *Knowledge and Passion: Ilongot Notions of Self and Social Life*. Cambridge Studies in Cultural Systems, 4. Cambridge: Cambridge University Press.

———. 1984. Towards an Anthropology of Self and Feeling. *Culture Theory: Essays on Mind, Self, and Emotion*, Richard A. Shweder and Robert A. LeVine, eds., pp. 137–57. Cambridge: Cambridge University Press.

Rosen, Harold. 1985. The Voices of Communities and Language in Classrooms: Review of Shirley Heath's *Ways With Words*. *Harvard Educational Review* 55:448–56.

Rosenberg, Bruce A. 1970a. The Formulaic Quality of Spontaneous Sermons. *Journal of American Folklore* 83:3–20.

———. 1970b. *The Art of the American Folk Preacher*. New York: Oxford University Press.

Rubinstein, Donald and D. Carlton Gajdušek. 1970. *A Study in Nascent Literacy: Neo-Melanesian Correspondence From a Fore, New Guinea Youth*. Bethesda, MD: Section of Child Growth and Development and Disease Patterns in Primitive Cultures, National Institute of Neurological Diseases and Stroke, National Institute of Health.

Sacks, Harvey, Gail Jefferson, and Emanuel A. Schegloff. 1974. A Simplest Systematics for the Organization of Turn-Taking in Conversation. *Language* 50:696–735.

Sahlins, Marshall. 1957. Differentiation by Adaptation in Polynesian Societies. *Journal of the Polynesian Society* 66:291–301.

———. 1958. *Social Stratification in Polynesia*. American Ethnological Society Monographs, 29. Seattle: University of Washington Press.

Sampson, Geoffrey. 1985. *Writing Systems: A Linguistic Introduction*. Stanford, CA: Stanford University Press.

Sandersen, Vibeke. 1990. Letters from Danish Private Soldiers in the First Schleswigian War 1848–50: Communicative Functions, Norm, and Form. *Culture & History* 8:51–9.

Sapoaga, Enele. 1983. Post-War Development. In Laracy, ed., pp. 146–52.

Schieffelin, Bambi B. 1990. *The Give and Take of Everyday Life: Language Socialization of Kaluli Children*. Studies in the Social and Cultural Foundations of Language, 9. Cambridge: Cambridge University Press.

Schieffelin, Bambi B. and Marilyn Cochran-Smith. 1984. Learning to Read Culturally: Literacy Before Schooling. In *Awakening to Literacy*, Hillel

Goelman, Antoinette Oberg, and Frank Smith, eds., pp. 3–23. Exeter, NH: Heinemann Educational Books.

Schofield, R.S. 1968. The Measurement of Literacy in Pre-Industrial England. In Goody, ed., pp. 311–25.

Scollon, Ron and Suzanne B.K. Scollon. 1981. *Narrative, Literacy, and Face in Interethnic Communication*. Advances in Discourse Processes, 7. Norwood, NJ: Ablex.

Scott, James C. 1990. *Domination and the Arts of Resistance: Hidden Transcripts*. New Haven, CT: Yale University Press.

Scribner, Sylvia and Michael Cole. 1981. *The Psychology of Literacy*. Cambridge, MA: Harvard University Press.

Sennett, Richard and Jonathan Cobb. 1972. *The Hidden Injuries of Class*. New York: Alfred A. Knopf.

Sherzer, Joel. 1987. A Diversity of Voices: Men's and Women's Speech in Ethnographic Perspective. In *Language, Gender, and Sex in Comparative Perspective*, Susan U. Philips, Susan Steele, and Christina Tanz, eds., pp. 95–120. Studies in the Social and Cultural Foundations of Language, 4. Cambridge: Cambridge University Press.

Shlomowitz, Ralph and Doug Munro. 1992. The Ocean Island (Banaba) and Nauru Labour Trade, 1900–1940. *Journal de la Société des Océanistes* 94:103–17.

Shore, Bradd, 1981. Sexuality and Gender in Samoa: Conceptions and Missed Conceptions. In *Sexual Meanings: The Cultural Construction of Gender and Sexuality*, Sherry B. Ortner and Harriet Whitehead, eds., pp. 192–215. Cambridge: Cambridge University Press.

1982. *Sala'ilua: A Samoan Mystery*. New York: Columbia University Press.

1991. The Absurd Side of Power in Samoa. Paper presented at the Conference on Leadership and Change in the Western Pacific: For Sir Raymond Firth on the Occasion of his Ninetieth Birthday, London School of Economics.

Shuman, Amy. 1986. *Storytelling Rights: The Uses of Oral and Written Texts by Urban Adolescents*. Cambridge Studies in Oral and Literate Culture, 11. Cambridge: Cambridge University Press.

Shweder, Richard A. and Edmund J. Bourne. 1984. Does the Concept of Person Vary Cross-Culturally? In *Culture Theory: Essays on Mind, Self, and Emotion*, Richard A. Shweder and Robert A. LeVine, eds., pp. 158–99. Cambridge: Cambridge University Press.

Siegel, Jeff. 1981. Developments in Written Tok Pisin. *Anthropological Linguistics* 23(1):20–35.

1984. Current Use and Expansion of Tok Pisin: Tok Pisin in the Mass Media. In *Handbook of Tok Pisin (New Guinea Pidgin)*, Stephen A. Wurm and Peter Mühlhäusler, eds., pp. 517–33. Canberra: Pacific Linguistics C-70.

Silverstein, Michael. 1976. Shifters, Verbal Categories, and Cultural Description. In *Meaning in Anthropology*, Keith H. Basso and Henry Selby, eds., pp. 11–55. Albuquerque: University of New Mexico Press.

Simmel, Georg. 1950. *The Sociology of Georg Simmel*. New York: Free Press.

Smalley, William A., Chia Koua Vang, and Gnia Yee Yang. 1990. *Mother of Writing: The Origin and Development of a Hmong Messianic Script*. Chicago: Chicago University Press.

Smith-Rosenberg, Carroll. 1975. The Female World of Love and Ritual. *Signs* 1:1–29.

Smitherman, Geneva. 1977. *Talkin' and Testifyin': The Language of Black America*. Boston: Houghton Mifflin.

Spencer, Jon M. 1987. *Sacred Symphony: The Chanted Sermon of the Black Preacher.* Contributions in Afro-American and African Studies, 111. New York: Greenwood Press.

Spinks, C.W. 1991. *Semiosis, Marginal Signs, and Tricksters: A Dagger of the Mind.* Basingstoke: Macmillan.

Spiro, Melford E. 1993. Is the Western Conception of the Self "Peculiar" Within the Context of the World Cultures? *Ethos* 21:107–53.

Spolsky, Bernard, Guillermina Engelbrecht, and Leroy Ortiz. 1983. Religious, Political, and Educational Factors in the Development of Biliteracy in the Kingdom of Tonga. *Journal of Multilingual and Multicultural Development* 4:459–69.

Spolsky, Bernard, and Patricia Irvine. 1982. Sociolinguistic Aspects of the Acceptance of Literacy in the Vernacular. In *Bilingualism and Language Contact: Spanish, English, and Native American Languages*, Florence Barkin, Elizabeth A. Brandt, and Jacob Ornstein-Galicia, eds., pp. 73–79. New York: Teachers College Press.

Stephenson, Peter H. 1990. *The Hutterian People: Ritual and Rebirth in the Evolution of Communal Life.* Lanham, MD: University Press of America.

Stock, Brian. 1983. *The Implications of Literacy: Written Language and Models of Interpretation in the Eleventh and Twelfth Centuries.* Princeton, NJ: Princeton University Press.

Stout, Harry S. 1986. *The New England Soul: Preaching and Religious Culture in Colonial New England.* New York: Oxford University Press.

Stowers, Stanley K. 1986. *Letter Writing in Greco-Roman Antiquity.* Library of Early Christianity, 5. Philadelphia: The Westminster Press.

Street, Brian V. 1984. *Literacy in Theory and Practice.* Cambridge Studies in Oral and Literate Culture, 9. Cambridge: Cambridge University Press.

1988. Literacy Practices and Literacy Myths. In *The Written World: Studies in Literate Thought and Action*, Roger Säljö, ed., pp. 59–72. Berlin: Springer-Verlag.

1993. Introduction: The New Literacy Studies. In Street, ed., pp. 1–21.

Street, Brian V., ed. 1993. *Cross-Cultural Approaches to Literacy.* Cambridge Studies in Oral and Literate Culture, 23. Cambridge: Cambridge University Press.

Street, Brian V. and Niko Besnier. 1994. Aspects of Literacy. In *Companion Encyclopedia of Anthropology: Humanity, Culture, and Social Life*, Tim Ingold, ed., pp. 527–62. London: Routledge.

Street, Brian V. and Joanna C. Street. 1991. The Schooling of Literacy. In *Writing in the Community*, David Barton and Roz Ivanič, eds., pp. 143–66. Written Communication Annual, 6. Newbury Park, CA: Sage.

Stromberg, Peter G. 1990. Ideological Language in the Transformation of Identity. *American Anthropologist* 92:42–56.

Szwed, John F. 1981. The Ethnography of Literacy. In *Writing: The Nature, Development, and Teaching of Written Communication*, Marcia F. Whiteman, ed., vol. 1, pp. 13–23. Hillsdale, NJ: Lawrence Erlbaum.

Talmy, Leonard. 1985. Lexicalization Patterns: Semantic Structure in Lexical Forms. In *Language Typology and Syntactic Description*, Timothy Shopen, ed., vol. 3, pp. 57–149. Cambridge: Cambridge University Press.

Tambiah, Stanley J. 1990. *Magic, Science, Religion, and the Scope of Rationality.* The Lewis Henry Morgan Lectures Series. Cambridge: Cambridge University Press.

Tannen, Deborah. 1982. Oral and Literate Strategies in Spoken and Written Narratives. *Language* 58:1–21.

1985. Relative Focus on Involvement in Oral and Written Discourse. In *Literacy, Language, and Learning: The Nature and Consequences of Reading and Writing*, David R. Olson, Nancy Torrance, and Angela Hildyard, eds., pp. 124–147. Cambridge: Cambridge University Press.

Tedlock, Dennis. 1983. *The Spoken Word and the Work of Interpretation*. Philadelphia: University of Pennsylvania Press.

Tench, Paul. 1988. The Stylistic Potential of Intonation. In *Styles of Discourse*, Nikolas Coupland, ed., pp. 50–84. London: Croom Helm.

Teo, Noatia P. 1983. Colonial Rule. In Laracy, ed., pp. 127–39.

Thompson, John B. 1984. *Studies in the Theory of Ideology*. Berkeley, CA: University of California Press.

1990. *Ideology and Modern Culture*. Stanford, CA: Stanford University Press.

Tinilau, Vaieli. 1983. Nukulaelae. In Laracy, ed., pp. 97–100.

Titon, Jeff T. 1988. *Powerhouse for God: Speech, Chant, and Song in an Appalachian Baptist Church*. Austin, TX: University of Texas Press.

Topping, Donald M. 1983. Identity and Literacy: The Power of the Written Word. *Pacific Perspective* 12(2):41–50.

1992. Literacy and Cultural Erosion in the Pacific Islands. In *Cross-Cultural Literacy: Global Perspectives on Reading and Writing*, Fraida Dubin and Natalie A. Kuhlman, eds., pp. 19–33. Englewood Cliffs, NJ: Prentice Hall.

Turner, George. 1861. *Nineteen Years in Polynesia: Missionary Life, Travels, and Researches in the Islands of the Pacific*. London: John Snow.

1865. Narrative of Elikana [*sic*], a Native Christian of Manahiki. *The Juvenile Missionary Magazine* 22(255):338–43, 367–72.

1876. Journal. South Sea Journals 168, Records of the London Missionary Society, School of Oriental and African Studies Library.

Turner, G.A. 1874. Report of a Voyage Through the Tokelau, Ellice, and Gilbert Groups in the "John Williams," 1874. South Sea Journals 165, Records of the London Missionary Society, School of Oriental and African Studies Library. (On Pacific Manuscript Bureau Microfilm 129.)

Turner, Victor. 1967. *The Forest of Symbols: Aspects of Ndembu Ritual*. Ithaca, NY: Cornell University Press.

1969. *The Ritual Process: Structure and Anti-Structure*. Chicago: Aldine.

1992. *Blazing the Trail: Way Marks in the Exploration of Symbols*, Edith Turner, ed. Tucson, AZ: University of Arizona Press.

Tuvalu Language Board. 1980. Standard Orthography Policy. *Tuvalu News Sheet* 109:19.

1991. Tuvalu Language Board Review [*sic*] its Activities. *Tuvalu Echoes* 192:4.

Tylor, Edward B. 1874. *Primitive Culture: Researches into the Development of Mythology, Philosophy, Religion, Art and Custom*. Boston: Estes & Lauriat.

Urban, Greg. 1989. The "I" of Discourse. *Semiotics, Self, and Society*, Benjamin Lee and Greg Urban, eds. pp. 27–51. Approaches to Semiotics Series, 84. Berlin: Mouton de Gruyter.

van Gennep, Arnold. 1909. *The Rites of Passage*, Monika B. Vizedom and Gabrielle L. Caffee, trans. London: Routledge & Kegan Paul.

Vetter, Ronald. 1991. Discourse Across Literacies: Personal Letter Writing in a Tuvaluan Context. *Language and Education* 5:125–45.

Voloshinov, Valentin N. 1978 [1929]. Reported Speech. In *Readings in Russian Poetics: Formalist and Structuralist Views*, Ladislav Matejka and Kristina

Pomorska, eds., pp. 176–96. Michigan Slavic Contributions, 8. Ann Arbor, MI: Michigan Slavic Publications.

Vygotsky, Lev S. 1962. *Thought and Language*, Eugenia Haufmann and Gertrude Vakar, eds. and trans. Cambridge, MA: MIT Press.

Wagner, Daniel A., Brinkley M. Messick, and Jennifer Spratt. 1986. Studying Literacy in Morocco. In *The Acquisition of Literacy: Ethnographic Perspectives*, Bambi Schieffelin and Perry Gilmore, eds., pp. 233–60. Advances in Discourse Processes, 21. Norwood, NJ: Ablex.

Wallerstein, Immanuel. 1974. *The Modern World-System: Capitalist Agriculture and the Origins of the European World-Economy in the Sixteenth Century*. New York: Academic Press.

Ward, R. Gerard, ed. 1967. *American Activities in the Central Pacific, 1790–1870*, vol. 5. Ridgewood, NJ: The Gregg Press.

Watson-Gegeo, Karen A. and David W. Gegeo. 1991. The Impact of Church Affiliation on Language Use in Kwara'ae (Solomon Islands). *Language in Society* 20:533–55.

Weinstein-Shr, Gail. 1993. Literacy and Social Process: A Community in Transition. In Street, ed., pp. 272–93.

Wetherell, David. 1980. Pioneers and Patriarchs: Samoans in a Non-Conformist Mission District in Papua, 1890–1917. *Journal of Pacific History* 15:130–54.

1993. From Samuel McFarlane to Stephen Davies: Continuity and Change in the Torres Straits Churches, 1871–1949. *Pacific Studies* 16:1–32.

White, Geoffrey M. 1992. The Discourse of Chiefs: Notes on a Melanesian Society. *The Contemporary Pacific* 4:73–108.

Whitmee, S.J. 1871. *A Missionary Cruise in the South Pacific, Being the Report of a Voyage Amongst the Tokelau, Ellice, and Gilbert Islands, in the Missionary Barque "John Williams," During 1870*. Sydney: Joseph Cook.

[n.d.] Recollections of a Long Life. South Sea Bound Volumes, Records of the London Missionary Society, School of Oriental and African Studies Library.

Williams, Maslyn and Barrie Macdonald. 1985. *The Phosphateers: A History of the British Phosphate Commissioners and the Christmas Island Phosphate Commission*. Melbourne: Melbourne University Press.

Willis, Paul. 1977. *Learning to Labour: How Working Class Kids Get Working Class Jobs*. Farnborough: Saxon House.

Wilmsen, Edwin. 1989. *Land Filled With Flies: A Political Economy of the Kalahari*. Chicago: University of Chicago Press.

Wit, Nico. 1980. Migration. In Iosia and Macrae, eds., pp. 50–60.

1984. *Migration and Socio-Economic Change: The Case of Tuvalu*. Groningen Demographic Reports, 8. Groningen: Geographical Institute, Groningen State University.

Wolf, Eric R. 1982. *Europe and the People Without History*. Berkeley, CA: University of California Press.

Wuthnow, Robert. 1987. *Meaning and Moral Order: Explorations in Cultural Analysis*. Berkeley, CA: University of California Press.

Zinsser, Caroline. 1986. For the Bible Tells Me So: Teaching Children in a Fundamentalist Church. In *The Acquisition of Literacy: Ethnographic Perspectives*, Bambi Schieffelin and Perry Gilmore, eds., pp. 55–71. Advances in Discourse Processes, 21. Norwood, NJ: Ablex.

INDEX OF TUVALUAN WORDS

The following list provides glosses and index references for the more important Tuvaluan words discussed in this book. Only translations that are relevant to the discussion are provided here. In many cases, verbs (including adjectives) can function as nouns without undergoing any internal morphological change (e.g., *salamoo* "[to feel] remorseful" or "remorse"). In the following, only the verbal or adjectival translation is provided if the nominal translation can be easily derived from it.

GENERAL INDEX

paulvk @ ucla.edu

Kyoto Kanita